Voting Madness

A SAPIENT Being's Guide to Election Irregularities, Voter Fraud, Mail-In Ballots, HR1 and More

By

Corey Lee Wilson

Voting Madness

Fratire Publishing books can be purchased in bulk with special discounts for educational purposes, association gifts, sales promotions, and special editions can be created to specifications. All inquiries for such can be made below.

FRATIRE PUBLISHING LLC
4533 Temescal Canyon Rd. # 308
Corona, CA 92883 USA
www.FratirePublishing.com
FratirePublishing@att.net
1+ (951) 638-5502

FratirePublishing
Relevant Books for **SAPIENT** Beings

Fratire Publishing is all about common sense and relevant books for sapient beings. If this sounds like you and you can never have enough common sense, wisdom, and relevancy, then visit us and learn more about the 50 *MADNESS* series of book titles at www.fratirepublishing.com/madnessbooks.

Printed paperback and eBook ePUB by Ingram Spark in La Vergne, Tennessee, USA
Copyright © 2021: First Edition May 2021
ISBN 978-0-9994017-4-3 (Paperback)
ISBN 978-1-953319-45-6 (eBook)
VotingMadness-01-PDF (pdf)
LCCN 2021909863

Special thanks for the cover design by Jenny Barroso, J20Graphics, j20graphics@gmail.com and ebook conversion by Redeemer SoftTech, redeemer.softtech@gmail.com.

Contents

Acknowledgements

I owe a debt of gratitude to the following for "heavily" borrowing at times pieces of their and/or outright sections. I do this unashamedly to use the sapient phrase, "if it ain't broke—don't try to fix it." Most of the borrowed works and research cannot be improved upon—so why try? It's better to assemble these meaningful parts, profound messages, and eloquent arguments into a cohesive whole, told with high school and college students in mind, and that's what I've done and where my talent lies.

Below in alphabetical order are the major contributors to *The SAPIENT Being* that I borrowed verbatim, quoted, and conceptualized much of their content from a little to a lot. Wherever this happened, I did my best to acknowledge my source. If I didn't at times within the 15 chapters, I did so intentionally because doing so would have distracted from their message. Nonetheless, they are more than acknowledged in the References and Index sections of this textbook.

Convention of States (COS): Professor Robert Natelson is a Constitutional leader and journalist in support of the Convention of States Project; a national effort to call a convention under Article V of the United States Constitution, restricted to proposing amendments that will impose fiscal restraints on the federal government, limit its power and jurisdiction, and impose term limits on its officials and members of Congress.

Judicial Watch: Led by President Tom Fitton since 1998, is a conservative, non-partisan educational foundation, which promotes transparency, accountability and integrity in government, politics, and the law. Through its educational endeavors, Judicial Watch advocates high standards of ethics and morality in our nation's public life and seeks to ensure that political and judicial officials do not abuse the powers entrusted to them and also fulfills its educational mission through litigation, investigations, and public outreach.

Navarro, Dr. Peter: Is the author of *The Navarro Report* and he holds a Ph.D. in economics from Harvard University and was a professor emeritus of economics and public policy at the University of California-Irvine for more than 20 years. He served as Assistant to the President and Director of the Office of Trade and Manufacturing Policy at the White House during the Trump Administration.

Public Interest Legal Foundation (PILF): Founded in 2012, J. Christian Adams serves as President and General Counsel, Public Interest Legal Foundation (PILF) is a 501(c)(3) public interest law firm dedicated entirely to election integrity. The Foundation exists to assist states and others to aid the cause of election integrity and fight against lawlessness in American elections. Drawing on numerous experts in the field, PILF seeks to protect the right to vote and preserve the Constitutional framework of American elections.

The Epoch Times: Is the SAPIENT Being's most trusted election information news source and deserves special mention for their sapient editorial and stance: Why The Epoch Times Won't Call the Presidential Race Until All Challenges Are Resolved. Add their truthful and unbiased journalism team, Jack Phillips gets special mention, and up-to-date reports—they're consistently the number one go-to-source for the *MADNESS* series of textbooks content.

The Heritage Foundation: Has provided the lion's share of book content for most every chapter of *Voting Madness*. For the third year in a row, they ranked as the No. 1 think tank in the world for "Significant Impact on Public Policy," according to the latest edition of the University of Pennsylvania's annual report on think tanks. Heritage also ranked first again in the "Best Use of the Internet" category, the think tank's second consecutive year at the top of that category.

Thomas More Society: Phill Kline, Director of the Amistad Project of the Thomas More Society at this not-for-profit, national public interest law firm is dedicated to restoring respect in law for life, family, and religious liberty. Based in Chicago, the Thomas More Society defends and fosters support for these causes by providing high quality pro bono legal services from local trial courts all the way to the United States Supreme Court.

von Spakovsky, Hans A: Is a Senior Legal Fellow and Manager of the Election Law Reform Initiative in the Edwin Meese III Center for Legal and Judicial Studies at The Heritage Foundation and former Commissioner on the Federal Election Commission for two years and am a former career Counsel to the Assistant Attorney General for Civil Rights at the U.S. Department of Justice (DOJ). At the DOJ, he coordinated enforcement of federal voting rights laws including the VRA. Hans von Spakovsky is also a former member of the Presidential Advisory Commission on Election Integrity; the Board of Advisors of the U.S. Election Assistance Commission; the Registration and Election Board of Fulton County, Georgia; the Electoral Board of Fairfax County, Virginia; and the Virginia Advisory Board to the U.S. Commission on Civil Rights. His extensive works dominate the content of *Voting Madness*.

Some readers of *Voting Madness* will accuse me, without knowing the facts of course, of being a closet Republican and Trump supporter. The first claim is false and the second is misstated. For the record, I'm an independent and centrist voter who has never registered for a political party and abstained from voting for the most "sapient" presidential candidate in the 2016 and 2020 elections on ethical principles as being the Founder and CEO of the SAPIENT Being.

However, prior to that, I have voted for five presidential Democratic Party candidates and four Republican Party candidates in my lifetime as follows: D-Carter in 1976, R-Reagan in 1980 and 1984, no vote in 1988 (as I had a hot date that election night), D-Clinton in 1992 and 1996, R-Bush in 2000 and 2004, and finally D-Obama in 2008 and 2012.

A SAPIENT Being's Preface

The Heritage Foundation has so far documented 1,328 proven cases of voter fraud since America's founding. Nonetheless, these numbers are miniscule compared to the millions of legal votes cast. Even if they likely represent the tip of an iceberg of voter fraud—there are not enough "proven" cases in the 2020 election to alter the seven million plus Joe Biden election victory margin. Or are there?

Is there some truth to Donald Trump's claims of a "stolen election" and "massive voter fraud" to justify his 2020 election loss when you analyze huge pro-Biden vote dumps after election night in key battleground states? If we replace the phrases of "stolen election" and "massive voter fraud" with "gamed" election and massive voter "irregularities"—does he have a case?

Furthermore, if we quantify these 2020 election gaming and irregularities by including the effect from election law changes enacted during the pandemic; combined with the subliminal leftist influence of big tech; a tsunami of fake news and false narratives, or voter fraud news suppression by mainstream media; and record setting funding by left leaning groups—yes, Trump has a case!

As you will discover in *Voting Madness*, the combined impacts of "gaming" and "irregularities" and perhaps outright voter "manipulation"—could have influenced millions—perhaps tens of millions of American votes—mostly Millennials—to the overwhelming benefit of Biden and Democratic candidates.

Trump's legal team submitted more than 800 sworn eyewitness statements across six states consisting of affidavits, whistleblower accounts, witnesses, expert testimony, video and photographic evidence, statistical anomalies, and mathematical analyses to provide respective state and federal courts with innumerable demonstrations of mismanaged ballots, voting machine irregularities, due process transgressions, equal protection violations, actual fraud, and more.

The vast majority have been dismissed due to improper legal procedures, lack of evidence or legal precedent, and some have been debunked and withdrawn. Yet others cannot be explained away—and until they are/or not—ongoing election integrity will be in doubt.

And what about further scrutiny of the myths of voter suppression, ID requirements, and the 'so-called' election integrity measures HR1 and NPV to restore voter confidence?

Like all *MADNESS* textbooks, *Voting Madness* offers an opportunity to be part of the solution to these many problems. For some of you this *MADNESS* book will be a revelation, an epiphany, a sapient being moment. For others, it will be a triggering event, denial of truth, and a painful intervention.

Are you interested in learning about the depth and breadth of voter fraud, election irregularities, manipulation, and assaults on American democracy and how to work together to reform them before they destroy our republic? If yes, please read on and if you also believe in the message of this book and willing to fight for it—please considering joining or participating in one of the three SAPIENT Being programs below.

Make Free Speech Again On Campus (MFSAOC) Program

Provide high school and college students the opportunity to start SAPIENT Being campus clubs, chapters, and alliances where independent, liberal, and conservative minded students can meet, discuss, and debate important issues and develop sapience in the process. Learn more about the process of practicing, protecting, and promoting viewpoint diversity, freedom of speech, and intellectual humility as part of the Make Free Speech Again On Campus (MFSAOC) program for on or off site campus groups at https://www.sapientbeing.org/programs.

World Of Writing Warriors (WOWW) Program

Return free speech, open dialogue and civil discourse to high school and college students and journalists without the cancel culture against those with differences in opinion, ideologies, and practices. Encourage open debate, dialogue, and the free expression of alternative and non-orthodox viewpoints with the goal of creating a World Of Writing Warriors (WOWW) program at https://www.sapientbeing.org/programs that upholds journalistic standards throughout all types of campus journalism and media.

Sapient Conservative Textbooks (SCT) Program

Relevant and current events textbooks program to help return conservative values, viewpoint diversity, and sapience to high school and college students and enlighten them on the many blessings to humankind that are the direct result of American exceptionalism, Western European culture, and Judeo-Christian values. The ethos for every textbook in the Sapient Conservative Textbooks (SCT) program is truth without bias and for more information on the 50 titles please visit the program website at https://www.fratirepublishing.com/madnessbooks.

Are You a Sapient Being or Want to Be One?

Sapience, also known as wisdom, is the ability to think and act using knowledge, experience, understanding, common sense and insight. Sapience is associated with attributes such as intelligence, enlightenment, unbiased judgment, compassion, experiential self-knowledge, self-actualization, and virtues such as ethics and benevolence.

Being a sapient being is not about identity politics, it's about doing what is right and borrows many of the essential qualities of Centrism that supports strength, tradition, open mindedness, and policy based on evidence not ideology.

Sapient beings are independent minded thinkers that achieve common sense solutions that appropriately address America's and the world's most pressing issues. They gauge situations based on context and reason, consideration, and probability. They are open minded and exercise conviction and willing to fight for it on the intellectual battlefield. Sapient beings don't blindly and recklessly follow their feelings or emotions.

Their unifying ideology is based on the truth, reason, logic, scientific method, and pragmatism—and not necessarily defined by compromise, moderation, or any particular faith—but is considerate of them.

Most importantly, per a letter written by Princeton professor Robert George in 2017 and endorsed by 28 professors from three Ivy League universities for incoming freshmen, "Think for yourself!"

George's letter continues:

Thinking for yourself means questioning dominant ideas even when others insist on their being treated as unquestionable. It means deciding what one believes not by conforming to fashionable opinions, but by taking the trouble to learn and honestly consider the strongest arguments to be advanced on both or all sides of questions—including arguments for positions that others revile and want to stigmatize and against positions others seek to immunize from critical scrutiny.

The love of truth and the desire to attain it should motivate you to think for yourself. The central point of a college education is to seek truth and to learn the skills and acquire the virtues necessary to be a lifelong truth-seeker. Open-mindedness, critical thinking, and debate are essential to discovering the truth. Moreover, they are our best antidotes to bigotry.

Merriam-Webster's first definition of the word "bigot" is a person "who is obstinately or intolerantly devoted to his or her own opinions and prejudices." The only people who need fear open-minded inquiry and robust debate are the actual bigots, including those on campuses or in the broader society who seek to protect the hegemony of their opinions by claiming that to question those opinions is itself bigotry.

So, don't be tyrannized by public opinion. Don't get trapped in an echo chamber. Whether you in the end reject or embrace a view, make sure you decide where you stand by critically assessing the arguments for the competing positions. Think for yourself. Good luck to you in college!

Now, that might sound easy. But you will find—as you may have discovered already in high school—that thinking for yourself can be a challenge. It always demands self-discipline, and these days can require courage.

In today's climate, it's all-too-easy to allow your views and outlook to be shaped by dominant opinion on your campus or in the broader academic culture. The danger any student—or faculty member—faces today is falling into the vice of conformism, yielding to groupthink, the orthodoxy.

At many colleges and universities what John Stuart Mill called "the tyranny of public opinion" does more than merely discourage students from dissenting from prevailing views on moral, political, and other types of questions. It leads them to suppose that dominant views are so obviously correct that only a bigot or a crank could question them.

Since no one wants to be, or be thought of as, a bigot or a crank, the easy, lazy way to proceed is simply by falling into line with campus orthodoxies. Don't do it!

To be sure, our overly-politicized culture has a hard time viewing any "verbal cacophony" as a sign of strength and vibrancy. And perhaps nowhere is this truer than on many college campuses where political correctness is rampant, groupthink is common, and social media "mobs" arise in a flash to intimidate anyone who openly strays from the prevailing orthodoxy.

At the SAPIENT Being we're not intimidated—and our primary purpose is to seek the truth by enhancing viewpoint diversity, promoting intellectual humility, protecting freedom of speech and expression while developing sapience in the process—no matter what the cost on the intellectual battlefield, campus classroom, and marketplace of ideas. This is our ethos! Is it yours?

Best regards and sapiently yours,

Corey Lee Wilson

S.A.P.I.E.N.T. Being

1 – Voter & Election Fraud Convictions Are a Fact and So Is the Data

Credit: WYKT.com.

The general consensus in mainstream media, big tech, and many Democrats regarding 2020 election and voting fraud claims: There's no evidence of widespread fraud in the 2020 election and voting officials from both political parties have stated publicly that the election went well, and international observers confirmed there were no serious irregularities. Any claims otherwise are considered "false" or "fake news" or "conspiracy theories" and it's time to move on.

Voter fraud has become an increasingly partisan issue in recent years and came to the forefront of the 2020 election. Republicans have warned that mail-in ballots, same-day registration and lack of voter ID laws create ripe opportunities for liberal mischief. Democrats counter that efforts to curb those things are part of a larger plot by the GOP to suppress voting from poor and minority communities, core Democratic constituencies.

The Democratic Party line treats voter fraud as little more than a Republican Party (GOP) fever dream—and if it is conspiracy theory labeled with false accusations—why did President Joe Biden spent decades of his career sounding the alarm about it. Biden, the Democratic standard bearer, consistently shared GOP concerns about voter fraud during his 36 years as a United States senator from Delaware per the September 2020 article in *New York Post* by Jon Levine titled "Joe Biden spent decades warning of voter fraud—now called a myth by Dems."

Throughout the 1980s and 1990s, Biden worked closely with now-Senate Minority Leader Mitch McConnell to stiffen penalties for voter fraud. "Should Voters Be Allowed To Register On

Election Day? No," Biden wrote in an op-ed to a now-defunct Wilmington, Delaware newspaper in 1977. He even chided President Carter at the time for proposing it.

A "reservation I have and one that is apparently shared by some of the top officials within the Department of Justice is that the president's proposal could lead to a serious increase in vote fraud," Biden wrote.

In 1988 Biden introduced the "Anti-Corruption Act," which McConnell co-sponsored. The bill would have enacted penalties for anyone who deprived anyone of "a fair and impartially conducted election process through the use of fraudulent ballots or voter registration forms or the filing of fraudulent campaign reports."

Biden and McConnell tried again in 1989 and Sen. Strom Thurmond was also a co-sponsor of the bill. "Current law does not permit prosecution of election fraud … This bill makes it a federal offense to corrupt any state or local election process," Biden argued on the Senate floor. McConnell noted in his own floor assessment that it would "raise the maximum penalty for both election fraud and public corruption to 10 years in federal prison and a $10,000 fine." Unfortunately for all voting Americans and safe elections, the bill failed.

The Right to Vote Defines the Essence of American Citizenship & Exceptionalism

Fast forward to 2020, and many of the most troubling 2020 voting irregularities took place in states that set aside laws enacted by state legislatures in favor of sweeping changes ordered by governors, secretaries of state, and courts during the pandemic. Many of these changes enabled the Democratic Party strategy of "stuffing the ballot box" to their advantage in the 2020 elections.

Before the pandemic, President Barak Obama's chief of staff Rahm Emanuel famously said in 2008, "You never want a serious crisis to go to waste. I mean, it's an opportunity to do things that you think you could not do before." In 2020, he was so right.

Our right to vote defines the essence of American citizenship and it provides the bedrock upon which our democratic form of government survives. The greatest social struggles in our history, from the emotional impetus for the American Revolution itself, to the struggle for women's suffrage and the battle for civil rights, have all had at their core the acquisition of the vote for those who were disenfranchised. To a democracy, there can be no greater crime than voter fraud. A single falsely cast vote corrupts the entire electoral process.

An independent, nationwide analysis of voter rolls in 42 states has identified thousands of probable deceased and duplicate registrants, as well as cases of individuals credited for voting more than once. The Public Interest Legal Foundation (PILF) has launched the Safeguarding America's Votes and Elections (SAVE) Database as an analysis tool to track voter roll deficiencies and potential problem areas across America. Per PILF, the groundbreaking findings in their national report indicates that the SAVE Database raises serious concerns over the integrity of states' voter files.

After PILF collected data from 42 states and put it into a format where it could be critically studied, it was rigorously compared to commercial and government databases to increase confidence in the conclusions with particular emphasis on validating identities matched across state lines. Their September 2020 report, which is covered in this section, is titled "Critical Condition: American Voter Rolls Filled with Errors, Dead Voters, and Duplicate Registrations."

Also included with the data were voter history fields, namely, data about when each registrant voted. The combination of state election data, commercial data, and federal sources such as the Social Security Death Index, provides researchers with perhaps the best platform ever constructed to analyze the health of the voter rolls and catalogue potential vulnerabilities.

The findings are a helpful starting point for state election officials to review the findings and make final determinations and take appropriate actions.

Notable Safeguarding America's Votes and Elections (SAVE) Database Findings:

- 349,773: total number of potentially deceased registrants across 41 states.

- Michigan, Florida, New York, Texas, and California account for roughly 51% of national dead registrants.

- In 2016, 7,890 registrants were apparently credited for voting after death.

- In 2018, 6,718 registrants were credited for voting after death.

- North Carolina leads the U.S. in dead registrants credited for voting after death.

- 43,760 likely duplicate registrants appear to have cast second votes in 2016 from the same address.

- 37,889 likely duplicate registrants appear to have cast second votes in 2018 from the same address.

- Thousands of these apparent double votes were exclusively mail ballots.

- 8,360 – Number of registrants apparently registered in 2 states and credited for voting in both states in 2018.

- 5,500 – Number of apparently duplicate registrants credited for voting twice in the same state from 2 different addresses in 2018.

- 34,000 – Number of registrants credited for voting from apparently non-residential addresses in 2018.

Protecting the American Electoral Process

As noted per The Heritage Foundation: Something as critical as election integrity can't be left to a simple honor system. In the freest nation in the world, our system of government and our very liberty depend on free and fair elections. Whether they're selecting a school board member, mayor or the president of the United States, every American must be able to trust the process, or the democratic system itself breaks down.

When someone commits voter fraud, the process is no longer fair, everyone's vote gets diluted, and in some cases, election results are changed.

For those of you who might say, "but it's only a few fraudulent votes," read on and you'll see local and municipal elections decided by a couple of votes, state assembly and Congressional house races decided by a dozen or so votes, governor and senate decided by a few hundred votes give or take.

Finally and most graphically, it took only 537 verified and certified votes out of almost six million cast in Florida in the 2000 presidential election to give George W. Bush the edge over Al Gore nationally with 271 to 266 electoral votes. Yes, 537 votes decided the 2020 president election! Please let that sink in whenever you hear "a few votes cannot make a difference!" Oh yes they can!

After an intense recount process and the United States Supreme Court's decision in *Bush v. Gore*, Bush won Florida's electoral votes by a margin of only 537 votes out of almost six million cast (9/1000 of 1%) and, as a result, became the president-elect winning the electoral vote 271 to 266. Let this historical voting lesson sink in.

Contrary to the claims of many on the left, voter fraud is a very real problem as shown by The Heritage Foundation. As the Supreme Court noted when it upheld Indiana's voter ID law, flagrant examples of voter fraud have been documented throughout this nation's history.

The National Commission on Federal Election Reform has said that in many close elections, fraud can absolutely change the outcome. Cases of local elections getting overturned because of fraud have occurred in New Jersey, Indiana, and other states.

Although hundreds of people have been convicted in recent years, voter fraud often goes undetected. And even when it's discovered, overburdened prosecutors rarely prioritize these cases. Fraudsters can steal votes and change election outcomes in several ways, including:

- Voting in someone else's name.
- Registering in multiple locations to vote multiple times in the same election.
- Voting even though they're not eligible because they're felons or noncitizens.
- Or paying or intimidating people to vote for certain candidates.

Unfortunately, many on the left and Democratic Party are attempting to make election fraud easier by fighting laws that require an ID to vote. They've pushed to get noncitizens and jailed inmates to vote. And they've sued states that have tried to purge their voter rolls of people registered in multiple states. These are examples of voting madness!

How Can We Fix the Problem?

Per the Heritage Foundation: Since states control much of the electoral process, they must pass laws requiring government-issued IDs to vote stresses the Heritage Foundation: That ensures people aren't stealing others' identities and their right to vote.

States should join voter registration crosscheck programs to identify voters registered in multiple places. One crosscheck program has identified hundreds of thousands of potential duplicate registrations across 30 states as well as evidence of illegal double voting.

States should also compare voter rolls with government records to identify convicted felons and noncitizens who should be removed from the rolls. And the federal government should cooperate with these efforts and make Department of Homeland Security and other databases available to state officials.

Preserving this great experiment that is America depends on having free and fair elections where all Americans can trust the process and the results. This is what defines us more than anything else as Americans.

Something as critical as election integrity can't be left to a simple honor system. One of the most important roles of government is to safeguard the electoral process and ensure that every voter's right to cast a ballot is protected. That not only protects our right to vote; that's how we protect the future of our very republic. This must be taken seriously.

Types of Electoral Fraud or Abuse

Absentee ballot vote fraud: A person attempts to fill out and turn in an absentee ballot containing false information. For example, this can occur when a person attempts to fill out and turn in an absentee ballot with the name of a false or non-existent voter. The term can extend to manipulation, deception, or intimidation of absentee voters.

Ballot stuffing: Casting illegal votes or submitting more than one ballot per voter.

Electioneering: Ignoring restrictions that usually include limiting the display of signs, handing out campaign literature or soliciting votes within a pre-determined distance of a polling place.

Felon vote fraud: The casting of a ballot by a person convicted of a felony who is not eligible to vote as a result of the conviction.

Fraud by election officials: Manipulation of ballots by officials administering the election, such as tossing out ballots or casting ballots in voters' names.

Vote-buying: Agreements between voters and others to buy and sell votes, such as a candidate paying voters to vote for him or her.

Votes cast in the names of deceased people: The name of a deceased person remains on a state's official list of registered voters and a living person fraudulently casts a ballot in that name.

Voter impersonation: A person claims to be someone else when casting a vote.

Voter registration fraud: Filling out and submitting a voter registration card for a fictional person or filling out a voter registration card with the name of a real person but without that person's consent and forging his or her signature on the card.

Voter suppression: A variety of tactics aimed at lowering or suppressing the number of voters who might otherwise vote in a particular election.

The Heritage Foundation's Election Fraud Database

America's leading election and voting think tank without equal is The Heritage Foundation and their Election Fraud Database, presents a sampling of recent proven instances of election fraud from across the country per Hans von Spakovsky. This database is not an exhaustive comprehensive list. It does not capture all cases and certainly does not capture reported instances that are not investigated or prosecuted.

The reported cases in the database represent just the tip of the iceberg, given many other potential cases of fraud that election officials and prosecutors have failed to investigate or prosecute. The database demonstrates the vulnerabilities in the election system and the many ways fraud is, and can be, committed. In addition to diluting the votes of legitimate voters, fraud can have an impact in close elections, and we have many close elections in this country.

Every fraudulent vote that is cast invalidates the vote of an eligible voter, effectively disenfranchising that voter. In addition to diluting the votes of legitimate voters, instances of fraud can have—and have had—an impact in close elections, altering the outcome. We have many close elections in this country.

There are people who claim that election fraud is massive, and those who claim it is exceedingly rare or doesn't occur at all. But as the U.S. Supreme Court said in 2008 in *Crawford v. Marion County Election Board*, "flagrant examples of such fraud … have been documented throughout this Nation's history by respected historians and journalists … [that] demonstrate that not only is the risk of voter fraud real but that it could affect the outcome of a close election."

As von Spakovsky notes: The big problem is that nobody really knows the extent of election fraud, including The Heritage Foundation. While we are not making any definitive claims about the extent of election fraud in our country, we are confident in saying that there are far too many vulnerabilities in our current system. The important thing is that people must have trust in the outcome, which is difficult to do, in large part, because of the vulnerabilities that currently exist.

To be clear, this database is not an exhaustive or comprehensive list of all election fraud in the states. It does not capture all cases and certainly does not capture reported instances or allegations of election fraud, some of which may be meritorious, some not, that are not investigated or prosecuted.

Because of vulnerabilities that exist in state's election laws, election fraud is relatively easy to commit and difficult to detect after the fact. Moreover, some public officials appear to be unconcerned with election fraud and fail to pursue cases that are reported to them. It is a general truism that you don't find what you don't look for.

This database is intended to highlight cases of proven fraud and the many ways in which fraud has been committed. This fraud, committed by Democrats, Republicans, and independents, happened because of vulnerabilities in the states' election laws.

Reforms intended to ensure election integrity do not disenfranchise voters and, in fact, protect their right to vote and their confidence in the fairness and integrity of election outcomes no matter who wins. Preventing, deterring, and prosecuting election fraud is essential to protecting the integrity of our voting process.

Per von Spakovsky: Winning elections leads to political power and the incentives to take advantage of security vulnerabilities are great, so it is important that we take reasonable, common-sense steps to make it hard to cheat, while making it easy for legitimate voters to vote.

As these cases and the database demonstrate, the threats to election integrity and instances of election fraud throughout the country continue to jeopardize fair and free elections for the American people.

Americans Deserve an Electoral Process They Can Trust and Count On

The Heritage Foundation's Election Fraud Database tracking list started in 2017, has to this date (June 2021), over 1,300 proven cases of voter fraud, and it's their estimation that this number is only "the tip of the iceberg." However, if we look for proven cases of voter fraud that could have impacted the 2020 election results, the results are statistically insignificant and show little or no effect in altering election results.

Nonetheless, if we look at voting irregularities from mail-in and absentee ballots, how votes were accepted and ballots counted during pandemic influenced 2020 election, election law changes immediately prior to the 2020 election, and other factors such as the influence of mainstream and social media as well as non-profit organizations, ballot harvesting, voter ID requirements—that yes—we have a whole textbook full of issues to explore and analyze in *Voting Madness.*

Going back to "the tip of the iceberg" scenario, no one knows for certain at this point in time, the depth and extent of voter fraud, so let's make some assumptions based on the most likely scenario that these proven cases are the tip of an iceberg, as many independent organizations have demonstrated. But how big an iceberg we might ask, knowing that 90 percent of the mass of an iceberg is below the water line and only ten percent is exposed above water?

If only ten percent of an iceberg is visible but the rest, 90 percent is not and concealed below the water line, extrapolating from the iceberg example, there could be 900% more undiscovered cases, or 11,700 plus. Depending on your point of view, this number could be unimportant—or as history has shown using the current 1,300 plus proven cases—it could be relevant as it doesn't take a large number of fraudulent votes to alter an election.

So, with that established premise—suppose for conjecture and learning purposes only—the number of unknown cases of voter fraud is much higher than 11,700. Suppose we use instead the odds of being struck by lightning in your lifetime which is 1 in 3,000 chance?

If we now speculate (and calculate for example and discussion purposes only) the number of voter fraud incidences occurred at the same rate of being struck by lightning, that is 1 out of 3,000 voters (equals 0.033 percent, or 3/100 of one percent) in the 2020 election committed some form of voter fraud, the 2020 election impact scenario becomes more noteworthy and possibly alarming!

If we use the same 0.033 percent figure from above to estimate (more like guestimate) out of the 159 million registered voters that cast ballots in the 2020 general election (out of 239 million eligible voters)—then mathematically, the number of "guesstimated" voter fraud incidences could be 86,333 using this hypothetical voting fraud factor.

If each of these 86,333 incidences of voter fraud in turn were responsible for 10 fraudulent votes cast, the total number of fraudulent votes cast "nationally" as a total from all states could by 863,333 (close to a million)!

Compare that with the 311,899 vote advantage Biden had over Trump in the final vote totals for the six contested swing states, and if half of these national total fraudulent votes, were cast in these six contested swing states in Joe Biden's favor, and they were somehow magically removed by an omnipotent sapient voting god—431,666 fraudulent votes would have been removed from Biden's total and Trump would have carried those six contested swing states and won the electoral vote by a razor thin margin of 270 to 268 votes—and reelected to a second term.

Pure fantasy some may think—or it's possible say others. Please remember, these are hypothetical numbers and a learning case scenario to show the multiplying impact of voter fraud and also how a relatively insignificant vote advantage, like the 537 votes that won Bush the presidential election over Gore in 2020.

Why Safeguarding Our Elections Matters and the Risks That Threaten Them

Per Hans von Spakovsky's November 2020 "Why Safeguarding Our Elections Matters" article in The Daily Signal: The survival of our democratic republic depends on Americans' belief that their vote counts and their continued faith in the fairness and security of our electoral process.

Americans throughout history have made tremendous sacrifices to safeguard our democratic republic—and with it, the right to vote. Today, the threat to our voting system is election fraud. This is a very real issue, as recognized by the Supreme Court. Steps must be taken to combat fraud and other weaknesses in our electoral system that could result in stolen votes and elections.

Americans throughout history have made tremendous sacrifices to safeguard our democratic republic—and with it, the right to vote. We cannot disregard their sacrifice or squander their precious gift and legacy to us. And when we say "us" (think US)—we mean the entire rainbow of Americans of every race, creed, color, sex, ideology, religion, etc.—e pluribus unum, out of many, one (the motto of the US).

Per von Spakovsky, steps must be taken to combat fraud and other weaknesses in our electoral system that could result in stolen votes and elections. Failure to do so—is un-American!

Nobody knows for sure how much election fraud actually is committed. But it is beyond dispute that American elections are vulnerable to fraud and administrative errors that could make the difference in a close election—especially in state and local elections, and even federal elections. Example: the 9th Congressional District race in North Carolina that was overturned in 2018 due to absentee ballot fraud and illegal vote harvesting.

Election Fraud Denial Also a Serious Threat

Despite the threat that fraud poses to our democratic republic, the Democrats consistently deny the existence of election fraud. Even after being presented with case after case after case of evidence, those on the left often dismiss the problem as "not widespread" enough to warrant action.

Per Hans von Spakovsky, saying that "widespread" is the only criteria worth considering is absurd and he should know from his unequaled career as a Senior Legal Fellow and Manager of the Election Law Reform Initiative in the Edwin Meese III Center for Legal and Judicial Studies at The Heritage Foundation and former Commissioner on the Federal Election Commission for two years and am a former career Counsel to the Assistant Attorney General for Civil Rights at the U.S. Department of Justice, where he coordinated enforcement of federal voting rights laws including the Voting Rights Act (VRA).

The Heritage Foundation's Election Fraud Database demonstrates that there are many ways to engage in election fraud, and that it occurs often enough that we should be concerned about it and should try to address it. Liberal media and fake news attacks on the database have not been able to find a single instance of an error.

Instead, media attacks try to diminish the culpability of those found guilty of fraud despite the fact that every single case represents an instance in which a public official, usually a prosecutor, thought the offense serious enough to act upon it.

A 2005 report by the Commission on Federal Election Reform, a bipartisan commission led by former President Jimmy Carter, was clear that election fraud does exist, that it must be deterred to preserve election integrity, that it could make the difference in a close election, and that absentee ballots "remain the largest source of potential voter fraud." We have an obligation to secure our elections against these vulnerabilities.

In fact, one has to consider: Why has a legion of election fraud deniers so suddenly and so rapidly materialized at this moment in history? And why are they against commonsense reforms that the vast majority of Americans support, such as voter ID and maintaining the accuracy of voter registration rolls?

Tragically, election fraud has become a politicized topic. Americans—especially those in vulnerable communities who are the most susceptible to fraud—will suffer if we let partisanship come before what should be our shared goal of ensuring our elections are secure, accurate, and transparent.

The Vote Fraud That Democrats Refuse to Acknowledge

Per the *New York Post* article "The vote fraud that Democrats refuse to see" by Deroy Murdock in July 2017: An example of the Democrats new math could be: 265 + 742 + 765 + 953 + 7,474 = 0.

This fuzzy math sums up Democrats' orthodoxy on vote fraud: As the bulletproof evidence of fraud adds up, they still claim, "There's nothing to see here." Not even these hard numbers, based on verified vote-fraud cases, move their acceptance of this reality into the realm of positive integers.

This pathological denial is even more intense. Not since the outcome of the Carter-Baker Commission on Election Reform in 2005 has this topic been a national priority—until then President Trump in 2017 addressed vote fraud seriously enough to appoint a bipartisan panel, the Presidential Advisory Commission on Election Integrity, to get to the bottom of it, after his 2016 election win.

Never mind, leading Leftists insisted. The issue is bogus, and the commission is evil.

According to Sen. Bernie Sanders (Socialist-Vermont), "The sole purpose of this commission is to propagate a myth and to give encouragement to Republican governors and state legislators to increase voter suppression."

The Brennan Center for Justice's Michael Waldman believes that President Trump "set up a probe of an imaginary threat." Chris Carson, chief of the League of Women Voters, predicts that the Pence-Kobach commission will "undermine our elections by spreading falsehoods."

"The truth remains that it is more likely for someone to be struck by lightning than for someone to have committed voter fraud," Rep. Raul Grijalva (D-Arizona) said in May. "Voter fraud is a non-issue in our country."

These and other Democrats ignore concrete proof that vote fraud exists but when Democrats add up the values below (bolded)—they still arrive as the same sum of zero as if they don't exist:

- In May 2016, CBS2 Los Angeles identified **265** dead voters in southern California. Many cast ballots "year after year."

- The Heritage Foundation's non-exhaustive survey confirms, since 2000, at least **742** criminal vote-fraud convictions.

- North Carolina announced in April 2014 that 13,416 dead voters were registered, and 81 of them recently had voted. Among 35,750 North Carolinians also registered in other states, **765** voted in November 2012, both inside and outside the Tarheel State.

- South Carolina's attorney general concluded in January 2012 that **953** people "were deceased at the time of their participation in recent elections."

- The Public Interest Legal Foundation recently discovered that Virginia removed 5,556 non-citizens from its voter rolls between 2011 and last May. Among these non-Americans, 1,852 had cast a total of **7,474** illegal ballots across multiple elections.

Craftier liberals have inched away from the baseless "Vote fraud = Loch Ness Monster" argument. Now, some claim, vote fraud is not "widespread." What will they say after they read *Voting Madness*?

Why Do Democrats Pretend Voter Fraud Doesn't Exist?

From the November 2018 *Investor's Business Daily* article "Why Do Democrats Pretend Voter Fraud Doesn't Exist?" they point out how Texas State Attorney General Ken Paxton decided to crack down on voter fraud before the 2018 midterm elections. So far, he's prosecuted 33 people for 97 counts of voter fraud that year alone. Among the discoveries was a voter fraud ring that had received financial support from the former head of the Texas Democratic Party.

Yet there are those—mostly Democrats and mainstream journalists—who continue to insist that voter fraud is a myth. *The New York Times'* Glenn Thrush once declared, for example, that "there is essentially no voter fraud in this country."

When shown concrete examples, the response is usually "well, it's not widespread."

But that reflects a fundamental misunderstanding of elections. You don't need "widespread" voter fraud to change election outcomes, just small-scale efforts targeted on tight or consequential elections.

The fact is that committing voter fraud isn't all that difficult, but minimizing it is easy. Cleaning up registration rolls, enacting voter ID requirements, using paper ballots, and implementing better controls on early and absentee voting would make non-citizen voting and other forms of fraud virtually impossible.

Critics of such efforts say that they will only serve to suppress the vote of minorities and the poor—that is, voters who tend to vote Democratic. They want to make it easier and easier to register and vote.

But there's no evidence that voter ID laws suppress turnout. In fact, of 11 states that adopted strict voter ID laws, nine either saw increased turnout in 2016, or had turnout rates higher than the national average, the Heritage Foundation notes. The data are not on their side. Consider the latest from the Pew Research Center: In 2018, voter participation surged, and "last year's midterm voters [were] the most racially and ethnically diverse ever."

Nor does cleaning up registration rolls, aggressively pursuing voter fraud cases, using paper ballots, or other measures to ensure the integrity of the ballot suppress legitimate voters.

Those who say voter fraud is no big deal should realize something. Every single vote cast fraudulently cancels out one legitimate vote. They need to ask themselves how they'd feel if it was their vote being canceled.

U.S. Election Fraud is Real—And It's Being Ignored

Covered in "U.S. Election Fraud is Real—And It Is Being Ignored" article in October 2020 by Hans von Spakovsky in *The National Interest*: Although talk of voter fraud increased to a fever pitch in the 2020 election, The Heritage Foundation's updated election fraud database is up past 1,300 proven instances of voter fraud.

The fact is, election fraud is real, and as many of the examples in Heritage's Election Fraud Database show, they can change the outcome of an election and it's important to remember that every fraudulent vote that is cast invalidates the vote of an eligible voter.

Heritage's database is by no means comprehensive. It doesn't capture all voter fraud cases and certainly doesn't capture reported instances that aren't even investigated or prosecuted. The database is intended to demonstrate the vulnerabilities in the election system and the many ways in which fraud is committed.

They to keep a close eye on public information about potential cases through local news stories, court documents, county records, and police reports. But even that is difficult to do in a country as large as the United States, with hundreds of elections every year.

This sampling of cases illustrates the existence and effect of voter fraud. Most importantly, the public must understand that fraud can occur throughout the entire process of registering and voting.

Examples include impersonation fraud at the polls; false voter registrations; duplicate voting; fraudulent absentee ballots; vote buying; illegal assistance and intimidation of voters; ineligible voting, such as by aliens; altering of vote counts; and ballot petition fraud.

Fortunately, we know what policies work to combat voter fraud and they are pointed out in the "More Proof That Voter Fraud Is Real, and Bipartisan" August 2019 article by Jason Snead in The Daily Signal. Sapient voter identification laws and programs to clean up wildly inaccurate voter rolls help to verify that only eligible individuals are voting, and that they are casting ballots in the jurisdictions where they actually reside.

Interstate cross-check programs, meanwhile, compare state voter rolls and help to identify duplicate registrations and single out double-voters.

These policies are not only common sense, they are urgently needed. A 2012 Pew study found that one out of every eight voter registrations were inaccurate, with 2.8 million people registered in two or more states.

Across the nation, hundreds of counties have more registered voters than residents. In June 2019, California began a process of removing a staggering 5 million inactive registrations from its rolls—but only after it was sued by Judicial Watch.

Unfortunately, unless it's a Republican committing the fraud, many liberal politicians and activists routinely insist that voter fraud is a figment of conservatives' imaginations—or they assert that it's so rare it's inconsequential.

Yet, elections have been overturned due to fraud—sometimes, because of only a small handful of illegal ballots. Liberals label policies such as requiring IDs at the polling place "racist," and casually extend that derisive label to anyone who supports them.

According to the Census Bureau, black, Hispanic, and Asian voter turnout all increased by double digits from 2014 to 2018. In Georgia—where Democratic gubernatorial candidate Stacey Abrams refused to concede defeat because of supposed "voter suppression"—black voter registration increased by more than 6 percentage points from the prior midterm, and actually topped white voters in percentage terms, 68.4% compared with 66.8%.

The bottom line? Accusations of voter suppression have no basis in fact—and they are lies, lies, and more lies! So why, then, do we keep hearing them?

For some politicians and activists, election integrity is just too politically valuable. Turning the sanctity of the ballot box into a racially charged wedge issue animates the base, tars their opponents, and provides a convenient scapegoat for Election Day defeats.

Voters deserve better than cynical gamesmanship, and that is especially true when it comes to protecting the integrity of the electoral process.

2 – The 5 Biggest Myths Regarding Voter Fraud, Suppression & Election Integrity

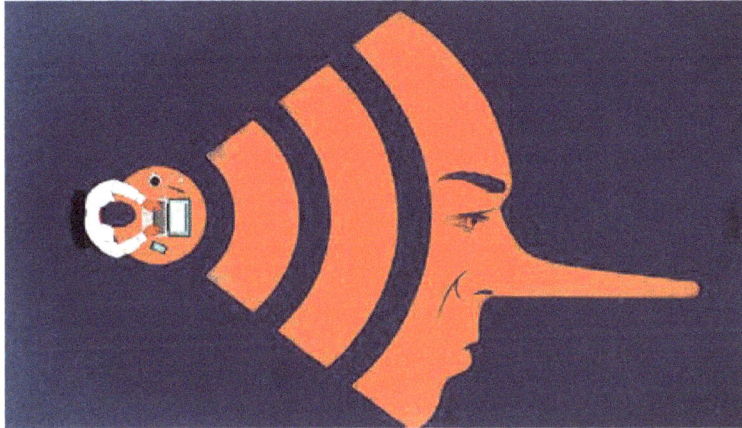

Credit: Science magazine.

Many readers of *Voting Madness* may not be aware of how prevalent and widespread the five common myths related to voter and election fraud are. That's why in this chapter we'll look at the hard facts, unbiased statistics, and overwhelming evidence—and let readers come to their own conclusions about each prevailing myth.

One of the refrains from those who oppose election reforms designed to protect the security and integrity of the voting process is that serious vote fraud is a myth. Downplaying the risks and vulnerabilities for election fraud in the current system exacerbates existing problems and compromises the most sacred right a free people have. One person—one vote.

The threat of vote fraud is real—and it could make a difference in a close election. Dirty voter rolls, mail-in voting, and ballot harvesting are three areas ripe for abuse. Strict voter-ID laws have long been denounced as voter suppression—but the overwhelming evidence shows it's not true. And do illegal aliens and non-citizens vote and affect outcomes? Yes, sometimes.

This chapter will cover and dissect the five common myths of: 1) there is no voter and election fraud in American elections, 2) requiring voter ID leads to or is a form of voter suppression, 3) cleaning up voter rolls is a right-wing conspiracy, 4) the 2016 election Russian interference and Trump, and 5) there is no voting by illegal aliens and non-citizens.

All of these five myths are perpetuated by leftist groups, liberal organizations, and leaders of the Democratic Party to one degree or another and none can be supported by unbiased facts, the truth, and sapience as we shall see in this chapter. We'll call out these myth perpetrators, so they register on your fact check radar screen and are easily spotted for their fake news and false narratives the next time you see, hear, or read them.

Myth 1: There Is No Voter or Election Fraud in America (Fact Check: False)

As documented in the Heritage Foundation Election Fraud Database, voter fraud has a long history in U.S. elections. Since the nation's independence, there have been 1,328 proven cases and counting (as of June 2021), resulting in 1,143 criminal convictions.

There's also overwhelming evidence that outcome-altering voter fraud, irregularities, and manipulations that occurred on and around the 2020 Election that are still under investigation and covered in later chapters in more detail.

Here is a sampling of 16 instances in which courts threw out an election result based in whole or in part on absentee voting fraud, from The Heritage Foundation's database and other sources.

17 Instances Where Courts Threw Out Many Close Elections and Why

Per Fred Lucas, Chief National Affairs Correspondent at The Daily Signal, Veteran White House reporter, Multi-media journalist, and author of the article "15 Election Results That Were Thrown Out Because of Fraudulent Mail-In Ballots," here is a sample below (of the tip of the iceberg) of but a few instances where courts threw out many close elections and the reasons why and also complemented with two more items from the SAPIENT Being:

1) In one of the most high profile cases, the North Carolina Board of Elections decertified the outcome of the 2018 race in the 9th Congressional District and ordered a new election after evidence of absentee ballot fraud emerged. About 61% of all mailed votes were cast for Republican candidate Mark Harris over Democrat Dan McReady, although only 16% of those requesting a ballot were Republicans. In the new election, Republican Dan Bishop stepped in as the party nominee and won.

2) In 2018, Dennis Jones beat Tracy Gray by one vote in a Republican primary in Texas for a seat on the Kaufman County Commissioners Court. Gray challenged the outcome, alleging a vote harvester submitted illegal mail-in ballots, while eligible provisional ballots went uncounted. After a hearing, a state judge invalidated the results and ordered a new election, which Gray won by 404 votes.

3) In another 2018 Texas case, Armando O'Cana seemingly won a run-off race for mayor in Mission, Texas, beating incumbent Norberto "Beto" Salinas. But after strong evidence emerged that O'Cana's campaign had bribed voters, tampered with absentee ballots, and improperly "assisted" voters at the polls, state Judge J. Bonner Dorsey invalidated the result, saying: "I hold or find, by clear and convincing evidence, that the number of illegal votes was in excess of 158."

4) In 2017, Eatonville, Florida Mayor Anthony Grant was convicted of a felony charge of voting fraud and misdemeanor absentee voting violations. Prosecutors said that as a candidate in

2015, Grant coerced absentee voters to cast ballots for him. In at least one case, prosecutors said, Grant personally solicited an absentee vote from a nonresident. Grant, a former mayor, lost the in-person vote but won the election with more than twice the number of absentee ballots that incumbent Bruce Mount got. After Grant's indictment, then-Gov. Rick Scott suspended the mayor. After his conviction, he was sentenced to 400 hours of community service and four years' probation.

This case was more than a decade after the Florida Department of Law Enforcement concluded: "The absentee ballot is the 'tool of choice' for those who are engaging in election fraud."

This 1998 report came after the department concluded an investigation of Miami's mayoral election the year before. A judge had thrown out the result after prosecutors brought a massive fraud case that involved more than 5,000 absentee ballots.

5) In 2017, an Alabama state judge reversed the result of a race for Wetumpka City Council in which incumbent Percy Gill appeared to have won by three votes. Gill's opponent, Lewis Washington, contested the outcome. A trial showed eight absentee ballots cast for Gill either had a forged signature or weren't notarized or signed in front of the requisite number of witnesses.

6) In the 2016 race for mayor of Gordon, Alabama, Elbert Melton won by just 16 votes. Melton later was convicted on two counts of absentee ballot fraud and removed from office. He was sentenced to a year in prison and two years' probation.

7) In 2016, Missouri state Rep. Penny Hubbard won the 2016 Democratic primary in the state's 78th House District by just 90 votes. Her opponent, Bruce Franks Jr., contested the outcome over a lopsided absentee vote tally. Judge Rex Burlison ruled that enough improper absentee ballots were cast to change the results and ordered a new election. Franks won by 1,533 votes.

8) In 2016 in Texas, former Weslaco city commissioner Guadalupe Rivera pleaded guilty to one count of providing illegal "assistance" to a voter in a 2013 race he won by 16 votes. Rivera admitted filling out an absentee ballot "in a way other than the way the voter directed or without direction from the voter." A judge determined that 30 ballots were cast illegally and ordered a new election, which Rivera lost. He initially faced 16 related charges, but 15 were dropped as part of a plea deal. He was sentenced to a year of probation and ordered to pay a $500 fine.

9) In 2015, Fernando Gonzalez clinched a win by 10 votes over Sergio Dias for a seat on the city council of Perth Amboy, New Jersey. After a determination that at least 13 absentee ballots were cast illegally, a state Superior Court overturned the results and ordered a new election. The second time, Gonzalez won by nine votes.

10) New York State Assembly candidate Hector Ramirez pleaded guilty to one count of criminal possession of a forged instrument during his 2014 campaign. Prosecutors charged Ramirez

with deceiving voters into giving their absentee ballots to his campaign on the false premise that it would submit them. Instead, Ramirez's campaign inserted his name on at least 35 absentee ballots, prosecutors said. Ramirez initially won, but a recount determined that he lost by two votes. Bronx Supreme Court Justice Steven Barrett ruled that Ramirez could not run for office again for three years.

11) In 2014 in Pennsylvania, Richard Allen Toney, the former police chief of Harmar Township, pleaded guilty to illegally soliciting absentee ballots to benefit his wife and her running mate in the 2009 Democratic primary for town council. Prosecutors said Toney applied for the ballots, then had them filled out illegally by individuals who were not expected to be absent on Election Day. The absentee ballot count flipped the primary results, securing a victory for his wife's running mate. During a subsequent FBI investigation, prosecutors said, Toney attempted to prevent two grand jury witnesses and others from testifying. He was sentenced to three years' probation.

12) After a 2012 federal investigation of a voter fraud conspiracy in West Virginia, Lincoln County Sheriff Jerry Bowman and County Clerk Donald Whitten pleaded guilty to stuffing ballot boxes and falsifying absentee ballots to try to steal a Democratic primary election in 2010. Lincoln County Commissioner Thomas Ramey pleaded guilty to lying to investigators. Bowman and Ramey were involved in helping Whitten get re-elected. He won the primary, but a judge overturned the election, tossing out 300 fraudulent ballots.

13) One of the more complex cases arose in a rural jurisdiction when the Justice Department brought a civil suit against Noxubee County, Mississippi over a massive absentee voter fraud operation run by the local Democratic Party machine. Prosecutors said notaries paid by the machine took ballots from mail boxes and voted the ballots in place of the intended voters.

On June 29, 2007, U.S. District Judge Tom S. Lee issued an opinion finding that county Democratic Party Chairman Ike Brown worked with the county's Democratic Executive Committee to manipulate the process. Lee determined that Brown violated Section Two of the Voting Rights Act through racially motivated manipulation of ballots, obtained and improperly counted defective absentee ballots, and allowed improper "assistance" of voters to ensure that his favored candidates won.

The 5th U.S. Circuit Court of Appeals affirmed the judgment. The Justice Department entered into a consent decree with Noxubee County's superintendent of general elections, administrator of absentee ballots, registrar, and county government to prohibit discriminatory and illegal voting practices and require officials to report such incidents.

"Dozens of contests were overturned there by the state courts," said Adams, who was involved in the case as a Justice Department civil rights lawyer at the time.

14) In 2004, the Alabama Supreme Court overturned the results of a mayor's race in Guntersville after finding that absentee ballots were cast without proper identification and should have been discarded.

15) In the 2003 mayor's race in East Chicago, Indiana, challenger George Pabey defeated eight-term incumbent Robert Patrick on Election Day, but lost by 278 votes after about 2,000 absentee ballots poured in.

Evidence of voter intimidation and vote buying emerged, and the Indiana Supreme Court ordered a new election. Pabey won with 65% of the vote, as detailed in the 2008 book *Stealing Elections* by journalist John Fund. The fraud led to at least seven convictions or guilty pleas in 2008, according to the Heritage database.

In 2008, when the U.S. Supreme Court upheld Indiana's new voter ID law, the ruling noted that America has a long, well-documented history of election fraud. The court cited the 2005 report of the bipartisan Commission on Federal Election Reform headed by former President Jimmy Carter and former Secretary of State James Baker, which said the "electoral system cannot inspire public confidence if no safeguards exist to deter or detect fraud."

16) At the conclusion of the 2008 Minnesota Senate race, incumbent Republican Senator Norm Coleman was the winner on Election Day by a little over 700 votes out of 2.9 million cast in his race against Al Franken. Franken, represented by Marc Elias along with a huge legal team and backed by millions of dollars, swarmed the recount, aggressively demanding that absentee ballots which had been disqualified and rejected for failing to meet state legal requirements be added to Franken's count, while at the same time arguing that others be denied to Coleman.

Eventually, Elias and his legal team were able to come up with enough absentee ballots to have Franken declared the winner by a 312-vote margin. The Minnesota Supreme Court ultimately stamped its approval on what Elias had accomplished—using litigation to reverse the election results.

17) A Mississippi judge ordered a new 2021 runoff election for a local election in Aberdeen after more than three-quarters of absentee ballots cast in the June 2020 Democratic runoff election were found to be invalid, while a notary involved in the election was arrested.

Myth 2: That Voter ID Requirements Cause Voter Suppression (Fact Check: False)

The progressive left has created a false hue and cry about a supposed loss of voting rights. It claims that support for reforms intended to improve the integrity of the election process, such as voter identification requirements and effective maintenance procedures for statewide voter registration lists, amount to widespread, systemic "voter suppression" of poor and minority voters.

Per J. Christian Adams is the President and General Counsel for the Public Interest Legal Foundation, former Justice Department lawyer who also served on the Presidential Advisory Commission for Election Integrity: It has never been easier to register to vote—or to vote—in America. Adds Adams from his March 2020 Inside Sources article "The Myth of 'Voter

Suppression': But you'd never know it if you listened to all the cries about so called "voter suppression."

Hans von Spakovsky, a former Federal Election Commissioner and currently a senior fellow at the Heritage Foundation, told *The Epoch Times* in May 2021 the voter suppression argument is a ridiculous claim. "There's no voter suppression going on. In fact, we have seen turnout in U.S. elections consistently go up in the last few elections that we've had, while the states have been doing things like putting in voter ID laws" states von Spakovsky.

Public intellectual Dinesh D'Souza, an author and filmmaker, has criticized the Democrat argument that ID requirements suppress voters. "Requiring an ID for airline travel doesn't "suppress travel." Nor do ID requirements for marriage licenses "suppress marriage." So why does the Left insist ID requirements for voting "suppress the vote?" D'Souza challenged on Twitter.

You could search long and hard in the lawbooks containing the United States Code and nowhere will you find one single law that mentions voter suppression. That's because voter suppression is a myth. It is a term made up to smear perfectly legal activities—like voter ID laws—by suggesting it is illegal. However, you can plenty of fake ID sires on the internet like the example below.

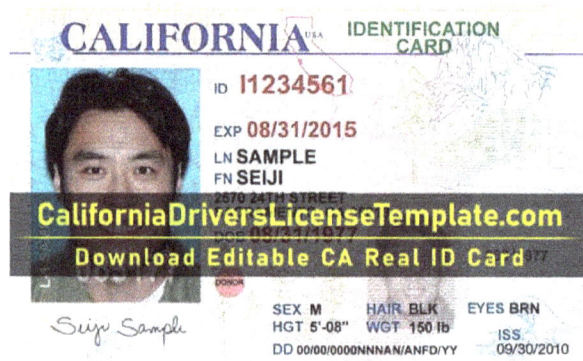

Credit: http://californiadriverslicensetemplate.com/ fake ID kit.

Every election year when you hear someone use the term voter suppression, pay attention. The user almost always has an agenda. Sometimes they want to scare minority voters into believing Jim Crow is returning. Other times they want to criticize perfectly legal practices that have protected the integrity of our elections—like registering to vote, in-precinct voting or citizenship verification.

All of this brings us to a teaching moment about language and the law of elections. The correct terms for suppression are "voter intimidation" or "vote denial." Both are illegal. Vote denial on the basis of race is illegal under the Voting Rights Act. It is what Mississippi election officials did back in the 1950s and, believe it or not, as recently as 2005.

In the latter case of *United States v. Ike Brown*, a case Hans von Spakovsky litigated when he was an attorney at the U.S. Department of Justice, election officials refused to count absentee ballots of some voters on the basis of race. In this case, the victims were white, and the election officials were African American, showing that vote deniers can come in many forms.

Polls show the real concern most Americans have about our elections is voter fraud. A Hill-HarrisX poll shows that voter fraud was the top fear of Republicans, Democrats, and independents alike. So-called voter suppression didn't even come in second or third in the poll.

If laws exist that deny someone the right to vote—such as a poll tax—that's vote denial. If laws exist that make it impossible for minorities to elect a candidate of choice, that's vote dilution. If someone objectively threatens or intimidates a voter, that's voter intimidation. So called voter suppression does neither.

Poll Shows Overwhelming Support for Photo ID Voting Requirement

Shown in the April 2021 *Epoch Times* article "Poll Shows Overwhelming Support for Photo ID Voting Requirement" by GQ Pan: Nearly three-quarters of Americans agree that voters should show photo identification before being allowed to vote, an Associated Press poll suggests.

And yet, fake news media, big tech, academia—and left-leaning organizations like the Brennan Center, George Soros, Center for American Progress, a cornucopia of left leaning groups like Fair Fight, and leaders of the Democratic Party continue to deny that common sense voter ID requirements do not lead to voter suppression, particularly among minorities. As you will see from multiple studies the opposite is true!

Seventy-two percent of Americans participating in the survey, conducted between Mar. 26 and 29, 2020, said they are in favor of requiring all voters to provide photo ID in order to vote. Another 14 percent said they neither support nor oppose the measure, while the remaining 13 percent said they are against such a requirement.

Characterizing Election Integrity Efforts as 'Voter Suppression' Is a False Narrative

According to GQ Pan: A popular claim among election fraud deniers is that working to ensure the integrity of our elections is simply a cover for making voting more difficult—presumably for those who will vote for leftist candidates. This is a complete misunderstanding of our election integrity efforts, and likely a willful one.

Every eligible American citizen should have the opportunity to participate in our electoral system. One of the greatest gifts of American citizenship is political participation. But that gift is subverted when election integrity is not taken seriously and safeguards to protect it are not put in place.

When election fraud or administrative errors by election officials occurs, that means someone else's vote was stolen, diluted, or rejected.

Commonsense protections help promote election integrity. Simple steps such as witness signatures on absentee ballots, official postmarks, in-person voting by all who are able, and photo ID at your polling place and with absentee ballots ensure that every American's vote counts.

These reforms do not make it more difficult to vote and do not "suppress" anyone's vote, as election turnout data over the past decade proves in states that have implemented such reforms. The reforms are intended simply to ensure that we have fair and secure elections. Any claims to the contrary are wrong and deceitful.

Election fraud deniers are signaling that they intend to do nothing about this very real problem. In fact, Democrats in the House are constantly pushing for changes that would make election fraud more likely.

The survival of our democratic republic depends on Americans' belief that their vote counts and their continued faith in the fairness and security of our electoral process.

New Study Confirms Voter ID Laws Don't Hurt Election Turnout

Voter ID laws don't "suppress" anyone's vote as noted in the "New Study Confirms Voter ID Laws Don't Hurt Election Turnout" by Hans von Spakovsky and Caleb Morrison in in the February 2019 edition of The Daily Signal. Among a variety of minority groups and political affiliations, no significant change in turnout occurred after voter ID laws went into effect.

Less than one week after Georgia Democrat Stacey Abrams made inflammatory claims in her 2019 State of the Union response about an epidemic of "voter suppression" jeopardizing the character of our nation, the National Bureau of Economic Research released a study that demonstrates once again that voter ID laws have no measurable impact on voting behavior.

In other words, voter ID laws don't "suppress" anyone's vote.

This latest study echoes the conclusion of others, including a landmark report by The Heritage Foundation in 2007 finding that voter ID laws don't reduce voter turnout, including among African-Americans and Hispanics. These voters were just as likely to vote in states requiring photo identification as in those that don't.

Researchers for the National Bureau of Economic Research found that between 2008 and 2016, voter ID laws had "no negative effect on registration or turnout, overall or for any specific group defined by race, gender, age or party affiliation."

The new study also concluded that these results "cannot be attributed to mobilization against the laws," contradicting critics who say election turnout has been sustained only by such campaigns.

Georgia On My Mind: The Left's "Jim Crow" Rhetoric Is Absurd, Insulting, and Dishonest

The Democrats' taunts are directed toward two of the bill's provisions, one that extends the state's decade-old ID requirement to absentee ballots, and another that attempts to prevent campaigns and party activists from trying to corruptly influence voters by providing them with money, gifts, food, and water in polling places.

Let's take a look at the first provision, which requires voters to provide an ID to receive an absentee ballot per "The Left's 'Jim Crow' Rhetoric Is Absurd, Insulting, and Dishonest" March 2021 article by Hans von Spakovsky in the Daily Signal:

Georgia has had a law in place since the 2008 presidential election that requires a voter to show a government-issued, photo ID when he or she votes in-person. When a federal judge threw out the lawsuit against the law in 2007 (amid similar "Jim Crow" comparisons), he specifically noted that in two years of litigation, the challengers could not produce a single resident of the state who would be unable to vote because of the new ID requirement.

Georgia provides a free photo ID to anyone who doesn't already have one. We have more than a decade's worth of Georgia's turnout data in election after election that graphically shows that the ID provision does not prevent anyone—including minorities—from voting. Simply extending the ID requirement to absentee ballots is a much-needed, common-sense reform that voters support.

But what does the provision actually say? Section 25 of the bill doesn't even require voters to provide a photocopy of their ID. Instead, the voter can simply write "the number of his or her Georgia driver's license or identification card" on the application for the absentee ballot.

Moreover, if the voter doesn't have such a Georgia ID card, she can "provide a copy of a form of identification listed" in another code section of Georgia law (§ 21-2-417(c)). And what does that code section say? That you can satisfy the ID requirement with a "copy of a current utility bill, bank statement, government check, paycheck, or other government document that shows the name and address of such elector." Besides used for voting, most every American has provided one of these docs without issue.

The language on voter IDs for absentee ballots in the new Georgia law is thus identical to the language in federal law, promulgated through the Help America Vote Act (HAVA) of 2002. And guess who voted to approve this federal law? Why, then-Sen. Joe Biden of Delaware. In fact, the vote was 92 to 2, and included in the "yes" votes were Sen. Dianne Feinstein, D-California; Sen. Dick Durbin, D-Illinois; Sen. Harry Reid, D-Nevada.; and Sen. Patrick Leahy, D-Vermont Wow! How times and political positions have changed in the Democratic Party.

Myth 3: There Are No Issues With Voting By Mail (Fact Check: False)

Voting by mail makes it easier to commit fraud, intimidate voters, and destroy the protections of the secret ballot. It puts elections into the hands of the Postal Service. Without the oversight of election and polling officials, ballots can be lost, disqualified, and even stolen.

Back in January 2020, Judicial Watch had some big news shared below: Their investigation of voter rolls nationwide turned up 2.5 million extra names and analysis of data from the U.S Election Assistance Commission found 378 counties that had a combined 2.5 million more voter registrations than citizens old enough to vote. Judicial Watch warned five states—California, Pennsylvania, North Carolina, Colorado, and Virginia—they intended to sue unless they cleaned up their voter rolls.

Three key articles below about or from Judicial Watch titled: "Judicial Watch Ballot Update: Judicial Watch Cleans Up Dirty Voter Rolls" in October 2020 by Micah Morrison; "Judicial Watch and Election Integrity Project California Both Work to Restore Voter Confidence Nationwide" May 2020 article by PRNewswire; and the April 2020 Judicial Watch article "Judicial Watch's Campaign for Clean Elections" by Micah Morrison bring us up to date with their cases to update outdated voter rolls in non-compliance states.

California

Judicial Watch and Election Integrity Project California joined forces in 2017 to challenge the failure of election officials in Los Angeles and the state capitol Sacramento to clean up Los Angeles County's voter rolls. A 2019 settlement of that lawsuit caused changes in California's statewide voter maintenance procedures and has the potential to result in the removal of some 1.5 million inactive registrations from Los Angeles County's voter rolls.

Judicial Watch uncovered 1.6 million inactive voters on California voting rolls. In 2017, and sued California and Los Angeles County to force a cleanup and their investigation found that Los Angeles County had more voter registrations on its rolls than actual voting age citizens in the county, and that the entire state had a voter registration rate of 101% of age-eligible citizens. In 2019, California capitulated, settling our lawsuit and agreeing to remove inactive voters from its rolls.

"Confidence in voter rolls is a civil rights issue," declared Judicial Watch President Tom Fitton. "If voters don't have confidence that voter rolls are updated regularly, it undermines the integrity of our elections."

Linda Paine, President of Election Integrity Project California, added, "Our Election Integrity Project® recently served notice on the California Secretary of State for violations of the National Voter Registration Act, after identifying hundreds of thousands of registration irregularities. Our work has exposed the urgent need to clean the voter lists, especially with potential all-mail elections on the horizon."

Pennsylvania

In April 2020, Judicial Watch sued Pennsylvania for failing to make reasonable efforts to remove ineligible voters from their rolls, as required by the National Voting Rights Act (NVRA). Earlier this month, Pennsylvania offered a limited capitulation: it admitted it had reported incorrect information to a federal agency on the removal of ineligible voters

The Pennsylvania numbers were pathetic. The state initially claimed that in one county of 457,000 registrants, it had found only eight inactive names eligible for removal under the NVRA; in another county of 357,000 registrants, five such names had been removed; in a third county of 403,000 registrants, four such names removed. The state has since revised its numbers, but even the new numbers are too small. Pennsylvania now admits that in eighteen other counties—which together contain twenty-five percent of the entire state's registered voters—it removed a grand total of fifteen inactive, ineligible voters. Voting madness!

Judicial Watch is keeping the pressure on Pennsylvania. "Pennsylvania's voting rolls are such a mess that even Pennsylvania can't tell a court the details of how dirty or clean they are," Fitton says. "The simple solution is to follow the federal law and take the necessary and simple steps to clean up their voter rolls."

North Carolina

In April 2020, Judicial Watch filed suit against North Carolina for the same reason—large numbers of ineligible voters on the state voter rolls and their lawsuit argues that North Carolina has about one million inactive voters on its rolls. That's about seventeen percent of the state's total voter registration.

The state has a terrible voter registration record, one of the worst in the nation. In nineteen North Carolina counties, twenty percent of the registrations were inactive. In three other counties, twenty-five percent or more were inactive.

Judicial Watch told the court that North Carolina failed to clean up its voter rolls and the state violated the National Voter Registration Act by not providing Judicial Watch with public records related to registration numbers.

And dirty voter roll numbers are not small. Here's what we have uncovered:

In North Carolina, a Judicial Watch investigation revealed nearly one million inactive voters on its rolls. That's about 17% percent of North Carolina's total voter registration. Earlier this month, we sued North Carolina to clean up its act.

Colorado, Maryland, Ohio, Kentucky, Iowa, Virginia, New Jersey, etc.

There are similar ongoing cases in the states of Colorado, Maryland, Ohio, Kentucky, Iowa, Virginia, New Jersey, and to learn more about Judicial Watch and the complete list of current lawsuits and their status, please follow the link in the Appendix.

Myth 4: That Non-Citizens Never Vote in Elections (Fact Check: False)

According to a Philadelphia elections official, hundreds of individuals who are not U.S. citizens have registered to vote in Philadelphia and nearly half of them voted in past elections. Since 2006, 317 registered voters have contacted the City Commissioners, which oversees Philadelphia elections, asking that their registrations be canceled because they are not citizens.

Both Meagan Devlin and Hans von Spakovsky highlighted in their September 2017 article "Hundreds of Illegal Voters Revealed in Philadelphia" in The Daily Signal that Philly.com reported that many non-citizens registered while either applying for or renewing their driver's licenses. All applicants were offered the option to register to vote even after providing documentation to DMV officials that although they were in the country legally, they *were not* citizens.

A major component of Philadelphia registering noncitizens involves the National Voter Registration Act, or "motor voter," which was passed in 1993. It requires state governments to offer voter registration to any eligible person who is applying for or renewing their driver's license or registration.

This requirement has been misinterpreted by state officials as supposedly prohibiting them from failing to offer everyone who applies for a driver's license the opportunity to register. This includes cases where the DMV official knows the individual is not a U.S. citizen.

Schmidt's office has obtained data on 220 of the 317 registrations. Of these 220, 44 voted in one election while 46 voted in multiple elections. It is unclear how many more noncitizens are registered and voting since Philadelphia election officials take absolutely no steps whatsoever to verify the citizenship status of individuals who register to vote. They only found out about the 317 because these registered noncitizens asked to be removed from the rolls (and congrats to every one of them for being honest!).

The Pennsylvania Department of State has a review underway; but has already reported that, since 1972, 1,160 voters statewide have requested their registrations be canceled because they were not citizens. There can be little doubt this is just the tip of the iceberg in this state and many others.

Two other cases of noncitizen registration and voting show that this is not solely a Pennsylvania problem. Earlier this month, Public Interest Legal Foundation published a report after a six-month review of New Jersey voter registrations. It found that 616 noncitizens registered to vote, 76 percent of whom admitted their non-citizenship status at the outset. Yet they were registered by election officials anyway. Some noncitizens were even asked if they wanted to register to vote after presenting a "Green Card" to get their driver's license.

Added to the Pennsylvania and New Jersey cases, Virginia has also faced a multitude of noncitizens registering to vote. In May 2017, Public Interest Legal Foundation published a report showing that between 2011 and May 2017, Virginia removed 5,556 noncitizens from its voter rolls. Those noncitizens cast 7,474 votes in multiple elections. And in the last 12 years in Virginia, there have been two statewide attorney general races that have been decided by fewer than a thousand votes.

Just more evidence of the kind of problems that exist in our voter registration and election process. How much of this is not reported or identified is "most likely" very extensive.

Noncitizens Discovered in New Jersey Voter Registration System

In September 2017, the Public Interest Legal Foundation (PILF) released their "Garden State Gotcha: How Opponents of Citizenship Verification for Voting Are Putting New Jersey's Noncitizens at Risk of Deportation" report and it is covered in this section as follows:

The Public Interest Legal Foundation (PILF) released Garden State Gotcha: How Opponents of Citizenship Verification for Voting Are Putting New Jersey's Noncitizens at Risk of Deportation. Their report was updated in October 2017 to reflect the review of Essex and Middlesex Counties.

Public Interest Legal Foundation (PILF) is a 501(c)(3) public interest law firm dedicated to election integrity. The Foundation exists to assist states and others to aid the cause of election integrity and fight against lawlessness in American elections. Drawing on numerous experts in the field, PILF seeks to protect the right to vote and preserve the Constitutional framework of American elections.

After a six-month review of New Jersey county voter registration files, PILF found numerous enforcement flaws for the National Voter Registration Act (Motor Voter) that unnecessarily expose noncitizens to future naturalization challenges and even deportation without clearly-justified reforms.

- Nine percent of aliens self-reporting their status also cast ballots prior.

- 76 percent of noncitizens found in the system admitted their immigration status at the outset.

- 1,069 admitted and officially recorded noncitizens in 11 counties engaged on some level with the NJ voter registration system.

- 37 percent of aliens self-reporting their status also cast ballots prior.

- 78 percent of noncitizens were invited to register while receiving driver's licenses or in other government transactions like community college admissions or public schools.

- Eight counties, including one "sanctuary county," claimed to have never seen noncitizens registered or applying to vote.

"New Jersey offers eye-opening lessons," PILF President and General Counsel J. Christian Adams said. "A limited inquiry found that hundreds of noncitizens are documented throughout voter records, typically because a bureaucrat offered them an application. Some were even asked after presenting a Green Card.

That broken system is propped up by an honor code proven repeatedly to fail. Many illegally voted. Some claimed they didn't know they were registered until an immigration agent called. All will likely face an inquiry if they decide to become Americans."

Per Adams, "It's time to have a serious discussion about modernizing our Motor Voter law and determine how we can verify citizenship in the process…"and "anyone who disagrees exposes Americans to vote dilution and helps write one-way tickets for deportees."

In the absence of regular data-sharing arrangements between federal officials and the State, the ability of election officials to identify aliens on the voter rolls in real time is almost nonexistent. Voter registrars are stuck waiting for noncitizens to contact them, usually in a panic, admitting to registering despite their ineligibility. Such reactionary maintenance was typically due to pending naturalization applications.

"New Jersey's only defense to alien registration is the hope that aliens who get on the voters rolls will self-report," the new PILF study notes. "Without proactive verification mechanisms built into the voter registration application process, cascading negative consequences are sure to follow for eligible and ineligible voters alike."

After reviewing thousands of pages of voter records, Motor Voter arises as a contributing factor for why so many alien residents are getting trapped in the voter registration system. Years of official and third party pressure on state agencies to register more voters has apparently driven some offices to become overly aggressive in offering applications to those that do not qualify.

No uniform protections were apparent for noncitizens to be shielded from voter registration after they presented identification clearly documenting their ineligibility.

The Senator Nobody Voted For Has Devious Plan for Joe Biden's America

Sen. Alex Padilla (D-California) was a city councilman in Los Angeles from 1999 to 2006, and a state senator from 2006 to 2014. The City of Los Angeles has the largest illegal alien population in California and California has the largest illegal alien population in the United States. The following year, Padilla became California's secretary of state, and after the 2016 election, Padilla refused to cooperate with a federal probe of voter fraud, a longstanding practice in California.

As documented in "The Senator Nobody Voted for Has Curious Plan for Joe Biden's America" *Epoch Times* article by Lloyd Billingsley in April 2021: A State Department investigation discovered, falsely documented illegals have been voting in local, state, and federal elections for decades. In 1996, 642 illegals voted for Democrat Loretta Sanchez, who defeated Republican Robert Dornan by fewer than 1,000 votes. In recent years, voter fraud has been surging through the state's imported electorate.

According to a study by scholars at the Massachusetts Institute of Technology and Yale, more than 22 million people are illegally present in the United States. Pew Research pegged the figure at 11 million, more likely the number illegally present in California alone. For example, when he announced a lawsuit against the Trump administration in 2019, then-California Attorney General Xavier Becerra displayed a sign claiming 10 million "immigrants" in the state.

When illegal aliens get driver's licenses, the California Department of Motor Vehicles automatically registers them to vote. In 2015, Padilla told the *Los Angeles Times*, "At the latest, for the 2018 election cycle, I expect millions of new voters on the rolls in the state of California." True to form, by March 2018, the DMV "motor voter" plan had given licenses to more than one million illegals. Padilla wouldn't say how many illegals voted in 2018, but his previous reference to "millions" provided a ballpark figure. Many more are on the way.

Myth 5: The 2016 Election Trump-Russian Collusion Claim (Fact Check: False)

The Senate Select Committee on Intelligence on Aug. 18, 2020, release the fifth and final volume of its report on Russian interference in the 2016 election. The nearly 996-page report is the culmination of a three-year-long investigation, which involved the interviews of 200 witnesses and the review of more than a million pages of documents.

Similarly to the conclusion of the report by special counsel Robert Mueller, the committee found no evidence of collusion between the Trump campaign and Russia. The report also concludes that Russia intervened in the election to harm Hillary Clinton's campaign and help the campaign of Donald Trump.

As covered in Ivan Pentchoukov's August 2020 *Epoch Times* article "Senate Intelligence Committee Releases Final Volume of Russia Report": Unlike the Mueller report, the committee's report thoroughly explores the FBI's use of the Clinton campaign-funded Steele dossier to obtain a warrant to spy on former Trump campaign advisor Carter Page.

"We can say, without any hesitation, that the Committee found absolutely no evidence that then-candidate Donald Trump or his campaign colluded with the Russian government to meddle in the 2016 election," the committee's acting chairman, Sen. Marco Rubio (R-Florida), said in a statement.

"What the Committee did find, however, is very troubling. We found irrefutable evidence of Russian meddling. And we discovered deeply troubling actions taken by the Federal Bureau of Investigation, particularly their acceptance and willingness to rely on the 'Steele Dossier' without verifying its methodology or sourcing," Rubio added.

The fifth volume of the report focused on the counterintelligence concerns surrounding the 2016 election. The prior volumes dealt with Russian efforts against U.S. election infrastructure, Russia's use of social media, the U.S. government's response to the interference and the creation of the January 2017 Intelligence Community Assessment on Moscow's interference in the presidential election.

Sen. Mark R. Warner (D-Virginia), the vice chairman of the committee, said in a statement that the report is "the most comprehensive examination of ties between Russia and the 2016 Trump campaign to date."

The Trump campaign responded to the release of the report shortly after it was made public. "The Russia Collusion Hoax is the greatest political scandal in the history of this country. As this report proves—yet again—there was no collusion between Russia and the Trump campaign," Tim Murtaugh, Trump 2020 communications director, said in a statement.

"The report does remind Americans that there was, however, political reliance on foreign assistance in 2016, since Hillary Clinton's campaign and the DNC paid for the bogus Steele Dossier assembled by a foreign operative using Russian disinformation."

3 – Sapient & Conservative Election Integrity Organizations Take Action

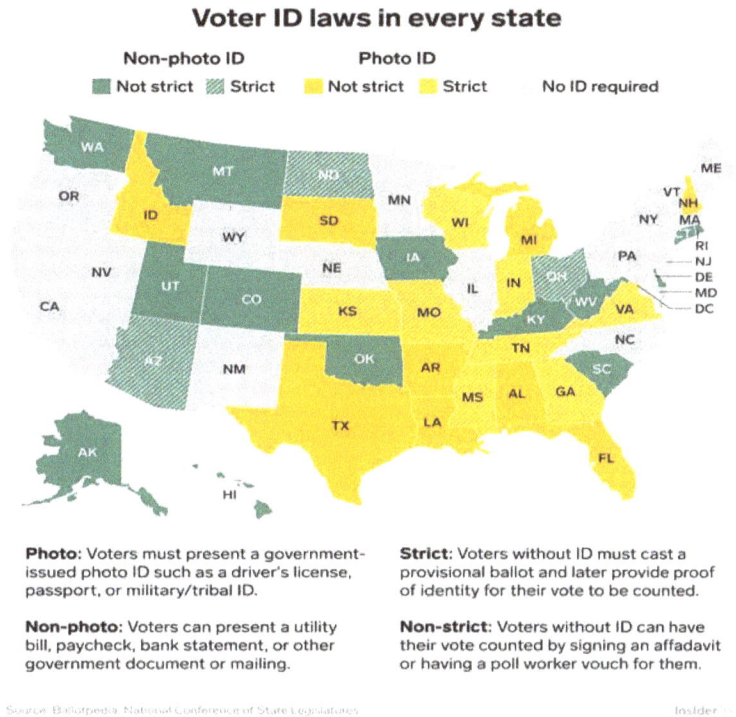

Voter ID laws in every state

Non-photo ID: Not strict, Strict
Photo ID: Not strict, Strict
No ID required

Photo: Voters must present a government-issued photo ID such as a driver's license, passport, or military/tribal ID.

Non-photo: Voters can present a utility bill, paycheck, bank statement, or other government document or mailing.

Strict: Voters without ID must cast a provisional ballot and later provide proof of identity for their vote to be counted.

Non-strict: Voters without ID can have their vote counted by signing an affadavit or having a poll worker vouch for them.

Source: Ballotpedia, National Conference of State Legislatures   Insider

To restore public confidence in our elections, our leaders should uphold the Constitution, reject congressional Democrats' plan to nationalize our elections, and get about the serious work of state-based reform that will protect the integrity of the vote for every American. The American people expect us to ensure that every eligible citizen is able to vote and also make sure that their vote is not stolen or diluted through errors, mistakes, or outright fraud.

Every citizen deserves the freedom to support, oppose, criticize, or promote the candidates and causes they believe in. And most importantly, the American people must have the utmost confidence that every voice matters, and every vote counts—or democracy cannot survive.

Some of the most prominent and sapient election integrity organizations who are fighting to ensure every voice matters, and every vote counts are utilized in *Voting Madness* for their factual, truthful, and in-depth reporting. These select few are The Heritage Foundation, Public Interest Legal Foundation (PILF), Judicial Watch, Thomas More Society, and The Navarro Report (actually three volumes). There are more noteworthy contributors covered throughout this textbook.

Americans deserve to have an electoral process that they can trust and that protects their most sacred right, and they have the right to know when the integrity of that process is imperiled—and the above organizations are committed to doing just that without prejudice, bias, or false narratives.

The most flagrant and unsapient liberal organizations (like the "current" Democratic Party, Brennan Center, American Civil Liberties Union, League Of Women Voters, Common Cause, Fair Fight and a vast of array of Soros funded groups) that propagate these myths, perpetuate lies, and spin false narratives with non-stop fake news—need to be challenged and each transgression held accountable for their own self interests.

Prominent and Sapient Election Integrity Organizations Take Action

There are a number of serious issues related to voter fraud, ballot irregularities and election integrity that these organizations focus on, and they are introduced below, along with their goals and strengths. You will find no leftist, liberal, or Democrat related organization on this list because each and every one of them—to one degree or another—promote and propagate at least one of the five myths covered in Chapter 2.

To make this sapient list you have to earn it.

All of the conservative organizations, their leaders, and teams below are working effectively towards election integrity and voter rights by selflessly focusing on the many issues covered in *Voting Madness* and using the Constitution as their yardstick, foundation and purpose for the benefit of "all" Americans—instead of applying or misdirecting their allegiance and goals to only "some" Americans that belong to a particular political party, voting group, or ideology that weakens the Constitution and disrespects all American voters that it stands for.

The Constitution, Bill of Rights, and Amendments stand for us, *e pluribus unum*; out of many, one (the motto of the US). These five organizations are voting/election integrity champions because they recognize all five myths and are working diligently to expose and counter them.

The Heritage Foundation

As previously noted, as of December 2020, the Heritage Foundation's <u>Election Fraud Database</u> had topped 1,300 cases of confirmed voter or election fraud as reported on in "The Heritage Foundation's Election Fraud Database Tops 1,300 Cases" December 2020 article in The Daily Signal by Hans von Spakovsky and Kaitlynn Samali. As clarified in Chapter 1, the Heritage database is not an exhaustive, nor comprehensive list. It doesn't capture all cases, and certainly doesn't capture all reported instances or allegations of election fraud, some of which may be deserving of being investigated or prosecuted but aren't.

Their database makes clear, there are many ways to tamper with elections. Take the five local officials, including an alderman and fire chief, who were convicted for their efforts to rig the town's 2017 municipal election in Canton, Mississippi, in that scheme that involved everything from voter registration fraud to intimidating and bribing witnesses.

Regarding the razor-thin margins of some of our elections, the Ohio Secretary of State Office reported that between 2013 and 2017, fifty-six elections resulted in a tie vote and eighty-six were decided by only one vote. In close elections, where every vote counts, a handful of fraudulent votes can alter the outcome, and thwart the will of the people.

It is important to remember that every fraudulent vote that is cast invalidates the vote of an eligible voter. We have many close elections in this country, and plenty of people stand to gain financially or through increased access to powerful figures who have incentives to cheat, as well as some individuals who just want to provide a boost to their preferred candidate.

Public Interest Legal Foundation

One of the constant refrains from those who oppose election reforms designed to protect the security and integrity of the voting process is that serious vote fraud is a myth. But as a shocking new report from the Public Interest Legal Foundation (PILF) in the October 2020 edition of The Daily Signal titled "Tens of Thousands of Cases of Possible Vote Fraud Cited in New Report" by Hans von Spakovsky and Kaitlynn Samalis-Aldrich shows—the mediacrat naysayers could not be more wrong.

The foundation's report, "Critical Condition," highlights the severity of the problem: inaccurate voter rolls, duplicate registrations, dead voters, and incomplete registrations—all of which allow fraud by those willing to exploit vulnerabilities in the system.

The foundation discovered more than 140,000 instances of potential election fraud in the 2016 and 2018 elections, ranging from individuals illegally voting in multiple states to someone voting in the name of a deceased person.

The Public Interest Legal Foundation created the type of database that President Donald Trump's 2017 Presidential Advisory Commission on Election Integrity wanted to create but was prevented from doing so by numerous frivolous lawsuits filed by the left. Many state governors and election officials also refused to provide data to the commission, which is why it was shut down before it could even do any research.

The foundation obtained voter registration and voter history data from 42 states. It had to sue three states—Illinois, Maine, and Maryland—to get what is supposed to be public information after they refused to comply with their own laws.

All of this information was put into the Safeguarding America's Votes and Elections (SAVE) database. It was then supplemented with information from other commercial and government data sources, such as credit agencies, obituaries, and the Social Security Death Index.

By supplementing the voter registration information, the Public Interest Legal Foundation (PILF) was able to sift out as many "false positives" as possible.

A false positive in data comparisons occurs when two different individuals have the same name and birthdate. For example, "John James Smith" born July 4, 1976, appearing on two state voter registration lists may actually be two different people.

By leveraging other identifying information, such as commercial data, Social Security numbers, and credit address histories, one can eliminate most, if not all, false positives that have plagued prior reports from other entities.

The foundation now has what it says is "the best platform ever constructed to analyze the health of voter rolls and catalog potential vote fraud vulnerabilities."

Judicial Watch

Judicial Watch is the national leader in election integrity education and litigation. The very notion of voter fraud is steeped in partisan bickering, but Judicial Watch President Tom Fitton insists electoral abuse is not "a Right-Left issue" at all. The Right may be leading the fight on election fraud, but "if you're a Leftist Democrat trying to take on an incumbent in a corrupt jurisdiction," Fitton says, "voter fraud can keep you from gaining traction as well."

Judicial Watch is cleaning up dirty voter rolls across the nation. States are required by the National Voter Registration Act (NVRA) to remove so-called "inactive voters" from registration rolls if they do not respond to an address confirmation notice and then fail to vote in the next two general federal elections. Many "inactive voters" do this because, well, they're dead. Or they have moved away.

Why does this matter? Leaving the names of inactive voters on registration rolls creates opportunities for fraud, such as dead people voting or double voting. Critics argue that these concerns are overblown, but sometimes it only takes a few votes to swing an election.

Thomas More Society

Using the COVID-19 flu pandemic as justification and the excuse that local elections lacked funding to facilitate safe elections, a well-funded network of foundations and non-profit organizations gave hundreds of millions of dollars of private funding directly to counties and municipalities across Michigan, Wisconsin, and Pennsylvania for electoral purposes.

The illegitimate infusion of private funding and third-party promotion of training, equipment, security, staffing and reporting programs by a network of private nonprofits at the local level bypassed state administrative processes, violated legislative prerogatives codified in state Help America Vote Plans (HAVA), and resulted in questions about the integrity of the US electoral system.

The Thomas More Society report 'The Legitimacy and Effect of Private Funding in Federal and State Electoral Processes" prepared by Phill Kline in charge of the Amistad Project of the Thomas More Society Findings, places in context and raises substantive questions about last minute gifting of private funding by five progressive, non-profit foundations and ten non-profit organizations into the local elections of swing states.

The Navarro Report

Another benefit of the Sapient Conservative Textbook (SCT) Program by the SAPIENT Being is providing opportunities for further exploration, critique, and research on a variety of topics that many readers who may be a victim of fake news influences and developing their opinions from 'so-called' progressivism points of view. The Navarro Reports are covered in more detail in Chapters 7, 9, and 10 of *Voting Madness* is to provide alternative viewpoints and welcomes a full and thorough analysis of each report.

The three volumes of The Navarro Report provide a demonstration and "what if" analysis of voter fraud, irregularities, and manipulations (gaming) that President Trump had a good faith belief the November 3, 2020 Presidential election results, were, indeed, the poisonous fruit of widespread fraud and election irregularities.

Evidence used in the preparation of The Navarro Report includes more than 50 lawsuits and judicial rulings, thousands of affidavits and declarations, testimony in a variety of state venues, published analyses by think tanks and legal centers, videos and photos, public comments, and extensive press coverage. The author Dr. Peter Navarro produced the three volumes of The Navarro Report in his personal capacity to shed light on potentially illegal activity that may have occurred during the 2020 Presidential Election.

Dr. Peter Navarro holds a Ph.D. in Economics from Harvard University and was a professor emeritus of economics and public policy at the University of California-Irvine for more than 20 years. He served as Assistant to the President and Director of the Office of Trade and Manufacturing Policy at the White House during the Trump Administration.

Volume 1 of The Navarro Report: The Immaculate Deception, assessed the fairness and integrity of the 2020 Presidential Election by identifying and assessing six key dimensions of alleged election irregularities. These irregularities included: outright fraud, ballot mishandling, a wide range of process fouls, multiple violations of the 14th Amendment's Equal Protection Clause, voting machine irregularities, and statistical anomalies.

This assessment was conducted across six key battleground states—Arizona, Georgia, Michigan, Nevada, Pennsylvania, and Wisconsin. It was the outcomes in these six states that would ultimately be election-determinate—just as the strategy of the Democrat Party assumed.

Volume 2 of The Navarro Report: The Art of the Steal, examined the institutional genesis of the six types of election irregularities. One key finding: The Democrat Party efforts to strategically game the election process across the six battleground states began years before, and in many cases, shortly after President Trump was elected in 2016. A second key finding: the Democrat's gaming of the election process was implemented through a two-pronged Grand "Stuff the Ballot Box" Strategy designed to flood the six key battleground states with enough unscrutinized and potentially illegal absentee and mail-in ballots to turn a decisive Trump victory into a narrow alleged Biden "win."

Volume 3 of The Navarro Report: Yes, President Trump Won, is designed to serve as a capstone to what has been a comprehensive analysis of the question: Was the 2020 presidential election stolen from Donald J. Trump? Provided in this report, is the most up-to-date statistical "receipts" with respect to the potential number of illegal votes in each battleground state.

America's Hidden Voting Epidemic? Mail Ballot Failures

According to an April 2020 Fox News report "Adams & von Spakovsky: America's hidden voting epidemic? Mail ballot failures" by Hans von Spakovsky and J. Christian Adams:

Based on federal data from the U.S. Election Assistance Commission, millions of mail ballots were never counted as completed votes. If you vote by mail, in contrast to polling places, there is no one to help you and fix a mistake. Mail voting mistakes are fatal to your vote. Unsupervised mail ballots encourage vote-buying, intimidation, and absentee ballot fraud as previously seen in but a few examples in Chapter 1.

Taking into account the 2012, 2014, 2016, and 2018 federal general elections, 28.3 million mail ballots disappeared after officials gave them to the U.S. Postal Service. There are numerous problems to point fingers at and many explanations as to what happened to these ballots, but the bottom line is simple: tens of millions of ballots were lost in the mail voting system on a scale not seen at polling places.

Over the same time period, federal data show that 2.7 million ballots were sent to the wrong addresses. The causes are fewer here: as more states try to automate the mail participation process by mailing ballots to all registered voters, they become increasingly reliant on voter registration rolls that are highly inaccurate. If a state is not staying on top of registrants who die or move elsewhere, they are likely sending ballots to outdated addresses by default.

And to the extent that individuals are mistakenly registered more than once in the same state—and there is plenty of evidence that such errors occur—certain voters may be receiving multiple ballots.

The alarming trend is the rise in mail ballot rejections. These are cases where ballots are sent, completed (by someone at a particular address, not necessarily the voter), and returned to election officials—yet were rejected for various reasons, most commonly because the signature on the absentee ballot envelope does not match the signature of the voter on his or her registration form.

Voting By Mail in Contrast to Polling Places

The Census Bureau says that more than two-thirds of voters cast their ballots by mail or before Election Day for the 2020 presidential election.

The bureau, in a new report, found that 69 percent of voters nationwide took advantage of the expansion of mail and early-voting options in numerous states—a significant jump over the previous election. In 2016, about 40 percent of voters cast their ballots through these nontraditional methods, according to figures released this week.

"The 2020 election will long be remembered for having taken place during a pandemic," the Census Bureau said in its release. "As the above findings indicate, the methods of voting used by those casting a ballot were significantly different from prior elections, though the magnitude and nature of the changes varied from state to state."

The bureau, in a new report, found that 69 percent of voters nationwide took advantage of the expansion of mail and early-voting options in numerous states—a significant jump over the previous election. In 2016, about 40 percent of voters cast their ballots through these nontraditional methods, according to figures released this week. If you vote by mail, in contrast to polling places, there is no one to help you and fix a mistake as previously noted, and mail voting mistakes are fatal to your vote.

The U.S. Election Assistance Commission's (EAC) survey figures are, unfortunately, limited. Many local election officials simply ignore the questions posed to them and decline to fill out the survey. The City of Chicago's election department has been silent about mail ballot failures for eight years running, for example. So was the state of Oregon, which withheld data for "unknown" (the category where a state doesn't know what happened to a ballot) for the 2014 and 2016 elections.

In 2018, however, Oregon mailed out over 2.8 million ballots, according to the EAC report. Roughly 60,200 were "undeliverable," raising serious questions about the accuracy of the state's voter registration list. Almost 870,000 ballots are listed in the "unknown" category. That means the failure rate of Oregon's mail balloting system was more than 32 percent.

The most recent 2018 election data show counties in California and Arizona tipping the scales in terms of missing and undeliverable ballots. Eight of the top 10 counties in terms of missing ballots are in California alone. The Phoenix, Arizona, metropolitan area comes in second, while Seattle ranks fourth. Maricopa County, Arizona, also dominated the nation in undeliverable ballots in 2018 with more than 87,000. Hillsborough County, Florida, also had nearly 12,000 ballots sent to undeliverable addresses.

All-mail jurisdictions such as Oregon like to brag about the supposed "security" of their systems, which consists of almost nothing other than a rapid, superficial signature comparison.

As Melody Rose, an assistant professor of political science at Portland State University, told the *Los Angeles Times*: "I don't have much faith in that process. I can forge my husband's signature perfectly."

Rose conducted a survey of one county, Washington County, outside Portland. Five percent of registered voters admitted that other people marked their ballots, and 2.4% said someone else signed their ballots.

Rose suspected the actual number was higher, given that most people would not want to admit to being "party to a crime." That would mean that tens of thousands of mail-in ballots are being cast in Oregon by individuals other than the registered voter.

The data demonstrate the danger of putting the presidential election into the hands of the U.S. Postal Service, as well as the problems with inaccurate and out-of-date voter registration lists. It should alarm all who are pushing for all-mail elections based on federal data from the U.S. Election Assistance Commission, millions of mail ballots were never counted as completed votes.

According to the commission's 2016 report, for example, more mail ballots were misdirected and unaccounted for than the margin of votes between Hillary Clinton and Donald J. Trump. She had 2.9 million more votes, yet 6.5 million ballots were misdirected or unaccounted for by the states. In other words, for every vote that Hillary won over the eventual president nationally, more than twice as many mail ballots disappeared or went to the wrong addresses.

That included preying on first-time voters, those "less informed or lacking in knowledge of the voting process, the infirm, the poor, and those with limited skills in the English language." Ballots were filled out by campaign workers instead of voters; people were pressured to vote a particular way or were paid for their votes; and individuals who did not even live in the city or were registered at vacant lots voted illegally (but easily) using absentee ballots.

The federal Election Assistance Commission collects information from the states and files a report with Congress after every national election, including on absentee or mail-in ballots. In 2016, more mail ballots—6.5 million—were misdirected or unaccounted for than the margin of votes separating Donald Trump and Hillary Clinton.

"Unaccounted for" means state officials handed requested absentee ballots over to the Postal Service for delivery to voters but never heard another word about them. So election officials don't know what happened—whether the ballots were properly delivered, whether voters decided not to vote after all or whether the envelopes got lost when voters sent them back.

Thousands of absentee ballots were found in Wisconsin after its April 7 primary, including in a mail-processing facility, and were not delivered or counted.

Committing Voter Fraud Is Easy To Do

For example, Richard Davis was convicted of a felony in California after registering his four dogs to vote as Democrats over a four-year period. Davis said his goal was to draw attention to the flawed voter registration system in his state, and he did notify the local district attorney's office of what he was doing.

Disregarding several warnings to stop those false registrations, and after registering his deceased father, too, Davis was charged and pleaded guilty to voter registration fraud. He never submitted a fraudulent vote, but he could have done so easily using absentee ballots if he hadn't told officials what he was doing, since his "signature" for his dogs would have been a match on all of the forms.

Another case out of California demonstrates how voter fraud often hurts the most marginalized individuals in communities.

Norman Hall was involved in a scheme with eight other individuals involving the homeless on Skid Row. According to the Los Angeles District Attorney's Office, they "solicited hundreds of false and/or forged signatures on state ballot petitions and voter registration forms by offering homeless people $1 and/or cigarettes for their participation."

The ballot petitions for which Hall and others gathered fraudulent signatures included calling for reducing jail time, changing the authority of the sheriff's office, and increasing taxes on millionaires and other business owners.

Two other cases out of California include two individuals, Jentry and Bradley Jasperson, who forged the signatures of voters for a referendum initiative. They were each paid $5 per signature.

Another case from the Heritage Foundation's newest batch features Frank Rabia, a City Council candidate in Hoboken, New Jersey, who bribed voters with $50 payments for mail-in ballots to support his candidacy.

Heritage's Election Fraud Database has more than 60 instances of vote buying. Attempting to buy votes or signatures is entirely repugnant to the republic that America is so lucky to maintain. But purchasing votes is much easier with absentee or mail-in ballots.

The purchaser—such as Rabia—can see the voter's absentee ballot in the voter's home and ensure he is getting what he paid for. A purchaser can't do that when a voter goes into the privacy of a voting booth.

Another new case added to the Heritage Foundation's database arises out of Espanola, New Mexico, where Laura Seeds and Dyon Herrera falsified absentee ballots in favor of Seeds' husband, a Democratic candidate for City Council. This is the same state where a lawsuit has been filed to require election officials to automatically mail absentee ballots to all registered voters in the upcoming election.

The Public Interest Legal Foundation (PILF) pointed out in an amicus brief that it found more than 3,000 individuals registered multiple times in New Mexico; almost 1,700 registrants who are dead; 1,500 voters aged 100 or above (64 of whom are over 120 years old); and almost 200 individuals registered at commercial rather than residential addresses. All of these supposed voters would receive ballots automatically if the lawsuit were successful.

These cases demonstrate that election fraud does occur and can compromise the integrity of the election process. Another serious election integrity process issue is regarding ballot and vote harvesting that is covered in the next section per the April 2020 "Vote-by-Mail Makes Fraud and Errors Worse" article by Hans von Spakovsky and J. Christian Adams in *The Washington Times*.

Ballot and Vote Harvesting

In the Rio Grande Valley, for example, politiquerias roam colonias, preying on the most vulnerable voters and voting their ballots for them. In Cameron County, Texas, nine politiquerias were charged with voter fraud related to mail ballots. It is most often the poor and the elderly who lose their votes to the ballot harvesters.

It's not just one county in Texas either. When Hans von Spakovsky and J. Christian Adams were both at the Justice Department, we were involved in a case of systemic vote-by-mail fraud in Noxubee County, Mississippi. A federal court found that mail ballot fraud was very real, part of an organized scheme to disenfranchise voters.

It worked like this. The harvesters snatched mail ballots from the mailboxes of people they knew. They would then knock on their doors, ballots in hand, offering to "help" them vote. The harvesters would then fill in the ballots for their candidates, regardless of what the intended voters had told them.

The court ruling contains tragic testimony from one victim, Susan Wood. When asked why she allowed a harvester to fill out her ballot, Wood answered that the harvester "knows folks" better than she did—a classic case of trust betrayed.

In 2011 in Troy, New York, a local political operative was convicted for submitting fraudulent absentee ballots. When asked why he targeted voters who lived in low-income housing, he said it was because they were a lot less likely to complain or notice their ballot had been stolen.

Those who commit mail ballot fraud are often in positions of relative power over the voter. Victims are frequently reluctant to speak with law enforcement officers because those committing the crime—the harvesters—live among them and are often politically well-connected. It took significant Justice Department resources to crack the case in Noxubee and unearth the plot.

Vote-harvesting fraud isn't the end of the problems with vote-by-mail. States relying on this method inevitably send piles of ballots to obsolete addresses or to registrants who have died. That's because voter rolls are filled with errors. California voter rolls remain tainted with thousands of deceased registrants, as well as voters who say they live at commercial addresses. In Swissvale, Pennsylvania, one man had seven simultaneous active voter registrations at the same address. Vote-by-mail would send seven ballots to this house.

Advocates of vote-by-mail don't understand the extent of the snafus on American voter rolls. They don't understand the hundreds of thousands duplicate registrations that exist. They don't understand the problem of placeholder registrations—where many registrations don't even have full addresses. And those who do understand have chosen to turn a blind eye to these and other glaring problems.

Now, add to all these problems the simple fact that vote-by-mail is entirely dependent on the postal service—the same outfit that routinely delivers you your neighbor's mail.

Cleaning Up Voter Rolls Prevent Millions of Missing Mailed Ballots

Overall, *The Washington Post* found 534,731 ballots were disqualified in 23 states in the 2020 primary season. A similar analysis by NPR tracked 558,032 ballots that were rejected in 30 states. A large share of the rejected ballots tracked by *The Post* were in just two jurisdictions: California, which threw out more than 102,000, and New York City, which tossed more than 84,000.

As reported in the August 2020 "More than 500,000 mail ballots were rejected in the primaries. That could make the difference in battle ground states this fall" article in *The Washington Post* by Elise Viebeck: In eight battleground states, more than 125,100 ballots were rejected by election officials in the 2020 primaries, according to data compiled by *The Post*. The states were Florida, Maine, Michigan, Nevada, North Carolina, Ohio, Pennsylvania, and Wisconsin.

The Post totals include the number of ballots rejected in a primary held in each state this year, including several that took place before the novel coronavirus emerged as a serious concern in the United States. The figures almost certainly understate the number of rejections for several reasons, including failures by some counties to report their data.

Reasons for rejection vary across the country. The failure to provide a signature or to return the ballot on time tend to be the most common problems, according to state data. "A lot of people don't follow instructions," said Gerry Cohen, a member of the Wake County Board of Elections in North Carolina, which reviews every problematic ballot to determine whether it is valid.

28.3 Million Mail Ballots Went Missing from 2012 - 2018 Elections!

Even in times of relative tranquility and health, the U.S. mail voting system generates millions of errors and even more questions about what actually happens after an official puts a ballot in the postal system. In 2008, 3,900,000 requested ballots never arrived at their intended address targets. Another 2,900,000 ballots never made their way back to the election office. Roughly 1,000,000 ballots were rejected outright, typically due to signature match errors.

As noted in the "28.3 Million Mail Ballots Went Missing from 2012 - 2018 Elections" report by the Public Interest Legal Foundation (PILF): Expansion and automation during the pandemic will effectively guarantee even greater figures depicting failure and confusion during one of the most historic challenges facing the nation. Elections in 2012, 2014, 2016, and 2018 saw more than 28.3 million "unaccounted for" mail ballots and those types of errors are broken down below.

The 2020 data was not yet available as of the May 2021 publication of *Voting Madness*.

2016 Election

- 41.6 million ballots sent
- 568,412 undeliverable
- 318,716 rejected
- 5,951,992 "unknown"

2018 Election

- 42.4 million ballots sent

- 543,936 undeliverable
- 430,108 rejected
- 10,475,573 "unknown"

2018 Election – "Unknown" Ballots Location and Total

- Los Angeles County, CA 1,377,435
- Maricopa County, AZ 407,816
- Orange County, CA 374,264
- King County, WA 352,624
- San Diego County, CA 334,912
- Sacramento County, CA 324,312
- Riverside County, CA 273,458
- San Bernardino County, CA 242,870
- Alameda County, CA 226,761
- Santa Clara County, CA 208,037

2018 Election – Undeliverable Ballots Location and Total

- Maricopa County, AZ 87,045
- San Diego County, CA 69,770
- Orange County, CA 34,257
- Santa Clara County, CA 22,589
- Riverside County, CA 17,291
- King County, WA 13,338
- Multnomah County, OR 13,122
- Hillsborough County, FL 11,618
- Clark County, WA 9,427
- Kern County, CA 8,505

Enforcing Common Sense Voter ID Requirements

One thing is crystal clear amid the contentious fights occurring over the outcome of the 2020 presidential election: predictions that certain states would "backslide" into discriminatory voter suppression following the Supreme Court's 2013 *Shelby County v. Holder* decision were completely wrong as documented in a December 2020 issue of *Newsweek* titled "Despite Predictions, Shelby v. Holder Did Not Lead to Voter Suppression" by Hans von Spakovsky: In fact, turnout in both presidential and congressional elections in those states has risen significantly since that decision.

When the Supreme Court handed down its ruling, the Shelby County decision was unjustly criticized and misunderstood by many who claimed the decision abrogated the Voting Rights Act (VRA). That claim was simply not true. The act's main provision—a permanent, nationwide ban on racial discrimination in the voting context—is alive and well today. It has been so effective that discriminatory practices by state and local officials have become a rare exception rather than the rule.

What was at stake in Shelby County was Section 5, an emergency provision passed in 1965 that was only supposed to last five years but was successively renewed by Congress. Under Section 5, certain jurisdictions could not make any changes to their voting laws without first getting the approval—referred to as "preclearance"—of the U.S. Justice Department or a federal court in Washington, D.C.

The coverage formula was designed to capture those states, and only those states, that were engaging in blatant discrimination. In determining which states would be covered by the preclearance requirement, Congress took into account the low registration and turnout caused by discriminatory practices. Specifically, it covered states that had maintained a test or device as a prerequisite to voting and had voter registration or turnout of less than 50 percent in the 1964, 1968, or 1972 presidential elections. Those states were Alabama, Alaska, Arizona, Georgia, Louisiana, Mississippi, South Carolina, Texas, and Virginia.

No one disputed that Section 5 was needed in 1965, and hence the Court upheld its constitutionality because of the widespread and extensive discrimination in the segregationist South. But the majority rightly said in Shelby County that the preclearance requirement—an extraordinary intrusion into state sovereignty—was no longer constitutional because it had not been updated to reflect modern conditions.

Many Liberal Positions Are Grossly Outdated and Rooted in the Distant Past

In an opinion by Justice Ruth Bader Ginsburg, the four dissenting justices claimed that Section 5 was "vital to protecting minority rights" and predicted that without it, there would be "backsliding" by state and local governments returning to their old ways of discriminating. As several national elections have taken place since the decision, we can now evaluate whether Ginsburg's prediction was justified.

Since Congress thought voter turnout was an appropriate measure of discriminatory practices when it passed Section 5, it is still a relevant measure to show how wrong the four SCOTUS dissenters were about what would happen without Section 5 in place. As the 2020 turnout numbers show, the dissenting justices were wrong to view these states through a lens that saw only the decades-old past.

The United States Election Project (USEP) calculates turnout based on the Voting Eligible Population (VEP), which begins with the voting-age population of each state and subtracts individuals who are ineligible to vote, such as non-citizens and felons who have not yet had their ability to vote restored. The following numbers are the VEP turnout rate from USEP for the highest office on the ballot.

The national VEP turnout in the 2012 presidential election—before Shelby County—was 58 percent. The national VEP turnout in 2016—after Shelby County—was 59.2 percent. So turnout went up nationally that year and went up again in this year's election, which the USEP pegs at 66.6 percent.

The VEP turnout also either went up or stayed virtually the same in the nine formerly covered states:

- Alabama's turnout in 2012 was 58.6 percent; in 2016 it was 58.8 and in 2020 it was 63.1, steadily rising after Shelby County. Over the same three elections Georgia went from 59 to 59.1 to 67.7.

- Alaska from 52.6 to 54.9 to 68.8. Louisiana went from 60.2 to 60 to 64.4. Mississippi went from 59.3 to 55.2 to 60.2.

- South Carolina went from 56.3 to 56.7 to 60.4.

- Texas climbed steadily from 49.6 to 51.4 to 60.4.

- Even Virginia jumped from 66.1 in 2012 and 2016 to 73 in 2020.

Note that all of these turnout rates are about or higher than Congress's key 50 percent measure. Similar increases happened in congressional elections (which have much lower turnout) in the USEP numbers. For example:

- The VEP turnout in Alabama in 2014 was 32.9 percent, rising to 46.9 percent in 2018.

- Georgia, which has been the subject of many recent claims of voter suppression, went from 33.4 percent in 2014 to 46.9 percent in 2018.

- Mississippi went from only 29 percent in 2014 to 42.7 percent in 2018.

4 – Best Practices & Measures to Ensure Election Integrity & Prevent Abuse

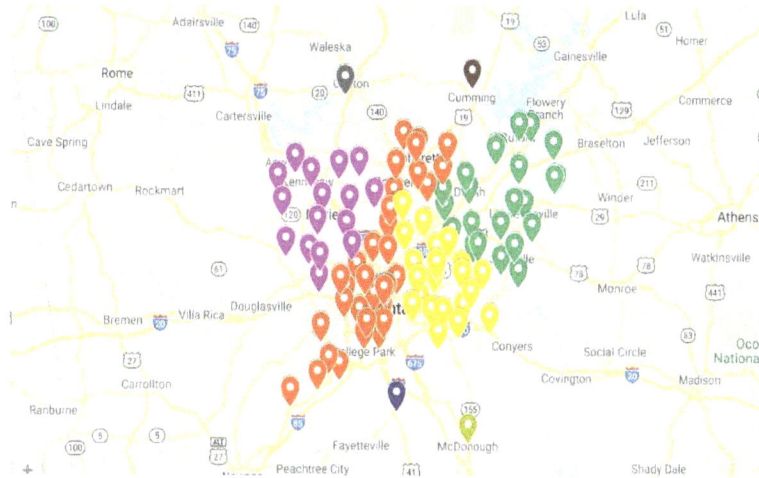

Credit: The Atlanta Journal-Constitution - Unsecure ballot drop boxes around Atlanta set up for Georgia's Nov. 3 election.

As noted in the conclusion to the Commission on Federal Election Reform, headed by former President Jimmy Carter and former Secretary of State James Baker, said in 2005:

The electoral system cannot inspire public confidence if no safeguards exist to deter or detect fraud or to confirm the identity of voters. Photo IDs currently are needed to board a plane, enter federal buildings, and cash a check. Voting is equally important and requires the same protections.

Is voter ID the only reform that states need to implement to ensure the integrity and security of the election process? Certainly not. But it is one of the many steps states should take to safeguard both voting in person and by absentee ballot.

The reality is, election fraud often goes undetected; even when it is discovered, investigators and prosecutors often opt to take no action. In other words, no reliable data exist on the true scope or frequency of fraud, and Heritage's database can't be treated as a proxy. Fake news and false narratives claims against the database should be treated with great skepticism.

Nor can voter fraud prosecutions be used to measure the overall scope of fraud. That reasoning was roundly rejected by the 7th U.S. Circuit Court of Appeals in *Crawford v. Marion County Election Board*, a decision that the Supreme Court affirmed when it upheld Indiana's voter ID law. The 7th Circuit opinion noted:

But the absence of prosecutions is explained by the endemic under-enforcement of minor criminal laws (minor as they appear to the public and prosecutors, at all events) and by the extreme difficulty of apprehending a voter impersonator. He enters the polling places, gives a name that is not his own, votes, and leaves. If later it is discovered that the name he gave is that of a dead person, no one at the polling place will remember the face of the person who gave that name, and if someone did remember it, what would he do with the information?

As the 7th Circuit said, such fraud "has a parallel to littering, another crime the perpetrators of which are almost impossible to catch."

When a lawbreaker is "almost impossible to catch," states are faced with two options, according to the court: States may "impose a very severe criminal penalty" or "take preventative action, as Indiana had done by requiring a photo ID." And that law has been in place for more than a decade, with none of the problems critics predicted.

Voting and Election Irregularities

This latest research confirms that states are justified in enacting voter ID laws to protect their electoral integrity. Such laws don't deter eligible voters from registering and voting, and they do not disenfranchise minority voters.

In reality, without rigid safeguards to prevent fraud, misuse, and voter intimidation, absentee ballot fraud—while it may occur sporadically—already has affected the outcome of elections in states and counties across the country as documented by the Heritage Foundation and others.

In 2012, before the current progressive love affair with absentee ballots and all-mail elections, *The New York Times* did a highly critical report on absentee ballots. They concluded that "votes cast by mail are less likely to be counted, more likely to be compromised, and more likely to be contested than those cast in a voting booth."

In fact, the *Times* said, the rejection rate for absentee ballots by election officials is "double the rate for in-person voting." More than half a million absentee ballots were ultimately rejected in 2020 primaries, including over 80,000–one out of every five ballots—in New York City alone–an enormous and unacceptable disenfranchisement rate.

The US Election Assistance Commission (EAC) reported that well over two million absentee or mail ballots sent to voters by election officials were returned as "undeliverable" by the U.S. Postal Service in the last four federal elections (before 2020). The fate of more than 28 million ballots is labelled as "unknown," defined by the EAC as those that "were not returned by voter, spoiled, returned as undeliverable, or otherwise unable to be tracked."

7 Ways the 2005 Carter-Baker Report Could Have Averted Problems With 2020 Election

The Commission on Federal Election Reform also called the Carter-Baker Commission was created in 2004 to address voting and election integrity issues raised by the tumultuous 36-day postelection battle of 2000, which was settled by the U.S. Supreme Court decision that resulted in awarding Florida's 25 electoral votes and the presidency to Republican George W. Bush over Democrat Al Gore.

As noted in the November 2020 article "7 Ways the 2005 Carter-Baker Report Could Have Averted Problems With 2020 Election" in The Daily Signal by Fred Lucas: Had Congress and state governments adopted many of the panel's recommendations, the 2020 postelection mess between President Donald Trump and former Vice President Joe Biden might have been avoided, said Carter-Baker Commission member Kay C. James, now the president of The Heritage Foundation.

"So many of the problems we're now hearing about in the aftermath of the 2020 election could have been avoided had states heeded the advice of the Commission on Federal Election Reform," she said.

Furthermore, 70% of Republicans do not believe the 2020 election was free and fair, according to a Politico/Morning Consult poll. Before the election, just 35% of Republicans didn't believe the election would be free and fair. The shift was different among Democrats, where 95% believed the election was free and fair afterward, compared with 52% who said the same before the election.

Here's a very brief outline of the 2005 Carter-Baker Commission panel's recommendations relevant to this 2020 elections:

1) Voter ID requirements.
2) Mail-In and Absentee Voting Risks.
3) Avoiding Duplicate Registration Across State Lines.
4) Election Observers for Integrity.
5) Reliable Voting Machines.
6) Media Calling Elections.
7) Prosecuting Voter Fraud.

Officials should look at the commission's recommendations and ensure they're doing everything possible to protect the integrity of our elections—one of the most sacred trusts of our republic.

For a more up to date overview of recommendations, we'll turn our attention to then President Donald Trump's 2017 Presidential Advisory Commission on Election Integrity and later to The Heritage Foundation's 2021 report titled <u>The Facts About Election Integrity and the Need for States to Fix Their Election Systems.</u>

President Donald Trump's 2017 Presidential Advisory Commission on Election Integrity

President Trump dissolved his voter integrity commission in January 2018 and ordered the Homeland Security Department to take up the job instead, in a move his backers said could speed up an investigation of the extent of voter fraud. The White House announced the president's decision bringing the 8-month-old effort to an end as covered in the "Trump cancels voter fraud commission, says cost of legal battles was too much Orders Homeland Security

Department to take up investigation" by Stephen Dinan in a January 2018 edition of *The Washington Times*.

Trump decided the commission had become mired in legal challenges and it was a waste of money to continue when much of the same work could be performed by existing federal agencies. Democrats and liberal activists claimed victory, saying they stopped a threat to democracy by derailing the panel, known officially as the Presidential Advisory Commission on Election Integrity.

But Kris Kobach, who was vice chairman of the panel, said Democrats come out behind because the commission's work will continue but will be completed without any input from Democrats, who had been part of the commission but won't have a say in Homeland Security's work. "It will get done faster, but the Democrats no longer have a seat at the table," Kobach said. "If they think this is a victory for the left, they are wrong."

"Despite substantial evidence of voter fraud, many states have refused to provide the Presidential Advisory Commission on Election Integrity with basic information relevant to its inquiry," press secretary Sarah Huckabee Sanders said. "Rather than engage in endless legal battles at taxpayer expense, President Donald J. Trump signed an executive order to dissolve the commission, and he has asked the Department of Homeland Security to review its initial findings and determine next courses of action."

Trump had set up the commission, chaired by Vice President Mike Pence, to investigate his postelection claims that voter fraud is a massive problem that cut into his 2016 vote margins. The panel struggled from the start, however, with Democratic state officials refusing to comply with requests for public voter roll data that in many cases can be easily bought.

At least eight lawsuits were filed to try to derail the commission, accusing it of violating open-records laws or breaking privacy protections by asking for the state voter data.

The commission, created in May 2017, held just two meetings—one in July and another in September. But the biggest job of the commission was to obtain voter data from states and compare it to Homeland Security databases to determine the extent of noncitizens' registration and voting.

Although the commission's work wasn't completed, Kobach who was vice chairman of the panel said, members were able to highlight some information, such as 8,500 documented cases of double-voting in elections in 21 states and 1,000 convictions for voter fraud since 2000.

Kobach said given the hurdles the commission faced, it made sense for the president to ask the department to complete the investigation. "DHS can do it more freely and efficiently than a commission can," Kobach said. "The most important info that only the DHS can provide is how many aliens we have on the voter rolls." However, such a count has been difficult to come by over the years, though efforts by some nongovernmental groups have exposed scattered instances.

The Public Interest Legal Foundation (PILF), run by J. Christian Adams, who was also a member of the Trump voter commission, found thousands of self-admitted noncitizens who registered to vote in Philadelphia, Virginia, and New Jersey. In many of the cases, the noncitizens cast illegal ballots.

Kobach said the commission wasn't a mistake but that the level of opposition made clear it was going to be a morass. "The fact that the commission encountered so many lawsuits and such resistance illustrates just how the partisan left is determined to obstruct the gaining of information about the extent of voter fraud," he said.

Heritage Foundation: 2020 Election Integrity and the Need for States to Fix Their Election Systems

The Heritage Foundation's Election Fraud Database shows that election fraud does occur in American elections. Errors, omissions, and mistakes by election officials and careless, shoddy election practices and procedures or lack of training can cause and have caused problems for voters and candidates.

The Heritage Foundation was ranked as the No. 1 think tank in the world for "Significant Impact on Public Policy" in 2020 according to the latest edition of the University of Pennsylvania's annual report on think tanks and their following report "The Facts About Election Integrity and the Need for States to Fix Their Election Systems" in February 2021 is one of many reasons why:

While there is no accurate information on the extent of these problems, the number of instances in which such issues have occurred and are occurring clearly demonstrates the vulnerabilities in our current patchwork system across the states.

The U.S. Supreme Court said in 2008 in *Crawford v. Marion County Election Board* that the "flagrant examples of [voter] fraud [that] have been documented throughout this Nation's history by respected historians and journalists…demonstrate that not only is the risk of voter fraud real but that it could affect the outcome of a close election." As The Heritage Foundation's database shows, election fraud does occur in American elections.

Errors, omissions, and mistakes by election officials and careless, shoddy election practices and procedures or lack of training can cause and have caused problems for voters and candidates. While there is no accurate information on the extent of these problems, the number of instances in which such issues have occurred and are occurring clearly demonstrates the vulnerabilities in our current patchwork system across the states.

In addition, the rules governing the conduct of elections, which are constitutionally entrusted to the various state legislatures, should not be changed shortly before an election, confusing voters, candidates, and election officials, and should not be changed by those with no constitutional authority to do so. Such behavior is anti-democratic and can lead to the manipulation of election rules to favor certain candidates or political parties. Examples are collusive lawsuits by partisans or state and local election officials who unilaterally alter or ignore the rules the legislature has adopted to govern elections.

Private interest groups of whatever partisan affiliation should not be allowed to provide funds to local election authorities to defray the cost of elections and, in exchange for the local election authority's accepting these funds, dictate, direct, and interfere in the conduct of the election or provide unequal opportunities to vote.

What States Should Do

Per The Heritage Foundation, the public must have trust in the outcome of our elections. That goal is elusive in large part because of the vulnerabilities that currently exist as previously noted.

The following recommendations of best practices have been developed by Heritage Foundation experts based on long experience in the area of election integrity. These recommendations are intended principally for state legislatures, which under our federal system have the primary responsibility for administering elections.

Voter Registration

- **Verify the accuracy of voter registration lists.** Computerized statewide voter registration lists should be designed to be interoperable so that they can communicate seamlessly with other state record databases to allow frequent exchanges and comparisons of information. For example, when an individual changes the residence address on his driver's license, that information should be sent to state election officials so that the voter registration address of the individual is also changed to his or her new department of motor vehicles (DMV) residence address.

- **Verify citizenship of voters.** Only lawful citizens can vote in federal elections. States should therefore require proof of citizenship to register to vote, as well as verify the citizenship of registered voters with the records of the Department of Homeland Security, including access to the E-Verify System.

In-Person and Absentee Voting

- **Require voter ID.** A voter should be required to validate his or her identity with government-issued photo ID to vote both in-person or by absentee ballot (as states such as Alabama and Kansas require). Government-issued IDs should be free for those who cannot afford one.

- **Limit absentee ballots.** Absentee ballots should be reserved to those individuals who are too disabled to vote in person or who will be out of town on Election Day and all Early Voting Days.

- **Prevent vote trafficking.** Vote-trafficking (also called vote harvesting) by third parties should be banned. This would ensure that candidates, campaign staffers, party activists, and political consultants are prohibited from picking up and potentially mishandling or changing absentee ballots and pressuring or coercing vulnerable voters in their homes.

- **Allow election observers complete access to the election process.** Political parties, candidates, and third-party organizations should all be allowed to have observers in every aspect of the election process because transparency is essential to a fair and secure system. The only limitation on such observers is that they cannot interfere with the voting and counting process. However, a representative of the election office should be present to answer the questions of the observers. They should be legally allowed to be in a position—exactly like election officials—to observe everything going on other than the actual voting by individuals. Election officials should be prohibited from stationing observers so far away that they cannot observe the process, including such procedures as the opening of absentee ballots and the verification process.

- **Provide voting assistance.** Any individuals providing assistance to a voter in a voting booth because the voter is illiterate, disabled, or otherwise requires assistance should be required to complete a form, to be filed with poll election officials, providing their name, address, contact information, and the reason they are providing assistance. They should also be required to provide a photo ID.

Counting Votes

- **Prohibit early vote counting.** To avoid premature release of election results, the counting of ballots, including absentee and early votes, should not begin until the polls close at the end of Election Day. However, if a state insists on beginning the count before Election Day, it should ban the release of results until the evening of Election Day, subject to criminal penalties.

Election Litigation

- **Provide state legislatures with legal standing.** State legislatures must ensure that they have legal standing—either through a specific state law or through a constitutional amendment if that is required—to sue other state officials such as governors or secretaries of state who make or attempt to make unauthorized changes in state election laws. For example, if a secretary of state extends the deadline set by state law for the receipt of absentee ballots, legislatures should have legal standing to contest that unilateral change that overrides state law. They should be classified as a necessary party in any lawsuit. And voters should be provided by state law with the ability to file a writ of mandamus against any state or local official who fails to abide by or enforce a state election law requirement.

What States Should Not Do

- **No same-day registration.** Registration should be required before Election Day to give election officials sufficient time to verify the accuracy of the registration information contained on a registration form and to confirm the eligibility of the individual seeking to cast a vote in the upcoming election.

- **No automatic voter registration.** States should comply with the National Voter Registration Act and provide registration opportunities at state agencies. However, all individuals should be asked at the time of the state agency transaction, such as the application for a driver's license, whether they want to register to vote. No one should be automatically registered without their consent or knowledge since this can lead to multiple registrations by the same individual as well as the registration of ineligible individuals such as noncitizens.

- **No private funding of election officials and government agencies.** States should prohibit election officials from receiving private funding from outside organizations or individuals. This prohibition prevents potential conflicts of interest. Such funding may influence the outcome of elections and violate principles of equal protection since it may lead to unequal opportunities to vote in different areas of a state.

Stolen Elections Due to the Vulnerabilities of Absentee and Mail-In Ballots

Pushing for more absentee balloting—even all-mail elections—is unwise. It would make election fraud far easier. All states ban electioneering in polling places, but there are no such bans on electioneering in voters' homes. This leaves at-home voters vulnerable. There is no reason we can't vote safely in our polling places in November, rather than hoping that someone else will deliver our ballot in time to be counted.

Per the July 2020 "Stolen Elections Show the Vulnerabilities of Absentee Ballots" by Hans von Spakovsky of The Heritage Foundation: No question about it, some people need absentee ballots—those with disabilities, those living abroad and others who can't make it to the polls on Election Day. But pushing for more absentee balloting—even all-mail elections—would make election fraud far easier.

In-person voting occurs under the supervision of election officials, with election observers there to make sure everything is on the up-and-up. This transparency is a vital hallmark of the democratic process. Mail-in ballots, however, are susceptible to being stolen, altered, forged, and forced—to say the least.

Listed below are four elections in California, Florida, Indiana, and North Carolina—stolen through absentee-ballot fraud—demonstrate some of the problems.

1. In 1991, school board elections in Fresno, California, were overturned due to "widespread illegal voting practices that permeated this election—including fraud and tampering" with absentee ballots. A local political organization took over the voter registration and absentee balloting process, completely controlling the application, delivery, completion and return of the absentee ballots of minority voters. Some were pressured to vote for specific candidates. Others had their ballots filled out without their consent or consultation.

2. Six years later, a court overturned a Miami mayoral election because of massive fraud involving 5,000 absentee ballots. A city commissioner and his chief of staff were among the 55 defendants convicted of fraud. Some voters were bribed for their absentee ballots. Some

somehow managed to submit absentee ballots from the grave, as did others who weren't even Miami residents. And many poor and elderly voters were coerced or had their ballots stolen and voted for them—effectively disenfranchising them.

3. In 2004, the Indiana Supreme Court threw out the results of a 2003 mayoral primary in East Chicago because the incumbent mayor and his cronies "perverted the absentee voting process and compromised the integrity and results of that election." Just as in Fresno and Miami, the fraudsters in East Chicago targeted "first-time voters" and others "less informed or lacking in knowledge of the voting process, the infirm, the poor, and those with limited skills in the English language" for their absentee ballots."

4. Just two years ago, a North Carolina congressional race was overturned by the state election board because of "concerted fraudulent activities related to absentee by-mail ballots." And the New Jersey attorney general has just charged four people in Paterson with engaging in absentee ballot fraud so pervasive that it has cast doubt on the results of the city's recent municipal, all-mail election.

This brief review doesn't even take into account the millions—yes, millions—of absentee ballots that the U.S. Election Assistance Commission reports were either misdelivered by the Postal Service or rejected by election officials after they were returned by voters in the last four federal elections.

Standards for Absentee Ballots and All Mail Elections: Doing It Right...and Doing It Wrong

Absentee ballots are vulnerable to intimidation, fraud, and chaos as all-mail elections move behind closed doors beyond the oversight of election officials, along with prolonged counting and potentially lengthy delays in certifying questionable results.

As per the "Standards for Absentee Ballots and All-Mail Elections: Doing It Right...and Doing It Wrong" May 2020 report by The Heritage Foundation, election officials must keep in mind that:

- Absentee ballots compromise the secret ballot process, a hallmark of U.S. elections for over 100 years.

- Voters are vulnerable to intimidation and pressure tactics by campaigns because these ballots are being filled out without the supervision of election officials.

- Absentee ballots are "the tool of choice" of vote thieves and those willing to compromise the election process.

- According to U.S. Election Assistance Commission surveys, millions of mailed ballots have been misdirected or gone missing in prior elections.

- Electronic signatures are too imprecise and easily duplicated and should not be accepted.

How Mailed Ballots Should—and Should Not—Be Handled

States should require voters to register prior to Election Day, with sufficient time to verify identity, residence, and citizenship status. Voter registration lists are notoriously inaccurate and out of date, with multiple registrations by the same individual; registrants who have died, moved, or are not U.S. citizens; and registrations lacking complete addresses.

States must review voter rolls to ensure accuracy, including verification through state and federal databases, such as the databases of state social service agencies, tax authorities, DMVs, corrections departments, the Social Security Administration, and the Department of Homeland Security.

States Must Prevent Fraudulent Voting Activities

Automatically mailing a ballot to all registered voters is an open invitation to fraud and abuse.

Not every new resident at an address throws out the ballot that is still being automatically mailed to a former resident, and third parties may canvass neighborhoods looking for those "extra" ballots—with some being tempted to cast those extra votes.

States should ban "vote harvesting" and not allow candidates, party activists, or political consultants who have a stake in the outcome, to collect absentee ballots from voters.

Ensuring Election Integrity by Mail

Voters should be required to request an absentee ballot with a signed form that can be authenticated. States should require a photocopy of an ID or the serial number of a driver's license or state ID card from all absentee voters.

If states insist on contacting all registered voters, active (not inactive) voters should be sent an absentee ballot request form by First Class mail, not an absentee ballot, which reduces the opportunity for an unauthorized person to complete an unsolicited ballot.

By sending the request via First Class mail, election officials will receive notice from the U.S. Postal Service if the voter is no longer at his registered address, providing valuable information for the accuracy of the registration list.

On Election Day

Only absentee ballots officially postmarked by the U.S. Postal Service by the end of Election Day should be accepted.

Simply requiring a signature by the end of Election Day provides no way for officials to verify that the ballot was actually completed before polls closed and preliminary results were being reported.

When processing returned absentee ballots, states must have strong authentication standards, including comparing signatures on ballot envelopes with voter registration signatures.

Absentee ballots should not be processed and tabulated until the end of Election Day; starting that process early risks leaks that could deter individuals from voting or provide information to candidates or vote harvesters that allows them to manipulate close races after the polls have closed.

Election Officials Must

Work with local U.S. Postal Service authorities to ensure integrity in the mail system and prevent delayed delivery of ballots.

Coordinate with federal, state, and local prosecutors to ensure that law enforcement is ready to move quickly to enforce federal and state laws against intimidation of voters, as well as other election crimes.

Florida, Texas, Georgia, and Arizona Lead the Way in 2021 Election & Voter Law Integrity

In the LifeNews.com article "Voters Should Have an ID to Vote and States are Leading the Way to Make Sure They Do" by Matt Carpenter in March 2021: Democrats have said that restrictions against mail-in ballot access are a ploy by Republicans in response to former President Donald Trump's election loss, while Republicans have said vote-by-mail leads to fraud. Unfortunately for the Democrats, voters very much believe in securing the integrity of elections.

In fact, a recent poll by Rasmussen Reports showed 75 percent of likely voters support laws requiring voters to produce a valid photo ID to vote—a number that has only increased in recent years, up from 68 percent in 2018. What is more, voters of all races agree: a clear majority of white voters (74 percent), black voters (69 percent), and other minority voters (82 percent) agree with voter ID laws. Only the most committed leftists think ID requirements to vote are discriminatory.

In addition to the states noted in this section, many others are considering similar legislation. All of this is happening at the same time the Senate is preparing to take up H.R. 1, the poorly named "For the People Act", which would codify many of the last-minute election policy changes implemented as part of the run-up to the 2020 election and ongoing pandemic that caused the crisis of confidence in our election system now being addressed by the states.

Democrats, their allies in mainstream and social media (i.e., mediacrats), and recently woke corporations, will undoubtedly keep up their allegations of voter suppression as governors and legislators in the states take up popular and common-sense legislation to protect the integrity of their state's elections.

Instead of tearing down efforts to secure the ballot box, voters should contact their legislators and governor and ask them to implement some of these proposals to ensure it is "easy to vote—but hard to cheat."

They should also contact their Senator and urge them to oppose H.R. 1. As the 2022 midterms approach, voters might wonder if the same potential for fraud and abuse we saw in the 2020 election will remain in future elections. Fortunately, states like Florida, Texas, Georgia, and Arizona are leading the way to ensure voters can have confidence in the integrity of their vote and others are sapiently following their lead.

Setting the Record Straight on Georgia's New Voter-Access Law

Per Brad Raffensperger, Secretary of State of Georgia: Ignore the partisan disinformation. Georgia remains a national leader in voting access and election security. Case in point is Georgia senator Raphael Warnock. In a fundraising email sent soon after SB 202—Georgia's new voter-access law—was passed, he falsely accused Georgia Republicans of waging "a massive and unabashed assault on voting rights" by "ending no-excuse mail voting" and "restricting early voting on weekends."

"I realize that Senator Warnock is a new lawmaker," states Raffensperger, "but he should at least read the bill in question before tossing out completely false claims. SB 202 leaves no-excuse absentee voting in place and expands early voting in Georgia by mandating an additional day of weekend voting in all Georgia counties. It also continues Sunday voting in counties that want it."

Not to be outdone, President Biden alleged that SB 202's new photo-ID-number requirement for absentee ballots "will effectively deny the right to vote to countless voters." He should tell that to the majority of Georgia voters, Georgia Democrats, and black voters in Georgia who supported the commonsense effort. Studies show that voter-ID laws don't decrease turnout. Georgia's voter-turnout numbers and percentages have hit records repeatedly since we introduced photo ID for in-person voting.

Georgia has the most successful automatic voter-registration program in the country. Automatically registering eligible voters through the Georgia Department of Driver Services, which confirms citizenship prior to registration, makes it easier for eligible voters to vote, and ensures that election officials have accurate, up-to-date information. Notably, President Biden's home state of Delaware does not offer this to voters.

The legislation moves Georgia from the subjective signature-match identity-verification process for absentee-ballot voting to objective ID numbers from photo IDs, free voter IDs, or other documents. I introduced this concept last year with the absentee-ballot-request portal, and it won bipartisan praise. With such close elections, moving to an objective standard takes pressure off of our local election officials.

It is also convenient for voters. Over 97 percent of Georgia's voters have a driver's-license number associated with their voter-registration record per the "Setting the Record Straight on Georgia's New Voter-Access Law" article by Brad Raffensperger in the April 2021 edition of the *National Review*.

After the 2020 election, we should all be able to agree that spreading disinformation about elections is wrong. Instead, the liberal outrage machine is running at full steam on SB 202, putting fundraising over facts. But I know better than most that truth matters in elections. I'll keep telling the truth about our election systems, even though I know President Biden, Senator Warnock, and Stacey Abrams care more about money and partisan outrage.

Further Georgia updates are covered in Chapter 13.

Florida Gov. DeSantis Signs GOP-Backed Election Bill Limiting Mail-In Voting, Drop Boxes

Florida Gov. Ron DeSantis on May 6, 2021, signed a Republican-backed election integrity law that places restrictions on ballot drop boxes and mail-in ballots. When signing the bill, the Republican governor said it would place Florida ahead of other states in preventing any potential voter fraud. "Right now I have what we think is the strongest election integrity measures in the country," he said. "We're also banning ballot harvesting. We're not going to let political operatives go and get satchels of votes and dump them in some drop box."

As per the May 2021 "Florida Gov. DeSantis Signs GOP-Backed Election Bill Limiting Mail-In Voting, Drop Boxes" by *Epoch Times* reporter Jack Phillips: The bill would require signature verification for voters; revise distance limits for people at polling places, early voting sites, and related sites; have election workers monitor ballot drop boxes; and include more identification requirements for dropping off ballots.

The legislation would place limits on who can return a finished mail-in ballot and prevent election officials from entering consent agreements; it would also require voters to submit yearly requests for mail-in ballots, according to the text of the bill.

"Drop boxes must be geographically located so as to provide all voters in the county with an equal opportunity to cast a ballot," the bill states, adding that they "must be monitored in person."

The "prohibition on the use of private funds for election-related expenses" is an apparent response to Facebook CEO Mark Zuckerberg and other groups having provided funding to some states and locals in 2020 to help run elections. Republicans have expressed concern that the funding mostly targeted Democrat-aligned areas and hurt the GOP.

The new measure dropped a "wet signature" requirement that was in earlier versions of the bill, whereby a physically signed signature is kept on file to verify a voter's signature. "Me signing this bill here says: 'Florida, your vote counts. Your vote is going to cast with integrity and transparency, and this is a great place for democracy,'" DeSantis said.

Several Democrat-aligned groups, corporate news outlets, and corporations panned the bill as being unfairly restrictive, while the NAACP and Common Cause have stated they would immediately file a lawsuit in court alleging that it disenfranchises black, Latino, and disabled people.

Minutes after DeSantis signed the bill, election attorney Marc Elias said his team filed a lawsuit challenging the bill on behalf of the League of Women Voters of Florida, the Black Voters Matter Fund, and the Florida Alliance for Retired Americans.

"SB 90 does not impede all of Florida's voters equally," the lawsuit alleged. "It is crafted to and will operate to make it more difficult for certain types of voters to participate in the state's elections, including those voters who generally wish to vote with a vote-by-mail ballot and voters who have historically had to overcome substantial hurdles to reach the ballot box, such as Florida's senior voters, youngest voters, and minority voters."

Texas House Passes GOP-Backed Election Integrity

The Texas state House passed a GOP-backed election overhaul bill in May 2021 that would add new penalties and rules, becoming the latest state Republican-led legislative body to pass similar legislation in recent days. The House passed Senate Bill 7 on a 78-64 mostly party-line vote. The bill, which was first passed in the Senate but was significantly reworked in the House, will now head back to the Texas state Senate for a vote.

In another *Epoch Times* article by Jack Phillips "Texas House Passes GOP-Backed Election Integrity Bill" in May 2021: Republican Texas Gov. Greg Abbott lauded the Republican state lawmakers for passing the bill in the House. "This bill will help ensure that we have trust & confidence in the outcome of our elections," Abbott wrote in a tweet. "One step closer to my desk & making it TX law."

The measure will make it a felony to provide voters with a vote-by-mail application if they hadn't already requested one. It would also bar the usage of public funds to facilitate the distribution of mail-in voting applications. "A person commits an offense if the person knowingly collects or possesses a ballot voted by mail or official carrier envelope from a voter in connection with vote harvesting services," the bill's text reads.

Also according to the bill, poll watchers can only be removed by a judge "if the watcher engaged in activity that would constitute an offense related to the conduct of the election." During the Nov. 3, 2020, election, numerous Republican poll watchers stated that they were treated unfairly or kicked out of polling places in areas like Philadelphia, Detroit, and Atlanta.

Democrats and "so-called" progressive groups criticized the bill and claimed it is tantamount to "voter suppression," deploying similar rhetoric used against election integrity bills that were passed and signed into law in Florida and Georgia in recent days. Texas Democratic Party chair Gilberto Hinojosa echoed claims made by Democrats in other states by saying the bill is an attempt to "silence voters in Texas, especially voters of color."

But Republicans, including Texas state Rep. Jeff Leach, said that the measure is a "strong [and] sensible election integrity legislation that ensures and protects full access to the ballot box while deterring and cracking down on illegal activity that undermines our elections."

Arizona Senate Republicans Audit Maricopa County Election Results

Biden won Arizona by about 10,000 votes, flipping the state after Trump's win in 2016, which led state Republicans leaders to halt the certification of the vote for alleged wrongdoing as reported in Poynter by Amy Sherman in May 2021 titled "Why Arizona Republicans are auditing election results."

However, judges rejected lawsuits on behalf of Maricopa County to half the certification and instead authorized a hand count audit of an 8,000 sample of ballots as required by state law and hired independent firms to conduct a forensic audit of tabulation equipment. The county found no abnormalities in November 2020.

However, five months later, Republican state senators wanted to do their own full audit of Maricopa County and per Senate President Karen Fann, "When you have got half the people that do not trust the electoral system anymore—rightly or wrongly so—if they have questions, who is responsible for answering these questions? How do we put election integrity back into our system? And that's only what this has been about."

In December 2020, Arizona state Senate Republicans sent subpoenas to Maricopa County seeking images of the ballots and election equipment, and a judge ruled in their favor. Senate Republicans hired a team including Cyber Ninjas, a Florida-based technology company lacking election audit experience. Regardless of the findings of the audit, they will not result in changing the outcome of the election won by President Joe Biden because the results were already certified.

As per the May 2021 "Arizona Lawmakers Tell Maricopa Officials to Turn Over Routers or Face Subpoenas" *Epoch Times* article by Zachary Stieber: May 2021, the Arizona Senate subpoenaed election materials, such as ballots, following the 2020 election; lawmakers also issued subpoenas for election machines, passwords, and other technology.

Maricopa County alleged in a lawsuit that the request for materials was overly broad and threatened voter privacy. A judge, though, ruled that the request was "the equivalent of a Court order." But the county says it won't turn over routers or router images, claiming that doing so poses a significant security risk to law enforcement.

Arizona lawmakers and officials in the state's largest county clashed anew over election audit subpoenas, with county officials refusing to hand over routers and claiming they don't have passwords to access administrative control functions of election machines. Arizona's Senate told Maricopa County on May 7, 2021 that it would issue subpoenas for live testimony from the county's Board of Supervisors unless it receives materials that are being withheld.

"We've been asked to relay that the Senate views the County's explanations on the router and passwords issues as inadequate and potentially incorrect," a lawyer for the Senate said in an email to county officials.

The county has also informed the Senate's audit liaison, former Republican Secretary of State Ken Bennett, that it doesn't have passwords to access administrative functions on Dominion Voting Systems machines that were used to scan ballots during the election.

The county board called an emergency meeting later on May 7, 2021 to consider legal advice and litigation regarding its noncompliance with the Senate subpoenas. Further Arizona updates are covered in Chapter 14.

5 – Unsapient & Leftist Policies Designed to Transform Elections & Politics

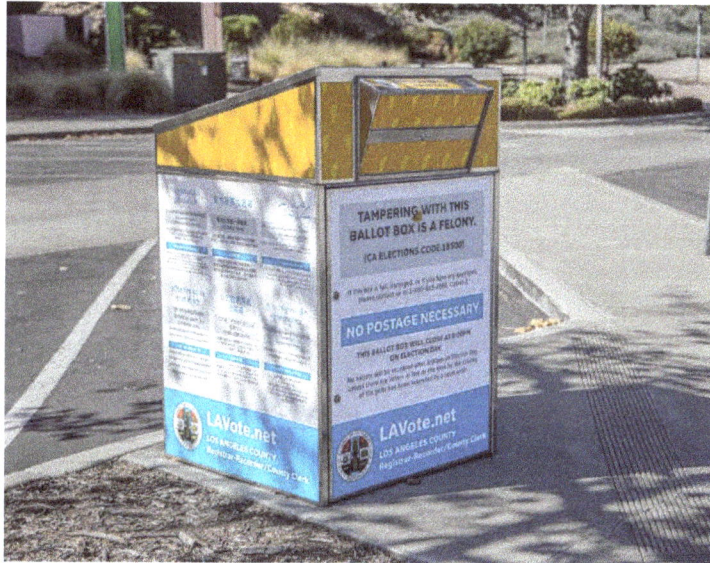

Credit: Bobby Block/The Signal - Official (and unsecured) ballot boxes are placed in public areas of Los Angeles County, including this one at the Santa Clarita Metrolink Station. October 12, 2020.

In the broader debate about election security, conservatives—and Republicans in general—have tended to argue that casting a vote is a privilege of citizenship that should be safeguarded with secure processes and restrictions, and that lowering requirements around voting opens the process up to fraud and abuse.

Progressives—and their Democrat allies—tend to state that barriers to casting a ballot should be as low as possible and that the kind of security measures pushed by conservatives, such as stricter voter ID or proof-of-citizenship laws, amount to disenfranchisement. Progressives often frame the debate as between voter suppression and expansion, while conservatives tend to see it as election security versus vulnerability to abuse.

In the wake of the 2020 election controversy, per the *Epoch Times* "Conservative Nonprofit to Launch $10 Million Campaign to Strengthen Election Integrity" article by Tom Ozimek in March 2021: Republican and Democrat lawmakers across the country have been pulling in opposite directions by introducing legislation that either reduces barriers—and guardrails—to voting or seeks to strengthen election integrity, which can also make casting a vote more effortful or burdensome.

Hopefully, by now, you're seeing a pattern where mostly sapient conservatives groups like The Heritage Foundation are working diligently to keep elections safe and voting secure. Equally important, you should also see a common theme amongst some Democrats and many leftists organizations like the Brennan Center who are enacting unsapient policies and pushing for new laws that undermine our election integrity and safety measures and make them more susceptible to tampering, fraud, and abuse.

10 Democrat and Leftist Tactics Versus the Vote

All of those lawsuits (and the COVID-19 response bills filed in the House by Speaker Nancy Pelosi and other Democrats) have similar goals that will give Democrat political actors the ability to game the system. This would be true of any actors trying to change the rules in this manner mid-game.

As per "The Left Versus the Vote" August 2020 article by Hans von Spakovsky in The American Mind: In state after state, almost all the lawsuits filed in 2020 prior to the November 3, 2020 elections have been filed by Democrats and liberal or progressive organizations, seeking to change election rules by judicial fiat. Their objective: force all-mail elections or huge increases in absentee balloting while simultaneously eliminating safeguards against abuse and fraud.

Professor Richard Pildes' count of at least 160 lawsuits filed by "party organizations, campaigns and interest groups," notes that the Trump campaign and the Republican National Committee "are involved" in only 40, "some in response to Democratic lawsuits." The rest are from the Democratic side of the political aisle and their end goals are not sapient in a variety of ways as covered in this chapter starting with "Here Are 4 Egregious Ways the Left Wants to Transform American Politics" in the March 2019 article by Elizabeth Slattery and Jason Snead in The Daily Signal.

1 – 'Sue and Settle' Changes to Mail-In Voting

Leftists and Democrats use various strategies to implement changes to voting laws in order to limit election integrity or make it more difficult for election overseers and observers to detect election fraud. One of the approaches is termed "sue and settle" as reported on by Mollie Hemingway in The Federalist in her March 2021 article "Media's Entire Georgia Narrative Is Fraudulent, Not Just The Fabricated Trump Quotes."

Perkins Coie, the law firm that also ordered what became the Russia collusion hoax against Trump in 2016, runs an extremely well-funded and highly coordinated operation to alter how U.S. elections are run. The firm will sue states and get them to make agreements that alter their voting practices.

Marc Elias, well known for his role in the Russia collusion hoax and other Democrat operations, runs the campaign to change voting laws and practices to favor Democrats. Perkins Coie billed the Democrat Party at least $27 million for its efforts to radically change voting laws ahead of the 2020 election, more than double what they charged Hillary Clinton and the Democratic National Committee for similar work in 2016.

In March 2020, Georgia Secretary of State Brad Raffensperger voluntarily agreed to a settlement in federal court with various Democrat groups, which had sued the state over its rules for absentee voting. The end result was a dramatic alteration in how Georgia conducted the 2020 election

Republicans were not party to the agreement, despite their huge interest in the case. The agreement explicitly states that neither Raffensperger nor the Democratic groups who sued him take a position on whether the laws and procedures being changed were constitutional or not.

Democrats' high-powered attorneys introduced several significant changes, such as the opportunity to "cure" ballots. That means that when an absentee ballot comes in with problems that would typically lead it to be trashed, the voter is instead given a chance to "cure" or correct the ballot. It also said Democrats would offer training and guidance on signature verification to county registrars and absentee ballot clerks.

Most importantly, the settlement got rid of any meaningful signature match. The law had previously required signatures to match the signature on file with the Georgia voter registration database. But the settlement allowed the signature to match any signature on file, including the one on the absentee ballot application. That meant a fraudulently obtained ballot would easily have a signature match and no way to detect fraud.

The ballot also could only be rejected if a majority of registrars, deputy registrars, and ballot clerks agreed to it, another burden that made it easier to just let all ballots through without scrutiny. It made a huge difference in how many ballots were rejected.

Raffensperger's decision to voluntarily agree to such a dramatic change in the rules of the game without input from the Republican Party of Georgia, much less the Republican National Committee, angered many Republicans, including Sens. Kelly Loeffler and David Perdue, as they learned about it following the November 2020 election. Other Republicans felt he harmed election integrity by mailing out millions of absentee ballot applications, ostensibly because of health concerns related to COVID-19.

2 – Vote Harvesting: A Recipe for Coercion and Election Fraud

Vote harvesting occurs when third parties—like campaign workers collect absentee ballots from voters and deliver them to election officials. Allowing individuals other than the voter or his immediate family to handle absentee ballots is a recipe for mischief and wrongdoing. Giving third parties who have a stake in the outcome of an election unsupervised access to voters and their absentee ballots is not wise.

Vote harvesting gives party activists, campaign consultants, and other political guns-for-hire the ability to manipulate election outcomes either through coercion of voters or outright ballot theft and forgery. Yet, in places like California and the District of Columbia, vote harvesting is perfectly legal as reported by Hans von Spakovsky in a October 2019 article in *The Washington Times* titled "Vote Harvesting a Recipe for Coercion and Election Fraud."

In 2010, Democrat Kamala Harris ran against Republican Steve Cooley, district attorney of Los Angeles County. Cooley held the lead on election night but the same Service Employees International Union (SEIU) drones who ran Harris's campaign dredged up enough provisional (vote harvested) ballots to give Harris a victory of less than 1 percent some three weeks later. If any Californian thought that was ballot fraud, it would be hard to blame them.

"The largest number of voter fraud cases involve absentee ballots," said Hans von Spakovsky, manager of the election law reform initiative at The Heritage Foundation, where he is a senior legal fellow.

"The problem with vote harvesting is that it destroys the secret ballot. It allows people to go into homes, pressure people," von Spakovsky, who also is a former Justice Department lawyer, member of the Federal Election Commission, and member of the 2017 Presidential Advisory Commission on Election Integrity.

3 – Eliminating the Senate Filibuster

Democrats have recently been more vocal about getting rid of the Senate filibuster, an action that prolongs debate and delays a vote on a measure as reported in the April 2021 *Epoch Times* article "Sen. Graham Supports Denying Quorum If Democrats End Filibuster" by Masooma Haq. Before 1917, Senate rules didn't provide a way to end a debate and force a vote on a measure, but that year they adopted a rule that enabled a two-thirds majority (67-votes) to end a filibuster via a procedure known as cloture, which later changed 60-votes.

Many top Democrats including President Joe Biden, Senate Majority Leader Chuck Schumer (D-New York), and Chair of the Senate Judiciary Committee Dick Durbin (D-Illinois) are calling for an end to the filibuster. Durbin, who previously supported the filibuster rule, has recently come out in opposition. Durbin in March argued that the filibuster was damaging the nation's democracy.

Senate Minority Leader Mitch McConnell (R-Ky.) said Republicans would fight back if Democrats eliminated the filibuster to push their agenda forward. Democrats are pushing for removing or reforming the filibuster to pass H.R. 1 in the Senate because the filibuster currently requires 60 votes to pass legislation.

McConnell threatened that if Democrats eliminate the filibuster, Republicans will fight back, and the Senate would be like "a 100-car pileup" with "nothing moving. It would not open up an express lane for the Biden presidency to speed into the history books, the Senate would be more like a 100-car pileup, nothing moving," McConnell recently said on the Senate floor.

To vote to rid the Senate of the filibuster rule, the Senate would need 51 votes, but two Democrat senators have committed to keeping the rule, Sens. Kyrsten Sinema (D-Arizona) and Joe Manchin (D-West Virginia). Manchin told Axios, if Democrats get rid of the filibuster, it will make the legislative process very weak.

"If you give up on democracy, if you give up on the Republicans, and you give up on filibuster, I tell you we're in serious problems," Manchin said. "This swing, and the yin and yang, will be so frequent every administration change, what goes around comes around."

4 – The Natural Disaster and Emergency Ballot Act of 2020

Senator Amy Klobuchar (D-Minn.) and Ron Wyden (D-Ore.) led a group of Democratic senators to introduce legislation on March 18, 2020 to promote mail-in and early voting to decrease the spread of the CCP virus. Their Natural Disaster and Emergency Ballot Act (NDEBA) would allow voters 20 days of early voting in all states and stipulates that all mail-in ballots received during the 21 days be valid and ensure that all voters have the option to request absentee ballots.

House Speaker Nancy Pelosi, D-California, unsuccessfully pushed to include provisions of the Wyden-Klobuchar bill in the $2.2 trillion coronavirus emergency relief bill that Congress passed in July 2020. The Democrats' unsuccessful NDEBA legislation would require every state to offer at least 20 days of early voting and "no excuse" absentee balloting.

The Klobuchar-Wyden legislation also states that local governments should begin processing absentee ballots up to two weeks before an election to avoid delay in certifying a winner. Currently, most jurisdictions don't count ballots until after Election Day, in part to prevent voting trends from leaking out to the public or campaigns.

These emergency plans would allow voters to vote by mail without a specific excuse and to vote early in person for a full day before an election. The ideas are to make voting as easy as possible for all voters. The unsuccessful bill would guarantee that all states automatically mail ballots to registered voters; voters can mail back those ballots for free, and voters should also be able to drop off ballots at predesignated locations. The ballots should be accepted as long as they are postmarked by Election Day and received within 10 days of the election.

Democratic party leadership stated in a recent op-ed that it will help states pay for these reforms, with the democratic leaders writing, "That's why any state that voluntarily complies with such reforms will receive payments equal to the costs they've incurred."

5 – Packing the Supreme Court

The last major attempt to alter the Supreme Court's composition was in the late 1930s. President Franklin Delano Roosevelt, upset with the conservative "Four Horsemen" of the Supreme Court thwarting parts of his New Deal agenda, tried to persuade Congress to allow him to appoint a "junior justice" for every sitting justice who remained on the Supreme Court beyond age 70.

That measure failed in the Democrat-controlled Senate. But Roosevelt got the last laugh—he got to "pack" the court the old-fashioned way and ended up appointing eight justices throughout his time in office. So while it's not unprecedented to alter the number of seats on the Supreme Court, proponents of "court packing" should explain why they want to do so and what kind of justices they would appoint.

Odds are, they would favor activist judges who don't understand the proper, limited role the judiciary is supposed to play in our government. That would end up compounding the problem of an activist Supreme Court that inserts itself into matters that should be handled at the ballot box and in Congress or statehouses across the country, not the SCOTUS.

6 – Granting Statehood to Washington, D.C.

There are good reasons why the District should not be made into a state—besides denying the Democrat' attempt to add two senate seats in a deep blue city.

The Founders settled on placing our nation's capital in a federal city that would not be unduly influenced by a state government. As James Madison explained in *The Federalist* No. 43, "dependence of the members of the general government, on the state comprehending the seat of government, for protection in the exercise of their duty, might bring on the national councils an imputation of awe or influence, equally dishonorable to the government and dissatisfactory to the other members of the confederacy."

It is not as though residents of the District are actually without representation, despite what the license plates say. In a way, people living in Washington, D.C. have 535 representatives from both houses of Congress who live and work there for a large part of the year.

The District also enjoys benefits from its unique status. For example, federal funds account for 20 percent of the District's budget, and Uncle Sam contributes more toward D.C. public school students than any other state. (As of 2018, the District spent roughly double the national average per student.)

7 – Lowering the Voting Age

In March 2019, a majority of House Democrats voted to lower the federal voting age to 16 as part of an amendment to H.R. 1's first attempt at passage. The motion, thankfully, failed by a wide margin and enjoys scant popular support.

But the idea of enfranchising children still won the backing of many leading Democrats, including House Speaker Nancy Pelosi, D-California, who said it was important to "capture kids" early. To hear Pelosi and others describe it, empowering 16-year-olds to vote is all about encouraging good habits of civic engagement, recognizing the intelligence of our youth, and giving them a voice. These kids are old enough to drive and work—shouldn't they also be able to vote?

That all sounds high-minded and empowering, but something far more cynical and manipulative is going on. Liberals know that young people tend to vote Democratic. It's with age and, dare we say, wisdom (sapience), that people tend to turn to the right, become more conservative and sapient and vote Republican.

Furthermore, half of young Americans now unsapiently favor socialism, probably because schools have utterly failed to teach them about the costs of collectivist ideologies. And when socialism is all about a free lunch, free health care, and free college tuition, it doesn't sound so bad. Generations X Y Z madness!

As a general rule, teens are impressionable, impulsive, and ill-informed about the real-world, and tend to be more liberal, vote Democratic and veer to the left—which is what happened in the 2020 election. That's not meant as derision. It's just biology: Teenagers' brains are still developing, and their hormones are surging. Many are bright and civic-minded, to be sure, and we've all met those rare teenagers possessed with maturity beyond their years. But they are the exception, not the rule.

On the whole, 16-year-olds know too little about the world—and often, virtually nothing about American history, government, or economics—to cast thoughtful and meaningful votes. If liberals truly care about raising the next generation to be engaged and informed, they should start by demanding civics education, not ballots, for America's youth.

The left is increasingly willing to cast aside any rule, any constitutional provision, and any political norm if they think doing so will lead to short-term partisan gains. That is a dangerous and short-sighted game to play—and voting madness!

8 – Allowing Felons to Vote While Incarcerated Is Reckless

The idea that felons should be allowed to vote while incarcerated is not just an unwise policy, it is a reckless one as noted in the October 2019 "Allowing Felons to Vote While Incarcerated Is Reckless" article by The Heritage Foundation's Hans von Spakovsky. In other words, felons are individuals who have chosen to violate the rules and norms of our society, rules and norms that are incorporated in our laws and that are intended to protect all of us and provide for the safety of our communities. Those who are not willing to follow the law cannot claim a right to choose those who will make and enforce the laws for everyone else.

Why would you want to allow those who have committed serious crimes against their fellow citizens to vote while they are still incarcerated? They have demonstrated by their action that they do not have the responsibility and commitment to our laws to make them trustworthy enough to vote.

Does anyone really think that someone like Richard Poplawski, who was convicted of the ambush-style killing of three Pittsburgh police officers, should be able to vote while he is sitting on death row?

9 – John Lewis Voting Rights Advancement Act

In the latest attempt to amend the Voting Rights Act, Senator Patrick Leahy (D., Vermont) recently introduced the John Lewis Voting Rights Advancement Act. It sounds great until you realize it will be used to achieve partisan political gains rather than prevent racial discrimination.

The real aim is to reverse the 2013 Supreme Court decision in *Shelby County v. Holder* and to give the political allies of Democrats—the radicals who inhabit the career ranks of the Civil

Rights Division of the U.S. Justice Department (where Hans von Spakovsky used to work), and advocacy groups such as the ACLU—control over state election rules.

It is a dangerous bill that violates basic principles of federalism. It also illustrates what could happen if Democrats gain control of Congress and the White House, to the detriment of secure, fair elections administered by the states. Utilizing the "Against the John Lewis Voting Rights Advancement Act" *National Review* article in October 2020 by Hans von Spakovsky, let's see why:

The Voting Rights Act of 1965 (VRA)

The Voting Rights Act (VRA) of 1965 is probably one of the most successful pieces of legislation ever passed by Congress. It helped eliminate the widespread discriminatory practices that were preventing African Americans from registering and voting in the 1960s.

There are no longer any such barriers or practices that block black Americans (or anyone else) from registering and voting, despite the mythical claims of "voter suppression" promulgated by the Left. In the 2012 presidential election, for example, blacks voted at a higher rate than whites nationally (66.2 percent vs. 64.1 percent), according to the U.S. Census Bureau.

The main provision of the VRA is Section 2, which prohibits any voting "standard, practice or procedure . . . which results in a denial or abridgment of the right of any citizen of the United States to vote on account of race or color" or membership in certain language-minority groups. It is permanent, applies nationwide, and can be enforced by the Justice Department as well as private parties. It was also completely unaffected by the *Shelby County* decision and remains in full force today.

VRA: Section 5

Shelby County v. Holder was—and the Leahy bill is—about another provision in the VRA: Section 5 saga.

Section 5 was originally an emergency five-year provision that required "covered" jurisdictions to get preapproval of any changes in their voting laws and practices (even simple changes such as the location of a polling place) from the U.S. Department of Justice or a federal court in Washington, D.C., a process known as "preclearance." Section 5 was renewed for an additional five years in 1970; for an additional seven years in 1975; for an additional 25 years in 1982; and finally for an additional 25 years in 2006. At the time of the Shelby County decision in 2013, Section 5 covered nine states and parts of six others.

Shelby County v. Holder dealt specifically with Section 4 of the VRA, which determined the states and smaller jurisdictions that were subject to Section 5 preclearance. The coverage formula was based on a jurisdiction's having voter registration and turnout by all voters of less than 50 percent in the 1964, 1968, or 1972 elections. The formula was designed to capture states engaging in blatant discrimination by taking into account black voters' low registration and turnout caused by those discriminatory practices.

Congress did not update the coverage formula in 2006. Why not? Perhaps because, if it had, all of the covered jurisdictions—mostly (but not exclusively) southern states—would have dropped out of the Section 5 preclearance requirement owing to the vast improvement of voting conditions since 1972. By 2006, the registration and turnout rates of black voters were on par with or even exceeded those of white voters in many of the covered states. So states such as Alabama, Georgia, and Mississippi remained under the onerous preclearance requirement based on information that was almost 40 years out of date. Voting madness!

But the Left loved Section 5 because of the central role played in its enforcement by its friends and political allies in the career ranks of the Civil Rights Division, many of whom were hired from the ACLU, the NAACP, and other groups allied with the Democratic Party. They could easily refuse to preclear any voting change opposed by the Left—such as voter-ID laws—without having to go to court with a Section 2 lawsuit, where they would have to prove that a law was discriminatory.

The Supreme Court Ruled That Section 5 Was Unconstitutional

The Supreme Court ruled that Section 5 was unconstitutional because it had not been updated in 2006 to reflect modern conditions. The Supreme Court said, "History did not end in 1965, . . . yet the coverage formula that Congress reauthorized in 2006 . . . kept the focus on decades-old data relevant to decades-old problems, rather than current data reflecting current needs."

There's another reason Section 5 preclearance was needed. Prior to 1965, states were actively evading federal-court decrees ordering them to stop discriminatory practices. And the only way a state could overcome an objection by the Justice Department was to file a lawsuit in the District of Columbia—no other federal court—because Congress did not trust federal judges in the southern states to enforce the VRA when it became law in 1965.

According to the Supreme Court in *Shelby County v. Holder* because Section 5 blatantly invades state sovereignty over elections, Congress would, in order to justify its continuation, have to show that there were still "blatantly discriminatory evasions of federal decrees," "voting discrimination on a pervasive scale," or "flagrant" or "rampant" voting discrimination.

None of that was present in 2013 when the case was before the Supreme Court, and there is no evidence of such behavior today, either.

Yet the Leahy bill would reimpose the Section 5 preclearance based on a new coverage formula even more onerous than the prior one and keep the Washington, D.C.-court requirement as if it were still 1965. States would be covered in their entirety for ten years if the attorney general determined that ten "voting-rights violations" occurred during a 25-year period, even if the state was responsible for only one of them and the rest were committed by city or county governments over which the state had no authority.

The Justice Department has a troubling history under Section 5

Voting-rights violations would include objections made by the attorney general, which don't require any finding of intentional discrimination. A claimed discriminatory effect based purely on a statistical disparity would count as a violation.

Such "disparate impact" liability has been misused in many areas besides voting. The Justice Department has a troubling history under Section 5 of making unwarranted objections and being castigated by courts for its behavior, as evidenced by a 2012 federal-court decision overturning the DOJ's frivolous objection to South Carolina's voter-ID law.

Consent decrees and lawsuit settlements would also count as voting-rights violations. This would provide an incentive for the Justice Department and advocacy groups to file as many lawsuits as possible against states, even if they had little or no merit, in order to obtain quick settlements that could then be used to trigger preclearance coverage.

Certain voting changes would automatically trigger preclearance requirements for jurisdictions. These would include any change in political boundaries during redistricting that resulted in reducing the population of a particular racial-minority group by three or more percentage points. They would also include any change requiring "proof of identity to vote" or "proof of identity to register to vote," as well as any "change that reduces, consolidates, or relocates voting locations" in jurisdictions with a certain minimum percentage of minority voters.

This is an obvious attempt to outlaw state voter-ID requirements.

In addition, the Leahy bill would make it almost impossible for any state or local jurisdiction to defend itself against a lawsuit filed by the Justice Department or an advocacy group such as the ACLU. It would create a unique and novel legal standard for injunctive relief. Courts would be directed to grant an injunction under the VRA if the plaintiff had "raised a serious question"—as opposed to providing actual evidence—about whether the challenged voting change violated the VRA or the Constitution.

This is like requiring a defendant in a criminal case to prove his innocence because the government simply claims he violated the law.

Since the *Shelby County v. Holder* decision, there has been a false clamor about a supposed loss of voting rights. That is a myth created by the Left and abetted by the mediacrats. That myth has been perpetuated as a way of opposing reforms intended to improve the integrity of the election process, such as voter-identification requirements and the cleanup of state-wide voter-registration lists, and to justify the reimposition of federal control over state election procedures by reviving the Section 5 preclearance requirement.

There is no voter-suppression epidemic. Americans today have an easier time registering and voting than at any time in our nation's history. On the increasingly rare occasions when discrimination actually occurs, Section 2 of the VRA provides a more than adequate remedy. The Leahy bill is unjustified and unneeded and would be a dangerous violation of state sovereignty.

10 – Replacing the Electoral College With the National Popular Vote (NPV)

The Electoral College can be a convoluted way to pick a president, but that's by design. The Framers rightly feared the tendency of pure democracy to descend into mob rule and run roughshod over the rights of disfavored minorities, so they created a Constitution chock-full of anti-majoritarian safeguards. That includes an Electoral College that can—though seldom does—seat a president who loses the popular vote.

There is a method to this madness. The nation is a diverse place, and voters living in rural Indiana quite likely have a different set of issues and concerns than do voters living in downtown San Francisco. The Electoral College gives greater weight to the former group, encouraging campaigns to focus on assembling broad coalitions that span regions and interests.

The alternative—election by pure popular vote—flips the tables. If pure turnout is the end goal, candidates will inevitably focus their efforts on the biggest states—California, for example—and major urban centers like Chicago and New York City.

That might not immediately sound so different than the status quo, in which campaigns spend nearly all their time and money on a small handful of key swing states. But the list of swing states changes with time, and they are called "swing" states for a reason. New York and California, meanwhile—to say nothing of most major urban centers—are solidly blue. It's no wonder, then, that the left wants to give these voters more power to select the president.

Democrats enjoy substantial competitive advantages in these areas

Democrats enjoy substantial competitive advantages in these areas, but there is another plus for them: Without the need to appeal to voters in "flyover country" to win national elections, candidates could run ever more leftward to satisfy the demands of coastal elites. The May 2020 "How the Electoral College Protects and Nurtures Our Republic" report by Bradley Smith, Josiah H. Blackmore II and Shirley M. Nault of The Heritage Foundation explains why:

Under the NPV interstate compact, signatory states would agree to award their electoral votes not to the winner of the popular vote in their states, but to the winner of the aggregated popular vote totals from across the 50 states and the District of Columbia. This proposal strikes at the heart of our constitutional system of government.

Our constitutional system aims not merely at majority rule, but at creating ruling majorities that are respectful of minority interests and values. To win the Electoral College, a candidate must appeal to a wide array of geographic, economic, and social interests. National Popular Vote strikes at the heart of our constitutional system of government and a process that has made the United States democratic republic the envy of the world.

NPV calls for states to join an interstate compact in which signatory states would agree to award their electoral votes not to the winner of the popular vote in their states, but to the winner of the aggregated popular vote totals from across the 50 states and the District of Columbia. The compact would become effective once states comprising an Electoral College majority—that is,

270 or more Electoral College votes—sign on, thus guaranteeing that the candidate with the most popular votes as aggregated from state vote totals would win the presidency.

As of the close of 2019, 15 states and the District of Columbia, with 196 Electoral College votes, had joined the NPV compact.

National Popular Vote (NPV) is the brainchild of Akhil and Vikram Amar

The National Popular Vote (NPV) is the brainchild of Akhil and Vikram Amar, brothers and law professors who proposed such a compact after the 2000 election in which George W. Bush won the presidency despite receiving fewer popular votes than Al Gore. John Koza, a California-based computer expert, took up the "sour grapes" proposal and in 2006 published the first edition of the NPV manifesto, Every Vote Equal, making a progressive attempt to justify the national popular vote scheme, but their arguments are weak and ineffective and fail to grasp the sapience and genius our Founding Fathers created in the electoral college.

The truth is that in the vast majority of democracies, a candidate who loses the popular vote can be chosen chief executive. Sometimes, typically in multiparty states operating under the curse of proportional representation, that has happened as a result of coalitions formed after the election. When no candidate gains a majority, the leaders of the various political parties gather after the election and negotiate a coalition designating a head of government (typically called a prime minister), whose party may or may not have won the most votes.

In 48 presidential elections since people began recording nationwide popular vote totals, the U.S. has had four in which the Electoral College winner did not win the aggregated state-by-state popular vote (1876, 1888, 2000, and 2016). In 1876 and 1888, however, the Democratic Party in the southern states engaged in so much fraud and violent vote suppression that it is hard to believe than a more honest election would not have caused the result in the Electoral College to match the result of the aggregated popular vote.

At odds with Constitutional principles

NPV would throw out our successful system and substitute a radically different one with no serious regard for the consequences and based on the abstract and highly contested principle that only the aggregated popular vote totals can bestow legitimacy on the winner. This principle is at odds not only with the Electoral College, but also with a host of other constitutional principles.

Our Constitution is democratic, but with numerous checks and balances to assure enduring majorities, moderation, and respect for minority rights and desires. These include separation of powers into three supportive but independent branches, a national government of enumerated powers, a bicameral legislature, staggered elections, presidential veto power, and federalism. Even then, the people ratified the Constitution only after assurances that further checks on the majority would be added to it. These additional checks became the Bill of Rights.

Our national legislative design also rejects raw majoritarianism. Not only do states have equal representation in the Senate, but in the House of Representatives, each state, no matter how small, is guaranteed at least one congressional representative. It is possible for a party to gain a House majority without winning a plurality of the aggregated national vote for House candidates (as happened as recently as 2012) and thus to elect the Speaker, who is second in line to the presidency. If the Electoral College is illegitimate simply because on rare occasions it yields counter-majoritarian results, so are the Senate, the House, and even the Bill of Rights.

Although our constitutional system draws its legitimacy from the people—again, it was ratified not by state legislatures, but by votes of the people in the states—it did not create and was not intended to create a system of pure majoritarianism. Rather, it was aimed at promoting good government based on a bedrock of popular consent for the form of government chosen.

The Constitution set up a structure intended to promote what the late Michael Uhlmann called "reasonable" majoritarianism.

6 – How the Pandemic's Impact Mostly Hurt Trump—But Helped Biden

Credit: Drew Angerer/Getty Images.

In the 2020 that might have been, nobody is sick, and politics is the center of the universe. The Democratic Party has just nominated Joe Biden and his running mate Kamala Harris at its mid-July convention in Milwaukee, while Republicans are gearing up to renominate Donald Trump in Charlotte, North Carolina At his usual rallies, Trump is pointing to the roaring economy to make his case for re-election, while Biden struggles to stir up crowds with his plea for a return to normalcy.

But in the 2020 scenario that happened, the COVID-19 pandemic changed everything–from how the campaign is conducted to how we vote to what we value. The pandemic has closed schools, offices, sports arenas, and limited social interaction for millions of people—perhaps an even bigger struggle for young people more used to being active.

It has canceled conventions, relegated fundraising, and campaigning to the digital realm, and forced many states to rapidly change how people get and submit their ballots, with unpredictable and potentially disastrous results.

In the August 2020 "How COVID-19 Changed Everything About the 2020 Election" article in *Time* by Molly Ball with reporting by Mariah Espada and Abby Vesoulis: The acute crises have refocused the nation's attention, bringing issues like public health and economic and racial inequality to the fore and prompting the public to revisit what characteristics it wants in its leaders.

For four years, Trump has been the dominant force and inescapable fact not only of national politics but also of American life. Now he finds himself displaced as the central character in his own campaign by a plague that answers to no calendar, ideology, or political objective.

Just as the virus has changed the way adults report to offices and children go to school, upending whole industries in the process, it has spurred a massive shift in the fundamental act of American democracy: how we select the President who will be charged with ending the pandemic's reign of destruction, dealing with its aftermath, and shaping the nation that rises from its ashes. And as with so many other changes wrought by the coronavirus, the practice of American politics may never be quite the same again.

On election day, a plurality of voters also said COVID-19 is their top issue—42% said so, while 27% said the economy and jobs, 9% said health care more broadly and 8% said racism. Americans also said it is more important to limit the spread of the coronavirus rather than limiting the damage to the economy by a whopping 61%-to-29% margin.

In a recent survey conducted by the Centers for Disease Control and Prevention, 63% of 18-to-24-year-olds reported symptoms of anxiety or depression (Interestingly, that rate almost matches exactly the 64% of Zillennials who voted for Biden) per the "Pandemic's mental health burden heaviest among young adults. In a recent survey, almost two-thirds of 18-to-24-year-olds reported symptoms" ABC News report by Dana Alkhouri in February 2021.

A High-Stakes Re-election Campaign at a Pivotal Moment in America

This was always going to be an unusual contest—the high-stakes re-election campaign of a historically divisive President at a pivotal moment for the nation, a referendum on his norm-shattering style and disruptive vision, a test for his scattered opposition to prove which side of a polarized political spectrum represents the mainstream.

Despite the pandemic, Trump had hoped to keep up the rallies central to his political mythology. But an attempted return to the stage in Tulsa, Oklahoma, on June 20 turned into a debacle, with a sparse, mostly mask less crowd that barely filled the bottom deck of the indoor arena.

In person, Trump's list of self-proclaimed success would draw a roar from Trump's throngs of admirers in person and at events—but online, the only feedback is the silent scroll of Facebook comments. Trump's political adviser Jason Miller says the tele-rallies have been a hit. "The genius of Donald Trump is that he knows how to foster and build one-on-one relationships with his voters," he says.

But it's clear the virtual gatherings are no substitute for the real thing. Lacking his usual source of mass adulation, the President has taken to touting the crowds that line the streets when he visits various states on official business.

Democrats decided early on that the planned July convention in Milwaukee would not be feasible; it was pushed back to mid-August and radically scaled down, with delegates staying home and voting remotely and Biden himself staying away.

The GOP has had a bumpier road. In June, Trump moved the convention from Charlotte, North Carolina, to Jacksonville, Florida, in a fit of pique over the North Carolina Democratic governor's insistence on safety protocols. As Florida's COVID-19 caseload surged this summer, party officials made a series of frantic adjustments, culminating in a last-ditch effort to hold the festivities in an outdoor stadium in the August heat.

Finally, in late July 2020, Trump announced the Jacksonville program would be scotched; the current plan, dramatically reduced in scale, was still held in Charlotte, such as "small, formal business meetings. The party held the rest of the events and festivities, including Trump's acceptance speech, remotely from various locations including Fort McHenry and the White House.

In a Fox News poll in July, 85% said they were extremely or very motivated to vote, and the percentage of respondents who told Gallup they were more enthusiastic than usual about voting was up 10 points from 2016. Despite the difficulties of pandemic voting, primaries in states such as Texas and Georgia have set turnout records.

The pandemic landed in the midst of America's primary-election season, forcing state election officials to adapt on the fly. The results offer a glimpse of the massive challenges the general election posed—and the disasters that ensued. Despite the negative impacts the pandemic had on Americans, they were more eager for political engagement in the 2020 presidential election as record breaking voting numbers proved.

Many states that have been administering elections in person for decades are now attempting to pivot to mail voting, allowing people to vote absentee without an excuse or by citing COVID-19 as a legitimate medical reason.

Trump's Approval Ratings With Dealing With the Pandemic Plummet

When the reality of the pandemic began to set in, Trump's approval rating initially went up, as often happens for Presidents in times of crisis. The percentage of Americans who approve of Trump—which has stayed within a narrow band throughout his term—reached 46% in late March 2020, the highest level since his Inauguration, according to the polling average maintained by FiveThirtyEight. Then it began to plummet.

In August 2020, with three months to go before the election, barely 40% approved of Trump's performance, while nearly 55% disapproved. Americans now disapproved of his handling of the pandemic by a 20-point margin.

Indicators that normally correlate to incumbents' political fortunes, such as the economy, may not apply this year, says GOP pollster Patrick Ruffini. The situation is simply too anomalous.

COVID-19 has changed the tenor of the election in unmistakable ways. Optimism has nosedived: the share of people who believe the U.S. is on the right track has declined 20 points since March. The pandemic has brought new urgency to issues like access to health care, inequality, and the social safety net, while driving Trump's preferred topics of immigration and trade out of the picture. "The voters are fundamentally the same, but the context of the 2020 election has changed," says UCLA political scientist Lynn Vavreck, author of *Identity Crisis: The 2016 Presidential Campaign and the Battle for the Meaning of America.*

Asked an open-ended question about Trump's vision for the country, about half the respondents in Third Way's surveys volunteered "self-serving" or "divisive." Respondents also rejected his calls for "law and order" in response to street protests. Asked who is hurt by Trump's vision, 30% of undecided suburban voters said, "all of us." "It used to be people would say LGBT people, or women, or people of color. Now, 4% say immigrants, 6% say minorities—but 30% say all of us."

Some focus-group participants were asked what they were looking for in the election. The responses were heavy on leadership qualities: people yearned for someone who was strong, compassionate, and listened to experts. People agreed that Trump was strong (and questioned Biden's strength) but rated the President abysmally on the other two.

As Trump's Worst Qualities Were Magnified—Biden's Strengths Matched the Moment

When Joe Biden announced his candidacy in 2019, he said he was compelled to run by Trump's equivocal response to Charlottesville. Some Democrats criticized his mantra of a "battle for the soul of the nation" as too puffy or vague at a time when his rivals were pumping out ambitious left-wing policy proposals. But a character-based campaign, tinged with nostalgia, now looks not just prescient but essential, whether or not you believe Biden has what it takes to deliver on it.

Trump's campaign insists he is positioned for victory despite the headwinds. Public polls are undercounting Republicans, says Tim Miller, the Trump political adviser, and the President's supporters are more enthusiastic about voting by a 2-to-1 ratio. "Are people going to stand in line for two hours to vote for someone they're not enthusiastic about?" he asks.

But analysts in both parties are skeptical. "Overwhelmingly, voters believe the pandemic and the resulting economic meltdown are the most important issues facing the country," says GOP pollster Whit Ayres. "Efforts to change the subject might work with people who are already in favor of the President, but there's no evidence they're working with the people who need to be brought into his coalition if he's going to win."

If the pandemic has revealed the fault lines in American society, it has exposed something else too: some things are still too important to get caught up in politics. Trump's attempts to make public health a partisan matter have mostly failed. Large majorities of Americans support their states' pandemic restrictions, believe it's more important to rein in the virus than to get the economy up and running, think more needs to be done and–by resounding margins–support mask wearing.

The national mood has undergone a wholesale shift in this most tumultuous of election years. In Third Way's studies, voters talked about feelings of sadness, anger, anxiety, and fear. Pollsters' response rates have skyrocketed because so many lonely, homebound people are answering the phone just to have someone to talk to. America is a divided nation, but also one that craves communion and solidarity.

When a Black man was unintentionally murdered on video by police in Minneapolis, people took to the streets in unprecedented numbers. Three-quarters of Americans said they backed the recent racial-justice protests, and support for the Black Lives Matter movement surged, stunning political observers. It's hard to imagine this happening without Trump. But it's hard to imagine it without COVID-19 too.

When one day Americans look back on this plague, the campaign it coincided with will be an inextricable part of the story. The U.S. has held elections under difficult circumstances before: wars, depressions, natural disasters. Each time, in the face of difficulty, we voted on schedule; each time, democracy gave us the opportunity to choose how we would steer out of the crisis.

But not this time in 2020!

How Much Did COVID-19 Affect The 2020 Election?

Enough time has passed since the 2020 presidential election that we can now ask: What effect did COVID-19, arguably the biggest event of the year—of the century, even—have on the election outcome?

The answer to this question probably seems straightforward considering how abysmally Americans thought then-President Trump handled the pandemic. But the evidence we have points in many directions as per the January 2021 "How Much Did COVID-19 Affect The 2020 Election? Not as much as one might expect" article by Seth Masket in FiveThirtyEight.com.

Let's start with what history can tell us. That is, given what we know about elections held in the middle of a pandemic, what effect should we have expected the novel coronavirus to have had? If you're scratching your head trying to think of a good comparison, that might be because we don't really have one.

The closest analogy to what we experienced in the U.S. in 2020 is the 1918-19 influenza pandemic, which also broke out during an election year and killed hundreds of thousands of Americans.

The effect of the pandemic on the 1918 midterms has been studied, too. But political scientists Chris Achen and Larry Bartels found that it had no particular effect on the election outcome; the Democrats (in control of the White House at the time) did no worse in congressional elections in places where the disease hit hard than in places where it didn't.

A somewhat different approach by Leticia Arroyo Abad and Noel Maurer found only a very small effect on the congressional vote in 1918 and no subsequent effect on the 1920 election. Now, that doesn't prove that a pandemic can't affect an election.

Maybe the fact that the 1918 election was a midterm election played a role here; that is, even if people did blame Woodrow Wilson's presidency for the pandemic, they didn't extend that to the rest of his party. And maybe the pandemic would have had a greater effect if the country hadn't been engaged in World War I at the time. It's also possible that many people didn't yet think of the federal government as responsible for matters of public health.

What Do We Know About the Role COVID-19 Played in the 2020 Presidential Election?

But returning to the present day, what do we know about the role COVID-19 played in the 2020 presidential election? One way to answer this question is to dig into state-level results and subtract Trump's vote share in 2020 from his vote share in 2016, measuring how much his vote improved or declined across those two elections. What we find, however, is no statistically significant relationship. That is, Trump did no worse—and possibly slightly better—in states with higher COVID-19 mortality rates. The same is true if we compare the vote against per capita COVID-19 cases.

It turns out that economic growth, measured as the growth in per capita real disposable income from the first through third quarters of 2020, may explain some of what we're seeing. That is, if we compare Trump's vote share from 2016 to 2020 with the amount of economic recovery a state experienced, we find that Trump did much better in those states where the economy bounced back, even controlling for COVID-19 death rates.

In other words, that $1,200 stimulus payment voters received back in the spring may have done a lot to help mitigate the political damage for Trump. In fact, had he and Congress been able to deliver some kind of additional economic relief prior to the election, that may even have saved his reelection bid.

Other researchers have also found this same pattern of Trump doing no worse, and possibly even better, at the county level in areas with higher COVID-19 mortalities. And, perhaps somewhat counterintuitively, the economy appeared to be somewhat weaker in states where there were more COVID-19 cases, and somewhat stronger where there were more COVID-19 deaths.

One possible explanation is that places with fewer health restrictions on businesses helped produce a stronger economy in those areas (helping Trump) even while spreading the disease, and in the end, the economy just had a greater effect on people's votes. Researcher Solomon Messing discovered an added wrinkle in that more COVID-19 deaths seem to have hurt Trump in very white counties, while the same wasn't true in counties where a large share of the population isn't white.

To be clear, we still don't have a great sense of why these patterns occurred, and none of this is to suggest that Trump did better in some areas because of the coronavirus. But, suffice it to say, this pattern is not the sort of thing many would expect given how poorly most Americans thought Trump handled the pandemic.

What also makes it difficult to detect the effect of COVID-19 on the election? Like so many other issues in American politics, the pandemic was quickly interpreted through partisan lenses. The fact that the initial fallout in March didn't give Trump much of a "rally-around-the-flag" effect, or a temporary boost in popularity given the crisis, is telling. But, then again, so is the fact that it didn't seem to hurt him all that much either.

So, what can we ultimately say about the impact of COVID-19 on the 2020 election? Most likely, it worked against Trump. Had there been no pandemic, he may have still lost the popular vote, but considering how close the election was, he may have had a decent chance of winning the Electoral College.

Yet the damage to his prospects was far from enormous, and that may have been mitigated somewhat by polarization. Indeed, a better response on Trump's part that either helped reduce the spread of the disease or limit its economic impact could well have secured his reelection bid.

Did the Pandemic Sink Trump's Chances? Not as Much as His Opponents Expected

The coronavirus pandemic was supposed to be the issue that doomed the Republican Party in the 2020 election, with President Donald Trump's poorly received response to the crisis leading to decisive and widespread losses up and down the ballot.

Now that the dust has settled—with Trump defeated but Democrats holding fewer seats in the House and the Senate than expected—the president's opponents realize it wasn't that simple as noted in the November 2020 "Did the pandemic sink Trump's chances? Not as much as his opponents expected" article by Alex Roarty in the *McClatchy* DC Bureau.

Democrats and Republicans alike are reconsidering what they thought they knew about the public's view of the viral outbreak and Trump's handling of it, convinced the issue wasn't as helpful politically for Democrats as they once expected.

Some strategists go so far as to say they think the president's insistent push to lift economic restrictions, compared with Joe Biden's emphasis on health and safety, even helped his cause with voters, leading to narrower-than-expected losses in battleground states and helping Republicans enjoy surprise success in congressional races.

"It's possible that the pandemic actually didn't accrue to Biden's benefit at all," said Tim Miller, the political director for the super PAC Republican Voters Against Trump. "And in certain areas, the open-it-up debate might have cost him votes."

Miller's view is a minority, even among anti-Trump operatives who think the pandemic wasn't as electorally beneficial as they expected. Many of them argue that although fewer voters were ultimately moved by the crisis, those who did were still crucial to Biden's margin of victory in closely fought states like Wisconsin and Arizona.

And few disagree that the pandemic, which since the spring has reshaped many facets of American life, was ever-present on voters' minds, or that large majorities viewed Trump's response to it negatively. But even if voters felt that way, it didn't necessarily mean they were compelled to vote for Biden or Democratic congressional candidates—at least not to the degree many expected.

"Clearly, we just missed something here in the data," said Jason Bresler, a Democratic strategist. "It just doesn't add up."

'I Wanted Them to be Madder'

It wasn't as if voters didn't receive serial reminders of Trump's handling of the pandemic. In September, a book from Bob Woodward revealed the president deliberately downplayed the danger of the coronavirus. Questions about the coronavirus were included near the start of every debate. And Trump's own hospitalization in early October 2020, the consequence of an apparent super-spreader event at the White House, received wall-to-wall coverage.

But Miller said that in his super PAC's focus groups of moderate GOP voters, many participants were unfailingly willing to cut the president slack, even if they thought his response had been poor.

"I remember seeing back in the spring and the summer these focus groups, where I wanted them to be madder about it than they were," Miller said. "They just weren't. They thought it was an outside, unprecedented, once-in-a-lifetime event that nobody could have done well with, that he shouldn't be held to account for it."

Bresler, the Democratic strategist, expressed his frustration that his party often focused on making a negative case against the GOP while failing to highlight their own agenda. It was a plan, he said, that would fall short with voters who didn't think Trump's response was so poor.

"I don't think that swing voters saw it so black and white that (Republicans) dropped the ball," he said. Some Democrats, even while acknowledging the issue might not have been as potent as they had hoped, say it was still the single biggest reason Trump lost.

"The voters who we saw swing toward us had consistently said that their number one issue was dealing with the coronavirus," said Patrick McHugh, the executive director for the pro-Biden super PAC Priorities USA. "And their number one concern about Donald Trump was his failure to do so."

Priorities USA consistently targeted Trump with pandemic-related ads, all the way through the end of the race when Biden's own campaign was highlighting ads that emphasized national unity and patriotism.

Holmes, the GOP operative, said in his view, even if the issue didn't move as many voters as widely thought, Trump would have won the election "by acclamation" absent the pandemic. "It definitely played a role," Holmes said. "It was by far and away the most significant impactful environmental piece of this election. The question is which way does it break amongst which parts of the electorate.

Coronavirus Is No Reason for the Feds to Take Over the Election Process

Ever since Democrats took over the House in 2018, they have been pushing bills to increase federal control of our elections. One such bill was S. 3529, the "Natural Disaster and Emergency Ballot Act of 2020" (briefly covered in 10 Leftist Tactics Versus the Vote section of Chapter 5 will be covered in much greater detail in this chapter) can serve as an example/lesson of unsapient legislation generated during the pandemic—even though it wasn't approved—it's important to know its pros and cons and why it wasn't approved.

Amid the coronavirus crisis, the Democrats in the House, led by Sens. Amy Klobuchar (D-Minn.) and Ron Wyden (D-Ore.) thought the time was ripe to create a bill to make it so the feds can tell the states how to run their elections. Under our Constitution, Congress sets the time, place, and manner of federal elections, but it is the states and particularly county governments that actually administer the elections.

Our Founders designed this structure because they understood that giving the federal government authority to run elections would also give that government—including the incumbents controlling Congress and the incumbent in the White House—he ability to manipulate election rules to ensure their desired election outcomes. Hans von Spakovsky at The Heritage Foundation explains further in the March 2020 article "Coronavirus Is No Reason for the Feds to Take Over the Election Process."

No Need to Impose a Federal Mandate to Existing State Requirements

Every state already allows absentee balloting, but the problem with the S. 3529, the "Natural Disaster and Emergency Ballot Act of 2020" bill goes beyond the fact that there is no need to impose a federal mandate on top of already-existing state requirements. The larger problem is that it would require changes in how absentee ballots are handled and processed—and the prescribed changes would increase the risk of election fraud.

While the health crisis may necessitate greater use of absentee ballots, no one should be happy about it. That's because absentee ballot fraud is one of the most common—and easiest—methods used to cheat and intimidate voters. Just look at what happened in the (ultimately overturned) 2018 Ninth Congressional District race in North Carolina. There, political operatives took absentee ballots from voters, then altered or filled them out before submitting them.

So, what are some of the changes the new bill would mandate? Well, currently, states require absentee ballots to be postmarked by Election Day. This is to prevent people from seeing voting results and then organizing an after-the-fact, get-out-the-[absentee-] vote campaign to try to change those results.

Yet S. 3529 would force states to accept absentee ballots as long as they have been supposedly "signed" by the voter before the polls close. Obviously, there is no way to verify that. This is very different from election officials accepting the official postmark of the U.S. Postal Service as evidence that an absentee ballot was cast before the polls closed. This change would give individual voters (or vote harvesters who collect their ballots) the ability to easily cheat by waiting until they see the results before voting.

Most States Don't Allow Early Votes to be Processed and Tabulated Before Election Day

The bill also orders states to begin processing votes cast during early voting or by mail 14 days before Election Day to "avoid delays" in the counting of votes on Election Day. Most states don't allow early votes to be processed and tabulated before Election Day for a very common-sense reason: to obviate the possibility of early results being leaked. If leaked to the media, early results could discourage some voters from casting ballots. If leaked to candidates or political parties that are trailing, it could give them information they can use to modify or refocus their strategy to change the results.

As for the provision to force states to allow 20 days of in-person early voting, how does that make sense at a time of social distancing, when we are limiting—even banning—public gatherings? Even if it were desirable, a federal mandate is hardly necessary. Fewer than a dozen states don't already allow some degree of early voting, and those that don't could surely change that on their own, should health concerns somehow make that advisable.

While the health advantages of early voting are dubious, at best, the electoral aspect has some shortcomings, as well.

Something similar can also happen during general elections. We all know that information about candidates, sometimes scandalous information, often comes out just before Election Day. If that information is relevant to a voter's choice and that voter has already early voted, there is nothing she can do to recall or change her vote. Moreover, studies have shown that early voting actually hurts turnout; it does not increase it.

Yet another bad provision in the Klobuchar/Wyden bill would "guarantee" that all voter registrations submitted 21 days before the election must be "deemed valid." States have varying registration deadlines, ranging from 30 days before an election to registration on Election Day. Those deadlines reflect the varying amounts of time it takes for states to check the validity and accuracy of voter registration information. (Typically, the larger the jurisdiction, the longer this process takes.)

But this bill apparently takes away the right of states to do any verification at all. Rather, it says states must consider as "valid" any voter registrations they receive—even if officials know the individual is ineligible to vote because he is a felon, an alien, or doesn't actually live where he claims to reside.

Hopefully, given all of the measures being put in place by the federal, state, and local governments, this health threat will have peaked and subsided long before the Nov. 3 election. A spokesman for the National Association of Secretaries of State says that the secretaries—who are in charge of administering elections in their respective states—are "closely monitoring COVID-19 public health alerts, working with their state public health departments, and assessing their state emergency preparedness plans."

State election officials already have all of the legal authority they need, as well as the detailed knowledge and experience to administer their elections even under extraordinary conditions. The last thing we need is federal interference from Washington bureaucrats and political know-it-alls who think they can do it better.

Coronavirus and Elections: Lessons From Liberia and Wisconsin

The "Natural Disaster and Emergency Ballot Act of 2020" tried but failed to justify a fundamental transformation of how an election should be run—*in six months*. Nonetheless, many of the provisions in one form or another, were implemented in a variety of ways, and they are covered in the next chapter.

Who says we cannot conduct a regular normal election even if the threat of COVID-19 is still an issue? One thing is for certain, one country in particular, Liberia in 2014 during Ebola epidemic—and one state in particular, Wisconsin in 2020 during Coronavirus—both conducted successful in-person elections during an epidemic.

Providing more insight on this question, the April 2020 Fox News program "von Spakovsky, Adams & Mitchell: Coronavirus and elections—changes increase risk of voter fraud" by Hans von Spakovsky. J. Christian Adams, and Cleta Mitchell shed more light on this topic below.

Lessons Learned From the Ebola Epidemic

Lessons can be learned from how elections have been conducted during other public health crises, such as the 2014 senatorial elections in Liberia in the midst of the West African Ebola epidemic.

While different in many ways from the COVID-19 virus in 2020, Ebola is an extraordinarily dangerous pathogen in terms of its infectiousness and fatality rates. Ebola symptoms include high fever, debilitating vomiting, and diarrhea, and perhaps most emblematic of the 2014 outbreak, internal and visible external bleedings from your eyes and pores.

Yet despite the devastating Ebola outbreak in the middle of the Liberian election, it was possible to create polling places that protected voter health with some help from outside organizations.

The International Foundation for Electoral Systems (IFES), headquartered in Washington, D.C., works in countries around the world to promote democratic elections. In 2014, they were instrumental in assisting Liberia to make its polling places safe despite Ebola. According to IFES President Anthony Banbury, that election was crucial in ensuring "continuity of government and to maintain Liberia's fragile peace" after a "devastating civil war."

So how did the National Elections Commission of the Republic of Liberia (the Commission) do it? What lessons can America learn from the Liberian experience with an epidemic? The "COVID-19 and Ebola: What We Can Learn from Prior Elections" May 2020 by Hans von Spakovsky and J. Christian Adams at The Heritage Foundation explain why:

According to the IFES, Liberian election officials worked closely with health experts to "integrate a range of practical health measures, such as social distancing and revised processing, to ensure the safe exchange of ballot papers, ID cards, pens, and other common voting materials." Poll workers were also trained in the "roll of queue controllers," and there was an extensive voter-education effort.

In other words, Liberia did the very same thing during the election that we are already doing today in dealing with the coronavirus: Businesses that are open to the public, such as grocery stores, drug stores, and chains like Lowes and Home Depot, have all incorporated social distancing and the use of face masks, gloves, and cleaning supplies into their business models—just as Liberia apparently incorporated the same tools, procedures, and distancing into the lines of voters waiting to vote and the clean-up and sanitation of poll locations and the voting materials being used to minimize the spread of any possible contamination.

And the Commission educated the public on the importance of using and applying all of these preventative measures. In fact, the Commission provided very specific guidelines "to prevent the spread of the Ebola Virus Disease," not just for polling places, but also for "Town Hall Meetings, Political Rally, and other Campaign Activities."

For political activities, that included "hand washing corners and temperature monitoring equipment" at all points of "entry/commencement of such campaign gatherings" with the exclusion of any individual whose temperature was above a certain point, and notification of public health authorities. All attendees were required to maintain "a non-contact distance of at least three (3) feet."

All polling and election officials were required by the Commission to undergo special training and health screening to be able to appropriately administer the election on Election Day with the health and safety precautions mandated by public health officials in place. All of those procedures were to be applied to the "deployment and retrieval of electoral materials and personnel" including the "washing of hands before entering vehicles" along with "temperature monitoring of individuals before boarding the vehicle."

Similarly, the same procedures were directed to be applied to the "tallying, tabulating, and collating of data from voting precincts across the country," including maintenance of the required three-foot physical separation requirement between all election officials

When it came to the actual polling locations, election officials were directed to immediately "isolate" any "visibly sick person" showing the "symptoms of Ebola Virus Disease." Voter's temperatures were also to be checked prior to admittance, with an additional check for voters with no visible signs of Ebola "at an interval of thirty minutes from the last check. Poll workers were directed to maintain the three-foot spacing between voters in the "queues" or voter lines, using white paint on the floor (similar to what we are all seeing these days at our grocery stores and pharmacies).

If there was more than one line of voters waiting to cast their ballots, a distance of four feet was to be maintained between the separate lines.

Normally in Liberia, a voter must hand his "voting card" to an election official when he enters a polling place in order that the information identifying that voter can be compared to the voter registration list. The Commission directed that voters would be "instructed to display their voting cards to the voter ID staff" so they could read them "without physical contact.

The IFES, working with the Commission, identified 40 points in the election process that constituted an Ebola transmission risk, including "items [that] moved between hands, such as voter registration cards, ballot papers, pens, and more." Those risks were mitigated through a "set of practical recommendations" that were "integrated into election-day operations."

Using all of the recommended precautions of health officials, Liberia held its election on December 20, 2014—in the midst of an epidemic. It was only the third election since the end of what the U.N. Secretary-General, who was in Liberia the day before the election, called a "brutal war." That election was conducted with *in-person voting*—not an all-mail election—and the U.N. congratulated Liberia on organizing a successful election "under challenging circumstances, particularly in the midst of difficulties posed by the Ebola crisis."

The CARE Act and Wisconsin's Successful Primary Election Lesson

The United States is vastly richer and wealthier than Liberia and has exponentially more resources than Liberia. In 2018, the U.S. gross domestic product (GDP) was over $20 trillion.25 Liberia's GDP in 2018 was only a little over $3 billion. As former Ohio Secretary of State Ken Blackwell, who is chairman of the bipartisan board of the IFES, says:

If Liberia was able to safely hold an in-person election amid an Ebola outbreak, there is no reason we cannot do so here in the United States in the wake of this pandemic. It will take planning, resources, and carefully developed protocols, but adhering to our existing set of electoral rules is well worth the effort.

Plus, state election officials have something that the Liberians did not have: a large amount of federal funds to implement polling place health protocols. On March 27, 2020, President Donald Trump signed the Coronavirus Aid, Relief, and Economic Security Act (CARE Act) into law. The Act provided $400 million in emergency funds that are being distributed to the states by the U.S. Election Assistance Commission to "prevent, prepare for, and respond to the coronavirus for the 2020 federal election cycle."

That preparation and response already started in Wisconsin and for a breakdown of their successful 2020 primary, consider these facts and measures below:

Voter Turnout. Wisconsin successfully held its primary election on April 7, 2020, with both absentee balloting and in-person voting. The voter turnout of 34.3 percent was virtually identical to the turnout of 34.9 percent in 2008, when there was a heavily contested race between Hillary Clinton and Barack Obama. And it was eight percentage points *higher* than in 2012 when turnout was only 26.1 percent.

Worker Training. Wisconsin's Elections Commission promulgated an extensive poll worker training manual (the Manual), providing mandated health procedures for the administration of polling places on Election Day. It included the placement of prominent warning signs stating the rules to be followed by voters, including a "Health Alert" telling them not to enter the building if they showed certain specific symptoms. Instead, they were given a phone number to call for a "curbside ballot."

Sanitizing Stations. The Manual required hand washing/sanitizing stations for all voters when entering and leaving a polling place, as well as before and after voting. Tables, door handles, pens, voting booths, voting equipment, and everything else being touched or handled in the polling place were to be sanitized regularly "or at least every ten minutes." There was a ban of "all non-election related activities in the polling location that could promote congregation and close personal contact."

Social Distancing. Pursuant to the Manual, voter lines had to maintain six-foot social distancing between voters, including using tape, floor markings, and chalk inside and outside the polling location to "establish appropriate gaps between voters and poll workers." Precinct officials were given authority to stagger voters "to limit the number of voters in a facility or voting area at the same time." Doors were to be kept open to "increase air flow and eliminate unnecessary touching of doors and door handles."

Health Screenings and Disposable Items. According to the Manual, all precinct workers were to be given health screenings prior to their shift. There were numerous procedures for avoiding personal contact. For example, Wisconsin is a voter ID state, but the ID could be reviewed and checked without the poll workers ever touching the ID presented by the voters. Voters were allowed to bring their own pens from home to mark their ballots and sign the registration poll book, and disposable items such as pens were to be sanitized or discarded after each use.

Curbside Voting. There were special procedures for "curbside voting" in the Manual for voters who could not come into a polling location. IDs could be checked through the car window, for example, while ballots were then passed through a slightly opened car window using a "privacy sleeve" and returned in the same way.

The Wisconsin Election Commission generated an Election Day checklist outlining all of these procedures for poll workers. In summary, Wisconsin put in even stricter, more careful procedures for its election workers and voters than those seemingly being followed by all of the businesses that have been allowed to remain open during the COVID-19 crisis. Additionally, those voters who did not want to vote in-person, including the elderly who may be more susceptible, could still vote by absentee ballot.

7 – How Democrats' Law Changes by State Legislatures Impacted the 2020 Election

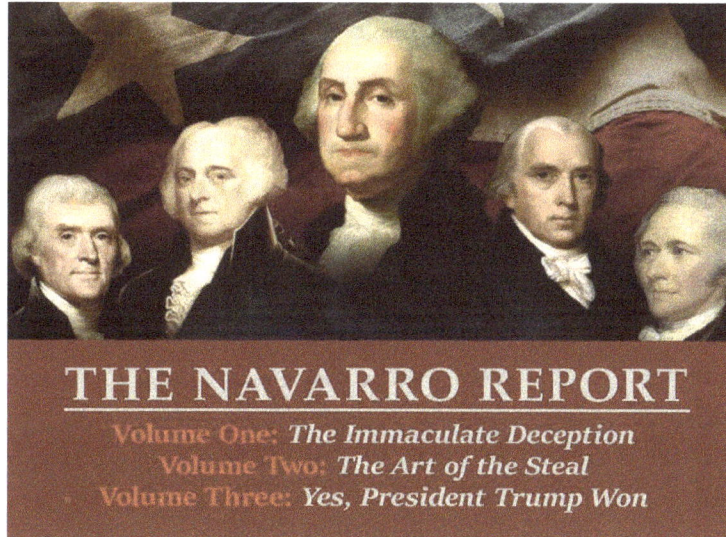

Credit: The Navarro Report.

White House trade adviser Dr. Peter Navarro released his first report titled *The Art of the Steal* on December 5, 2020, documenting what he considers evidence of the Democratic Party's years long effort to "steal" the election from outgoing President Trump. He then following up on his December report detailing 379,000 "possible illegal votes" with the *Immaculate Deception* released January 5, 2021.

This chapter is comprised primarily of "Volumes 1 and 2 of The Navarro Report—*The Immaculate Deception* and *The Art of the Steal*—and together make the strong case for a full investigation of the election irregularities and strategic gaming of our political process that in all likelihood have led to a stolen presidential election," Navarro concluded. "Any such investigation must begin immediately as this nation simply cannot risk the inauguration of a president who will be perceived by a large segment of the American people as illegitimate."

The Democratic Party's "Stuff the Ballot Box" strategy, according to Navarro, explains how relying on expanding voter access to absentee and mail-in ballots and relaxing ballot verification protocols and other impediments to registering to vote—was very effective as his report explains why.

The Democrat Party relied primarily on legal means such as legislative and rule changes at the state level to implement its Grand Strategy and thereby achieve its illegal outcome. However, at times, political operatives advancing the Democrat Party's Grand Strategy also bent, and sometimes broke, the laws and rules of that which is most sacred to our American public—our election system.

Based on this third and final volume of The Navarro Report—*Yes, President Trump Won*, it should be clear that there are far more questions raised about the potential illegality of the 2020 presidential election than have been answered.

Clearly, the case, evidence, and statistical receipts presented in this report provide a strong case that the 2020 election may well have been stolen not just from President Trump but also from the 74 million Americans who went to the ballot box in good faith in support of President Trump.

The Navarro Report, Vol. 1: The Art of the Steal

Per The Navarro Report, which the rest of this chapter is comprised of, the Democrat Party used a two-pronged Grand "Stuff the Ballot Box" Strategy to flood six key battleground states—Arizona, Georgia, Michigan, Nevada, Pennsylvania, and Wisconsin—with enough illegal absentee and mail-in ballots to turn a decisive Trump victory into a narrow and illegitimate Biden alleged "win."

Prong One dramatically increased the amount of absentee and mail-in ballots in the battleground states. Prong Two dramatically decreased the level of scrutiny of such ballots—effectively taking the election "cops" off the beat. This pincer movement resulted in a FLOOD of illegal ballots into the battleground states more than sufficient to tip the scales from a decisive legal win by President Trump to a narrow and illegitimate alleged "victory" by Joe Biden.

Democrat Party operatives frequently hid behind the shield of the Chinese Communist Party (CCP) virus (COVID-19) and resultant pandemic to further their goals of boosting the absentee and mail-in ballot counts in the key battleground states.

The Democrat Party's Grand Strategy

Per Peter Navarro, by implementing its Grand "Stuff the Ballot Box" Strategy, the Democrat Party, and its political operatives strategically gamed one of the most sacred elements of American democracy, our election system. This was brass knuckle politics played at the highest level which has delivered a brutal punch to the nose of the American people and a vicious kick to the groin of American democracy.

That the Democrat Party and its operatives have, up to this point, gotten away with their Immaculate Deception and Art of the Steal, represents a signal failure of the media, Republican state legislators, other Republican government officials across the battleground states, the US Congress, and our judicial branch of government at both the state and federal levels.

Key methods used by the Democrat Party to strategically game America's 2020 presidential election included changes in the law approved by State Legislatures; rule changes and new guidance initiated by Secretaries of State or other election officials; court rulings and interventions; and the aggressive use of so-called "public-private partnerships" to commandeer and manipulate the election process in key Democrat strongholds such as Wayne County, Michigan and Dane County, Wisconsin.

Prong One of the Democrat Party's Grand Strategy

This strategy used seven basic gambits to dramatically increase the flood of absentee and mail-in ballots: relaxing mail-in and absentee ballot rules; sending absentee or mail-in ballots or applications for such ballots to every voter (universal mailing); increasing both the legal and illegal use of drop boxes; ballot harvesting; and the use of corrupted voting machines.

Prong Two of the Democrat Party's Grand Strategy

This strategy used five additional gambits to dramatically decrease the level of scrutiny of the new flood of absentee and mail-in ballots into the battleground states: relaxation of ID verification; reduced signature matching requirements; illegally counting naked ballots to increase ballot curing–both legal and illegal; and reduced poll watching and observing.

The practical result of the Democrat Party's two-pronged Grand "Stuff the Ballot Box" Strategy as noted by Navarro was to flood the six key battleground states with enough illegal absentee and mail-in ballots to turn a decisive Trump victory into a narrow alleged Biden "victory."

Key political operatives assisting the Democrat Party included Wall Street oligarch George Soros, Silicon Valley oligarch and Facebook CEO Mark Zuckerberg, and Marc Elias, former Hillary Clinton Campaign General Counsel and one of the alleged architects and financial conduits for Fusion GPS and the Russia Hoax designed to topple a duly-elected President.

Soros money helped fund efforts to change election laws and rules through instruments such as referenda. Soros and his network of organizations such as the political action committee "Secretary of State Project" also helped to elect puppet Secretaries of State in Michigan (Jocelyn Benson) and Pennsylvania (Kathy Boockvar) who would play instrumental roles in bending or breaking election rules and thereby advancing the Grand "Stuff the Ballot Box" Strategy.

Zuckerberg money–nearly half a billion dollars–helped engineer what was effectively a hostile Democrat Party "public-private partnership" takeover of what should otherwise be a nonpartisan election process in key Democrat strongholds such as Wayne County, Michigan and Dane County, Wisconsin.

And they relied on the useful idiots for the Democrat Party that included Georgia's Republican Governor Brian Kemp and Republican Secretary of State Brad Raffensperger who entered into a Consent Decree that dramatically increased the number of absentee and mail-in ballots while dramatically decreasing the rejection rate of such ballots. Republican state legislators who voted for the bills that would help the Democrats advance its Grand Strategy likewise were unwitting dupes.

For a complete copy of The Navarro Report with all three volumes, please follow the link in the Appendix.

Democrat Party Strategically Games the 2020 Presidential Election	ARIZONA	GEORGIA	MICHIGAN	NEVADA	PENNSYLVANIA	WISCONSIN
State Law Changes – Bills & Referenda			✓	✓	✓	
Rule Changes – Secretary of State (SOS)		✓	✓	✓	✓	
Rule Changes – Other Officials				✓		
Guidance – SOS or Election Officials			✓	✓	✓	✓
Court Rulings	✓	✓	✓	✓	✓	✓
Court Interventions/Petitions				✓	✓	
Public-Private Partnerships (Zuckerberg/Soros Effect)	✓	✓	✓	✓	✓	✓
Propaganda/"Public Awareness" Campaigns	✓	✓	✓	✓	✓	✓

Credit: Figure Three — The Navarro Report.

Strategically Gaming America's Presidential Election

Per The Navarro Report, let's work our way now systematically through various means and gambits the Democrat Party used to strategically game America's presidential election. Per Peter Navarro, "the examples that we will offer throughout the remainder of this report are designed to be illustrative rather than exhaustive."

Figure three above summarizes the eight major means and gambits the Democrat Party used in its gaming of our presidential election as follows:

1 – Law Changes by State Legislatures

Three battleground states–Michigan, Nevada, and Pennsylvania–issued major changes to their individual State Election Laws in the year leading up to the 2020 General Election.

For example, after the Nevada State Primary Election, a Special Session of the State Legislature was called by the Democrat Governor Steve Sisolak of Nevada to change the state's voting procedures. Notably, the CCP virus pandemic was used as a justification for this action. Consequently, AB-4 was an omnibus measure modifying election procedures during periods of declared emergency in Nevada as currently exists due to the CCP Virus.

In Pennsylvania, on October 31, 2019, Democrat Governor Tom Wolf signed Act 77 after its passage in the Republican-Controlled State Legislature. This is the most drastic election law change Pennsylvania has made in modern history.

Act 77 made numerous major changes to state election law. In particular, the bill enabled "no-excuse" absentee ballot voting so voters no longer have to provide a reason for requesting absentee ballots; and it created a "new option" to vote by mail up to 50 days before an election and enabled voters to be placed on a list to "permanently receive a ballot application by mail."

This was a clear case where an unwitting "useful idiot" Republican legislature played right into the hands of the Democrat Party's Grand Strategy. Note: the term "useful idiot" is attributed to Vladimir Lenin. It describes naïve people who can be manipulated to advance a political cause.

This sweeping bill also extended the amount of time voters could register to vote; extended mail-in and absentee submission deadlines; and authorized a $90 million bond to "reimburse counties for 60 percent of their actual cost to replace voting systems."

2 – Rule Changes by the Secretaries of State

Secretaries of State in Georgia, Michigan, Nevada, and Pennsylvania bypassed their State Legislatures to issue rule changes that effectively allowed the counting of illegal ballots. They did so under the theory that the executive agency makes the rules while power is derived by legislation passed.

For example, on May 19, 2020, Michigan Democrat Secretary of State Jocelyn Benson, elected with the help of George Soros, announced that all registered voters in the August 4, 2020, primary and the November 3, 2020, General Election would receive mail-in ballot applications automatically. This was a sweeping change.

Regrettably, it wasn't just Democrat officials who were involved in promulgating such rule changes. As another useful idiot for the Democrats' Grand Strategy, Georgia's Secretary of State Brad Raffensperger played right into their hands. On March 24, he announced that election officials would mail absentee ballot request forms to all of Georgia's 6.9 million active voters for the primary election. This universal ballot measure was taken not just for the Presidential Primary Election on May 19 but also for the General Election on November 3.

3 – Rule Changes by Election Officials Other than Secretaries of State

Rule changes were also enacted by other election officials, effectively bypassing any chain of command running through either the Secretary of State or State Legislature. These changes likewise contributed to the expansion of absentee and mail-in ballot voting.

For example, in Georgia, the State Election Board approved a rule in April of 2020 to allow Georgia voters to cast ballots by drop boxes on a twenty-four hours a day basis, using the CCP Virus pandemic as justification. This was a clear case of bending or breaking the rules, as Georgia state law does not permit counties to collect ballots outside of the normal business hours of Election Offices. Moreover, as this expanded drop box capability was implemented, poll observers testified that they were obstructed from observing ballot counting and processing, meaning that fraudulent ballots could have been dumped into these 24/7 drop boxes prior to collection.

Similarly, on October 18, 2016, the Wisconsin Election Commission unanimously voted on a rule change for so-called "ballot curing" contrary to state law (specifically Wisconsin Statutes 6.84 and 6.86). With this illegal rule change, the Wisconsin Election Commission instructed that mail-in ballots with missing addresses should be cured, that is, fixed. However, Wisconsin Election Law states: "If a certificate is missing the address of a witness, the ballot may not be counted."

This may well be a case where the Republican Party was sleeping on the job. This change went unchallenged for eleven statewide elections until the Trump campaign took action following the November 3 election where mail in ballots played a crucial role. The lack of a more timely challenge notwithstanding, the action taken by the Wisconsin Election Commission was clearly illegal.

4 – Guidance Issued by Secretaries of State

As an additional gambit, Secretaries of State and other government officials in four of the six battleground states–Michigan, Nevada, Pennsylvania, and Wisconsin–pushed the envelope of their authorities and beat the rules to unilaterally bypass state legislatures and other election officials to issue so-called "guidance." Their goals are to effectively expand the universe of absentee and mail-in ballots while reducing scrutiny of such ballots. Moreover, they did so often in clear contradiction of State Election Codes.

The poster children for this problem–and two shining examples of the corrosive effects of the oligarch George Soros on the integrity of American elections–are Michigan's Secretary of State Jocelyn Benson and Pennsylvania's Democrat Secretary of State Kathy Boockvar. Both of these liberal extremist puppets were elected with the help of the so-called "Secretary of State Project," a political action committee funded by George Soros and members of the Democracy Alliance.

The goal of the Secretary of State project was to build a "Democrat Firewall" in key battleground states by placing progressive extremists in positions of authority where they would be willing to bend, and, at times, break the law. This is exactly what has happened in the 2020 Presidential Election.

Consider, for example, Boockvar's arguably unlawful guidance on September 15, 2020. She directed local election officials not to perform on-the-spot signature analysis for absentee and mail-in ballots. In effect, mail-in ballots could not be rejected even if election officials deemed there was an improper signature match. When it comes to outrageousness, this is about as outrageous as it gets in terms of decreasing the scrutiny of mail-in and absentee ballots.

More broadly, Boockvar appeared to exhibit a total disregard for the sanctity of our legal system when she submitted clearly unlawful guidance a few days before the November 3 election that allowed voters missing proof of identification to have their mail-in ballots cured until November

12–nine days after the election. This did indeed break the law; and the Pennsylvania Supreme Court agreed, finding that Boockvar lacked the statutory authority to take that step. Yet it was a clear and blatant attempt by a Soros puppet to rig the election.

George Soros certainly got his money's worth as Boockvar also sought to extend deadlines for mail-in ballots, citing concerns over delivery times involving the United States Postal Service. Republicans opposed the action. Said Pennsylvania Senate Majority Leader Jake Corman (Republican): "The issue is [that]...Secretary [Boockvar is] trying to influence this process by sending out guidance at the 11th hour." He also expressed that the (Pennsylvania) State Department had been "weaponized" and influenced by partisan attempts to sway the vote.

Not to be outdone, in September 2020, another Soros puppet –Michigan Secretary of State Jocelyn Benson–encouraged voters, along with Democrat Governor Gretchen Whitmer, to vote by absentee ballot and drop off ballots in drop boxes in order to "decrease the spread of COVID-19." She also urged voters "not to wait too long" to send in their ballots and to take the ballots directly to their clerks' offices for submission.

5 – Court Rulings

The American nation has been witness to the spectacle of our judicial branch likewise being used as a useful idiot for the Democrat Party's Grand Strategy to steal the presidential election. The problem here is that of judicial activism: far too often activist judges have let partisanship and their own ideology get in the way of a sober and clinical interpretation of the law.

Consider, for example, the ruling of September 10, 2020 by Obama-appointed Judge Douglas Reyes of the U.S. District Court of Arizona. He ordered an extension period for absentee ballots for the 2020 General Election and thereby allowed missing signatures to be added to vote-by-mail ballots. In this dramatic expansion of the rules for curing ballots, election officials were allowed to give voters until 5:00 PM on the fifth business day after the election to sign their vote-by-mail ballot envelopes if they failed to sign at the time they submitted the ballots.

Similarly, on August 26, 2020, Michigan Court of Claims Judge Cynthia Stevens, appointed by then-Governor and Democrat Jennifer Granholm, ruled that Michigan Secretary of State and Soros puppet Jocelyn Benson had the authority to mail all Michigan registered voters (7.7 million total) absentee ballot applications for the November 3rd election. This, likewise, was a dramatic expansion of universal mailing.

6 – Court Interventions

Democrat-backed and funded third-party groups during the 2020 Election would also intervene in court cases or submit petitions in order to coerce state government officials and judges into pushing Radical Left election law changes.

For example, the oligarch George Soros spent over $28 million on influence operations during the 2020 Election. He funded groups like the Brennan Center for Justice which intervened on behalf of powerful Democrats like his puppet, Michigan Secretary of State Jocelyn Benson.

During the *Davis v. Benson* case, three plaintiffs sued Secretary Benson for her decision to mail absentee ballot applications to all Michigan voters ahead of the 2020 Presidential Election. On August 25, 2020, the Michigan Court of Claims ruled in favor of Benson, granting her the authority to send ballot applications to all Michigan voters. Again, it is useful to note here that this was a dramatic expansion of universal voting through absentee and mail-in ballots, with such universal voting as one of the worst conduits for illegal votes.

Not to be outdone, the leftist organization Democracy Docket, founded by Marc Elias, former General Counsel to the 2016 Hillary Clinton campaign, intervened in court cases to push election law changes consistent with the Democrat Party's Grand Strategy across all six states. A case in point: Elias and Democracy Docket supplied lawyers as "Intervener Defendants" and filed a motion to intervene in the Election Integrity Project of *Nevada v. Nevada* case.

It is well worth noting here that Elias is also credited with hiring the dirty tricks group Fusion GPS to "compile the 'Russia dossier' to dig up dirt on Donald Trump in the 2016 race."

It is as remarkable as it is abhorrent that the Trump Administration's Department of Justice did not conduct a full investigation and issue indictments in a Russia Hoax that ended in a complete exoneration of President Trump. Effectively, the Elias-led effort has institutionalized the idea that it is perfectly acceptable to run propaganda campaigns for the purpose of toppling duly elected government officials, including the President himself.

7 – Petitions for Public Referenda

As Figure Three illustrates, the Democrat Party also used public referenda to change election laws in both Michigan and Nevada. The purpose of these referenda was to dramatically expand absentee and mail-in voting—just as the Democrat Party Grant Strategy dictates.

These referenda are financed in part by the Wall Street oligarch George Soros; and it is worth noting here that Soros, the consummate globalist, made billions by "breaking the Bank of England" while inflicting great harm on the British working class. It is equally worth noting that the Globalist Soros has a strong antipathy towards the Economic Nationalism of Donald J. Trump.

Proposal 3 in Michigan was one of the most radical and sweeping changes to election law ever witnessed in America. Changes consistent with the Democrat Party's Grand "Stuff the Ballot Box" Strategy included: straight-ticket voting, automatic voter registration, same-day voter registration, no-excuse absentee voting during the 40 days before an election, extended mail-in voter registration until fifteen days prior to an election, and the auditing of election results.

Proposal 3 was backed by Soros-financed far Left groups like Promote the Vote. Promote the Vote spent $2.5 million collecting signatures for the Proposal 3 petition and for consulting and marketing. The referendum wound up passing with sixty-six percent of the vote in the 2018 Midterm Election. Democrat Governor Gretchen Whitmer and Soros puppet Secretary of State Jocelyn Benson both heavily promoted this radical weakening of election laws in the mainstream media.

In fact, Proposal 3 was an encore to a similarly successful Soros-backed public referendum in Nevada. Shortly after the 2016 election, leftist organizations such as iVote and the ACLU of Nevada, both with ties to Soros, spent tens of millions of dollars in Nevada collecting 55,000 signatures to submit a petition for "automatic voter registration" law changes in Nevada.

The proposed legislation eventually passed by public referendum in 2018. It mandated that individuals would be automatically registered to vote when receiving select services from the Nevada Department of Motor Vehicles (DMV), such as obtaining a renewal or change of address for a license or identification card. In order to not be registered to vote, individuals would have to decline the registration by submitting a request in writing—an obvious strong incentive to be registered.

8 – Propaganda "Public Awareness" Campaign

Many of the gambits advanced by the Democrat Party, their operatives, and their useful idiots were done under cover of "public awareness" campaigns that often amounted to little more than propaganda. Such campaigns were designed to target voters through published statements, reports, and media stories. The goal was to influence–and soften–public attitudes towards the liberalization of absentee and mail-in voting.

For example, in leaked documents from Soros' Open Society Foundation (OSF), the Soros-funded Brennan Center was listed as the recipient of funds earmarked for the express purpose of "litigation to expand access to registration and improve ease of voting." As was common practice with the Democrats, the Brennan Center would use the shield of the CCP virus pandemic to advance its goals.

For example, in March of 2020, the Brennan Center issued a memo to influence mail-in ballot election law changes as a result of the CCP Virus pandemic. The memo stated: "All voters should be offered the option to cast their ballot by mail (with multiple submission options, as provided below), so as to enable voters to avoid lines at the polls and exposure to COVID-19."

Soros-funded Brennan Center memo also made five key recommendations aimed at expanding absentee and mail-in voting. These included: (1) polling place modification and preparation; (2) expanded early voting; (3) a universal vote-by-mail option; and (4) voter registration modification and preparation, including expanded online registration.

Democrat Methods to Dramatically Increase Absentee and Mail-In Ballot Voting

Per The Navarro Report, let's turn next to an examination of the various methods the Democrats used to dramatically increase absentee and mail-in ballot voting in the battleground states. As Figure Four below illustrates, there were seven principal methods, and they were identified from an analysis of the various modifications made to state election laws and rules and procedures in advance of the 2020 presidential election.

Note that a checkmark in a given cell in the matrix indicates that particular mechanism was present in a particular state. For example, universal mailing of absentee and/or mail-in ballots was observed in both Nevada and Wisconsin. Similarly, there is an increase in voting through the use of drop boxes in Georgia, Michigan, and Pennsylvania.

Of the six battleground states, Georgia and Wisconsin were subject to six of the seven methods of boosting absentee and mail-in ballot voting while at the other end of the scale Arizona was subject to three.

Dramatically INCREASE Absentee and Mail-In Ballots	ARIZONA	GEORGIA	MICHIGAN	NEVADA	PENNSYLVANIA	WISCONSIN
Relax Mail-In & Absentee Ballot Rules	✓	✓	✓	✓	✓	✓
Universal Mailing of Absentee & Mail-in Ballots				✓		✓
Universal Mailing of Absentee / Mail-in Ballot Applications		✓	✓			✓
Increase Voting by Drop Boxes		✓	✓		✓	
Illegal Use of Ballot Drop Boxes		✓	✓			✓
Ballot Harvesting	✓	✓		✓		✓
Use of Potentially Corrupt Voting Machines	✓	✓	✓	✓	✓	✓

Credit: Figure Four – The Navarro Report.

1 – Relaxed Mail-in/Absentee Ballot Requirements

The relaxation of absentee and mail-in ballot requirements was accomplished in a variety of ways. For example, on March 27, 2020, the Dane and Milwaukee County Clerks in Wisconsin issued guidance to voters that the pandemic was grounds for anyone to be considered an "indefinitely confined" voter. In effect, this gutted the ID verification process for anyone who chose to identify as indefinitely confined because it allowed these voters to cast their ballots without presenting proper ID as a condition for an absentee ballot.

As a result of this change, the number of indefinitely confined voters surged in Dane and Milwaukee counties–two Democrat strongholds–from 72,000 in 2019 to over 240,000 by November 3, 2020.60 Within the context of Democrat Party's Grand Strategy, this was a twofer. The guidance simultaneously expanded the universe of absentee and mail-in ballot voters while lowering the level of scrutiny of these ballots.

Similarly, in Pennsylvania, a lawsuit was filed by the Democrat Party on July 10, 2020, citing Act 77's provisions to expand absentee voting for all Pennsylvania registered voters. On September 17, the Pennsylvania Supreme Court ruled in favor of the Democrat Party, allowing a three-day receipt deadline for absentee ballots postmarked by 8 PM on Election Day (November 3). In other words, ballots with a "pre-election" postmark were counted as long as they were received by 5 PM on November 6th, three days after polls closed. 10,000 absentee ballots in Pennsylvania were received after 8:00 PM on November 3.

2 – Legalizing Universal Mailing of Mail-in/Absentee Ballots

Several states across the U.S. conduct all mail-in voting. These include Colorado, Hawaii, Oregon, Utah, and Washington. In other words, these states send mail-in ballots automatically without the voter's consent. However, universal mail-in ballots are historically subjected to higher rates of fraud due to lack of I.D. verification, individuals submitting ballots multiple times without being detected, and voting under the identity of another individual; and each of these examples are apparent during the 2020 Presidential Election.

As part of its Grand Strategy, the Democrat Party and its operatives were successful in pushing for universal mail-in voting in Nevada and Wisconsin. In both of these states, election laws were altered so that mail-in ballots could be sent automatically to every individual on the voter rolls.

For example, on August 3, 2020, Democrat Governor Steve Sisolak (D) in Nevada signed AB-4 legislation into law. It directed election officials to distribute mail-in ballots automatically to all active registered voters for the November 3, 2020, General Election. This bill also gave Sisolak the authority to bypass Republican Secretary of State Barbara Cegavske and command her to adjust election procedures during a declared State of Emergency.

Note that the CCP virus pandemic again was used to justify this power grab. This alleged "reform" has led to substantial fraud; for example, roughly 15,000 mail-in or absentee ballots were counted in Nevada from voters who had voted in other states.

3 – Legalizing Universal Mailing of Applications for Mail-in/Absentee Ballots

Closely related to the method of sending mail-in ballots to all registered voters is the technique of sending absentee ballot applications to all registered voters. This was done in Georgia, Michigan, and Wisconsin.

For example, as previously noted, on August 26, 2020, the Michigan Court of Claims ruled that Michigan Secretary of State Jocelyn Benson had the authority to mail all Michigan registered voters (7.7 million total) absentee ballot applications for the November 3rd election.

Similarly, on June 17, 2020, the Wisconsin Election Commission voted unanimously to send absentee and mail-in ballot applications automatically to 2.7 million registered voters for the November 3, 2020, general election, who had not originally requested mail-in ballots.

4 – Increase Voting by Drop Box

As discussed in Volume 1 of The Navarro Report, the use of ballot drop boxes raises huge chain of custody issues. As a further complicating issue, ballot harvesting, which is illegal in ten states, becomes much easier with the use of drop boxes.

Perhaps for this reason, prior to the 2020 election season, only thirteen states used ballot drop boxes. In this year's November General Election, however, that number skyrocketed to thirty-eight states and Washington, D.C.

Consider, for example Georgia. Ahead of the 2020 Presidential Primary Election held on June 9, the State Election Board required that "County registrars are authorized to establish one or more drop box locations as a means for absentee by mail electors to deliver their ballots to the county registrars." Drop Boxes were then installed in nineteen of Georgia's 159 counties.

Similarly, in Michigan, there appears to have been a conscious effort to stuff the ballot box by stuffing Democrat strongholds with drop boxes. Thirteen new drop boxes were established in Lansing, five in Ann Arbor,70 and nearly forty in Detroit. As of the November 3 Election, Michigan had a total of 700 drop-boxes statewide.

Both Governor Whitmer and Soros puppet Secretary of State Benson issued statements in September 2020 to encourage voters to vote by absentee ballot and submit ballots via drop box in order to "decrease the spread of COVID-19."73 Here again, we see the Democrats hid behind the shield of the CCP virus to advance their Grand Strategy.

5 – Illegal Use of Drop Boxes

In at least some cases, the expanded use of drop boxes was a clear violation of state law.

Consider, for example, Wisconsin. Drop boxes are clearly illegal according to state election law. Yet, the Wisconsin Election Committee nonetheless illegally issued guidance on August 19, 2020, to election officials in all municipalities throughout the state. It designated "drop boxes or mail slots set up for taxes, mail and public utilities as secure ballot drop locations" and suggested "partnering with businesses...such as grocery stores and banks" as places voters could cast their ballots.

For example, in Pennsylvania, ahead of the 2020 Presidential Primary, ballot drop boxes were established in violation of state law under Secretary of State Boockvar's knowledge and consent.

Similar problems arose in Pennsylvania. On June 29, 2020, the Trump Campaign filed a complaint to Secretary of State Boockvar and sixty-seven county officials in Pennsylvania, stating that the Secretary of State established drop boxes illegally by failing to provide adequate security, oversight, and supervision over the drop boxes. These conditions would thereby foster an environment that would encourage the legal ballot harvesting and/or tampering.

As indicated in Volume 1 of the Navarro Report, numerous abuses were indeed observed. For example, ballots were illegally dumped into drop boxes at the Nazareth, Pennsylvania, ballot drop box center, in violation of state law. Another witness in Pennsylvania with video and photo evidence caught a man coming out of an unmarked Jeep extracting ballots from an unsupervised ballot drop box to be brought into a ballot counting center.

It's not just that these drop boxes were illegally deployed. They were disproportionately deployed in urban areas with higher Democrat registration, favoring Joe Biden.

6 – Ballot Harvesting

"Ballot harvesting" is the practice of allowing individuals to collect ballots from voters and deliver these bundles of votes to polling stations or drop boxes. Given the obvious chain of custody issues associated ballot harvesting—and the equally obvious opportunities to engage in fake ballot manufacturing—it is no surprise that many states forbid the practice.

These dangers to our democracy notwithstanding, the Democrat Party successfully pushed for the passage of legislation to legalize ballot harvesting in the battleground states of Georgia, Nevada, and Wisconsin.

On August 3, 2020, Nevada Democrat Governor Steve Sisolak called a special session with the State Legislature and signed Assembly Bill 4. It legalized the practice of ballot harvesting.

Bill 4 passed on a party-line vote through both the state Senate and Assembly, with Democrats in favor and all Republicans opposed. Implementation of this bill took place over the strong objections of Nevada Republican Secretary of State Barbara Cegavske who warned that expanded ballot harvesting could fraudulently tip the scales in elections.

In both Georgia and Wisconsin, where ballot harvesting is illegal, Democrat operatives nonetheless pushed the envelope of the law to run ballot harvesting operations. For example, several Democrat non-profits took advantage of the Georgia ballot-curing extension deadline and conducted an absentee ballot-harvesting operation. This operation alone is suspected to have added enough Democrat votes to tip the scales in favor of Joe Biden.

To engage in this end run around the law, these organizations called themselves "Ballot Rescue Teams." They deployed Democrat volunteer activist operatives to call voters and knock on voters' doors as part of this operation.

As for Wisconsin, city officials in the Democrat stronghold of Madison assisted in the creation of more than 200 "Democracy in the Park" illegal polling places. These faux polling places were promoted and supported by the Biden campaign. They provided witnesses for absentee ballots and acted in every way like legal polling places—but weren't. Moreover, they received ballots outside of the limited fourteen-day period preceding an election that is authorized by statute for in-person or absentee balloting. These were all clear violations of state law that had the effect of propagating ballot harvesting. Gov. Bill Lee, a Republican, is expected to sign the measure.

Tennessee's Legislature approved a bill in May 2021 that requires the addition of a watermark on all absentee ballots in a nearly unanimous vote. Their Senate Bill 1314 passed the Senate in a 27-0 vote and the House adopted the state Senate version of the bill in a 92-1 vote.

7 – Installation of Potentially Corrupt Voting Machines

Much has been written about how vulnerabilities in voting machine systems may be exploited by cyber hackers and other bad actors to alter the count of actual ballots. A poster child for this problem is the dramatic malfunction that was observed with Dominion Voting Systems in Antrim, Michigan to the detriment of the count for President Trump.

In July of 2019, the nonprofit group Fair Fight Action issued a report claiming that another system—Election Securities and Software (ES&S)—has demonstrated "systematic disregard for basic security best practices and a complete lack of competence in the manufacturing of reliable voting machines." The report also cited "large-scale negligence [that] exposed personal data of millions of voters, left tens of thousands of names off rolls and led to massive delays in vote counts across the country." Moreover numerous US Senators "have expressed national security concerns after ES&S lied to federal lawmakers, refused to reveal which states were sent critically flawed machines, and vigorously fought attempts to reveal reliability information."

Despite such concerns and warnings, Dominion and ES&S were implemented in all six battleground states between 2017 and 2020. For example, in March of 2020, Georgia rushed to install 30,000 new electronic voting machines from Dominion. State evaluators warned that these machines were subject to vulnerabilities.90 Nonetheless, they were installed in all of Georgia's 159 counties.

In 2019, Pennsylvania installed Dominion in fourteen of Pennsylvania's sixty-seven counties, resulting from guidance issued by the Soros puppet Secretary of State Boockvar.92 In 2020, 33 counties in Pennsylvania also installed the ES&S system. These counties included the Democrat strongholds of Philadelphia and Montgomery. (Dane and Milwaukee in Wisconsin also use ES&S which were also found to be susceptible to vulnerabilities).

In March of 2017, the Michigan state government and twenty-two localities likewise awarded Dominion a $31.5 million contract to provide voting machinery statewide. The top-spending local governments included the cities of Detroit ($457,880), Dearborn ($22,975), and Livonia ($65,310) in Democrat-dominated Wayne County.

Dramatically Decrease Democrat Ballots Rejected Across Six Battleground States

Even as the Democrat Party sought to dramatically increase the amount of absentee and mail-in ballots, they also sought to dramatically decrease the level of scrutiny of such ballots. The practical effect of a reduced level of scrutiny–fewer "election cops" on the beat–was to significantly increase the level of illegal ballots able to flood into the six battleground states.

Figure Five below illustrates how the five major gambits used to reduce scrutiny of absentee and mail-in ballots were distributed across the six battleground states. You can see from the figure that the State of Georgia effectively ran the table on behalf of the Democrats–no small irony given the fact that Georgia has both as useful idiots, both a Republican governor and a Republican Secretary of State.

In studying this figure, it is important to note that all methods of reducing ballot scrutiny are not created equal. One of the most critical elements of a free and fair election is the transparency one gains through comprehensive poll watching and observing. While both Pennsylvania and Michigan are characterized by only this method of reduced scrutiny, this method alone affected hundreds of thousands of potentially illegal votes in both states.

Dramatically DECREASE Absentee and Mail-in Ballot Verification	ARIZONA	GEORGIA	MICHIGAN	NEVADA	PENNSYLVANIA	WISCONSIN
Relax ID Verification	✓	✓		✓		✓
Reduce Signature Matching Requirements	✓	✓		✓		
Illegally Counting Naked Ballots		✓				
Increased Ballot Curing	✓	✓		✓		✓
Reduced Poll Watching/Observing		✓	✓		✓	

Credit: Figure Five – The Navarro Report.

1 – Relaxed ID Verification Requirements

The Democratic push for lower voter identification requirements most notably occurred in Arizona, Georgia, Nevada, and Wisconsin.

For example, behind the shield of the CCP virus, Democrat stronghold counties in Arizona like Maricopa and Pima allowed and encouraged residents of long-term care facilities to vote by video chat. There is no way to verify voter identification by video call, and there is no oversight over special election boards to know, in fact, if ballots are being recorded accurately.

Similarly, as noted earlier, Wisconsin's Democrat-dominated Dane and Milwaukee counties allowed anyone to register as "indefinitely confined. These Wisconsin votes were thereby tabulated without verifying photo ID.

2 – Relaxed Signature-Match Requirements

A major way mail-in and absentee ballots can be verified is through a process called signature matching. All states require voters to provide signatures on their absentee and mail-in ballot return documents in order to verify identification.

Note that thirty-two states in the U.S. require election workers to match voter signature with a signature on record for the voter on their registration form.101 In this case, Arizona, Georgia, and Nevada all relaxed signature match requirements, bringing into question hundreds of thousands potentially illegal ballots.

Perhaps most egregiously, on March 6th of 2020, Georgia Secretary of State Brad Raffensperger, with the approval of Governor Brian Kemp, signed off on a secret legal agreement with the Democratic Party of Georgia, the Democrat Senatorial Campaign Committee, and the Democratic Congressional Campaign Committee to significantly alter absentee ballot procedures in Georgia. The Democrats' attorney for this secret deal was alleged Russia Hoax operative Marc Elias from Perkins Coie.

Originally, the signature-matching requirement in Georgia was such that the signature on the mail-in envelope had to match both the voter's signature stored in the State's E-Net system, as well as the absentee ballot application. The new guidance loosened these requirements; it only required that the signature on the absentee (mail-in) ballot envelope either must match the eNet signature, or the absentee ballot application, rather than both. Further, the State required that if the election worker found a signature to not match, it couldn't be rejected unless a majority of the registrars, deputy registrars, or absentee ballot clerks reviewing the signature agreed.

This wholesale gutting of the state's signature-match requirement resulted in a drastic reduction in Georgia's absentee ballot rejection rate from 6.8% in 2016, to 0.34% during the 2020 Presidential Election. Effectively, almost none of Georgia's 1.3 million absentee ballots were rejected. On top of this, Georgians were given the opportunity to "cure" or "fix" their ballot signatures on ballots incorrectly filled out for three days after November 3 (Election Day). If the flood of absentee ballots in the 2020 election had been rejected at the same rate as in the 2016 election, that would have been enough alone to flip the election to President Trump.

A similarly egregious problem reared its Grand Strategy head in Nevada. New legislation passed in August of 2020 allowed voters over sixty-five who have a disability or are unable to read or write to have someone assist them in physically marking signatures on their ballots. These relaxed rules thereby have called into question at least some of the 400,000 ballots cast by Nevadans aged 65 and older. This "reform" also likely contributed to the statewide absentee ballot rejection rate dropping from 1.6% in 2016 to 0.58% in 2020.

3 – Illegal Counting of Naked Ballots

A quick review of the Figure Five above indicates that the State of Georgia effectively cornered the market on the illegal counting of naked ballots. This was part of the bitter fruit of the aforementioned Georgia Consent Decree.

4 – Increased Opportunities for Ballot Curing

As a fourth method to decrease the scrutiny of absentee and mail-in ballots, Democrats pushed for ballot curing leniency, which increased the ability or timeframe for curing problematic ballots. Ultimately, this effort allowed for illegally submitted mail-in or absentee ballots to be counted.

For example, on September 10, 2020, Obama-appointed Judge Douglas Rayes of the U.S. District Court for Arizona ordered election officials to give voters five business days after Election Day to sign their vote-by-mail ballot envelopes. Voters had until 5 PM on November 10 to sign the envelopes even if they failed to sign at the time they submitted the ballots.

In the wake of this order, Democrat volunteers raced around the state texting, calling, and knocking on people's doors to make sure thousands of ballots would be cured. Without the ruling, such votes would otherwise have been deemed illegal.

Perhaps most egregiously, the Wisconsin Election Commission unanimously offered guidance for vote curing, notably in contradiction of Wisconsin Statutes 6.84 and 6.86. For example, the Wisconsin Election Commission instructed curing mail-in ballots with missing addresses. This was despite Wisconsin Election Law plainly stating: "If a certificate is missing the address of a witness, the ballot may not be counted." (Nevadans were also given a ballot-curing extension for up to a week after Election Day.)

5 – Reduced Poll Watching/Observing

Democrat Party officials and operatives repeatedly sought to reduce the meaningful access of Republican poll watchers and observers during the ballot counting process in half of the battleground states. At the same time, these officials and operatives also sought to reduce the actual number of poll watchers and observers, often behind the shield of the CCP virus.

For example, Act 12 was passed by the Pennsylvania State Legislature on March 27, 2020. It mandated a reduction in the amount of poll workers. Also in Pennsylvania, certified Republican poll watchers were not allowed within six feet of ballot counters, and even kept at distances between 50 and 100 feet. Despite the disenfranchisement of observers and legal voters, counties like Philadelphia asserted that these restrictions had to go into effect due to pandemic social-distancing guidelines. Such limitations would remain in place until a Pennsylvania Court Ruling went into effect on November 5, after hundreds of thousands of ballots had already been processed.

Michigan, likewise, was a hotbed poll watcher and observer abuses designed to reduce the scrutiny of potentially illegal absentee and mail-in ballots. For example, Republican poll workers were kept more than six feet from ballot counters, sometimes, on entirely separate floors. Like in Pennsylvania, this flagrant denial of ballot observation was justified under CCP pandemic guidelines.

The practical effect of the Democrat Party's Art of the Steal was to substantially increase the number of potentially illegal ballots across all six battleground states. The equally practical result of the Art of the Steal was to effectively tip the balance of the election through the strategic gaming of the electoral process. While much of what the Democrats did was not per se illegal, what they did enabled illegal activity, namely, stuffing the ballot box with illegal mail-in and absentee ballots.

8 – Private Funding, Facebook, Soros, PAC's & Non-Profits

Influencing Elections

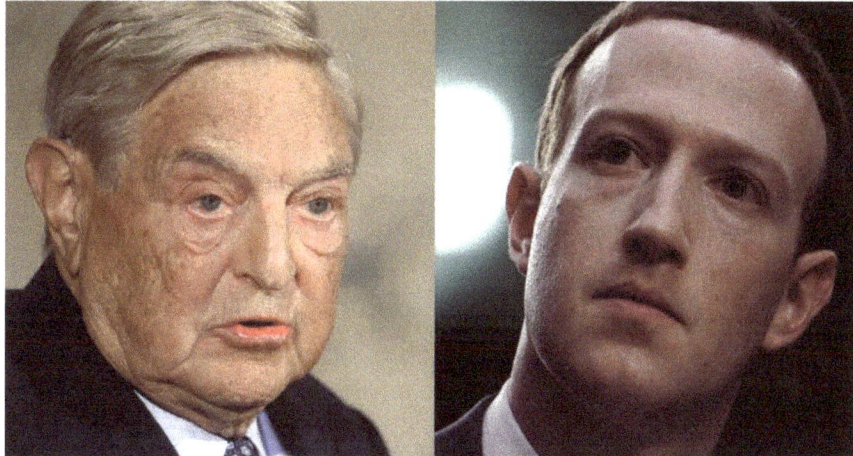

Credit: Mediaite.

For years we have watched deep-pocketed, liberal foundations spend hundreds of millions of dollars to change election process rules. They consistently advocate the federalization of election rules, which would allow Washington bureaucrats to dictate the terms of state elections.

Elections are decentralized because decentralization promotes liberty and stability. We will rue the day when federal bureaucrats command the rules of our elections. The Founders knew better because they understood the incremental invasiveness of tyranny and blessed us with a decentralized architecture of our electoral system. Let's keep it.

It is not difficult for even the most casual of observers to conclude that the presence of private funding in public elections simply is not a good idea. In fact, the use of public/private partnerships for elections is neither wise nor legal, and if allowed to continue unchecked will create a dependency of local governments on funding from a select group of people who can afford to promote their own causes.

Our particular concern lies not with the influence of foundations and their cooperating non-profits, but instead with the elected officials who accessed the funding and Secretaries of State who understood—even enabled—the influence of non-profits to take place within their states.

However, both the Wall Street oligarch George Soros and the Silicon Valley oligarch and Facebook CEO Mark Zuckerberg used their deep pockets to finance public-private partnerships that would help advance the Democrat Party's grand strategy of centralizing our elections (not just federal ones like the office of president) with the federal government.

Zuckerberg money—nearly half a billion dollars—helped engineer what was effectively a hostile Democrat Party "public-private partnership" takeover of what should otherwise be a nonpartisan election process in key Democrat strongholds such as Wayne County, Michigan and Dane County, Wisconsin, and Philadelphia County, Pennsylvania.

Zuckerberg's Center for Tech and Civic Life (CTCL) was founded in 2012 and is staffed by people that worked at the New Organizing Institute, a now defunct organization that was funded in part by George Soros' Open Society Foundation.42 During the 2020 Election, it would be Zuckerberg's CTCL that would spend hundreds of millions of dollars to fund cities, towns, and counties for "election administration."

Big Tech and PACs Gave 12 Times More Money to Democrats Than to Republicans

According to an original analysis by the Internet Accountability Project (IAP) released in April 2021, Facebook and Twitter employees and PACs donated more money to Democrats, at a ratio of 12 to 1, compared to the amount donated to Republicans in 2020. The PACs and employee donations to the Democrats from the companies in question were more than $5.5 million. Less than $435,000 went to Republicans.

"As Twitter and Facebook became more brazen in their politically biased censorship, Americans turned to Parler. By November 2020, Parler had the most downloaded app on Apple's U.S. App Store and on Google's U.S. Play Store, becoming more popular than TikTok, Zoom, and YouTube," said Mike Davis, the founder and president of IAP in a statement.

IAP, a nonprofit, states that its mission is to "lend a conservative voice to the calls for federal and state governments to rein in Big Tech before it is too late" according to the April 2021 "Big Tech Employees and PACs Gave 12 Times More Money to Democrats Than to GOP: Report" by Samuel Allegri and Bowen Xiao contributing at the *Epoch Times*.

"On January 8, 2021, the day after Facebook and Twitter banned President Trump from their platforms, Parler had 20 million users and was again the top-downloaded app and the obvious choice for President Trump and his 90 million followers. Parler's rising popularity made Parler a viable threat to Facebook and Twitter's dominance over social media. So together, they colluded with Amazon to destroy Parler and used the horrific attacks on the Capitol on January 6, 2021 as a shameful excuse. Why are Congressional Democrats on the House Oversight Committee investigating Parler? Just follow the money," Davis wrote.

In one example, the IAP says that in 2020, Alexandria Ocasio-Cortez received $36,346 while all Republicans on the House Oversight Committee combined only got less than $1,950, and that Twitter employees didn't donate "a single dollar" to Republicans on the Oversight Committee.

According to data from OpenSecrets, a nonprofit that tracks money in politics and campaign finance records, big tech companies have been major financial backers of the Biden campaign the election cycle.

The top five contributors to Democratic presidential candidate Joe Biden's candidate committee include Alphabet, which was the largest contributor; Microsoft Corp., the fourth-largest contributor; and Amazon, the fifth-largest contributor. Alphabet contributed just under $1.9 million to the committee, Microsoft contributed $997,226, and Amazon gave $931,821.

Other major technology companies that made it to the top donors list for the 2020 cycle included Apple and Facebook. Microsoft in particular has played an extensive role in supporting Biden's campaign, compared to other companies.

Microsoft's senior executives have donated more to the Biden campaign during the primaries than any other large tech company, according to data from the Revolving Door Project, part of the Center for Economic & Policy Research (CERP).

Soros Pours Record $50 Million Into 2020 Election

Leftist billionaire George Soros has flooded Democratic PACs and campaigns with $50 million the 2020 election cycle, shattering his personal record by tens of millions with four months to go before the elections as reported in the "Soros Pours Record $50 Million Into 2020 Election" article at The Washington Free Beacon by Joe Schoffstall in July 2020.

Soros ramped up his political spending through the Democracy PAC, which he created in 2019 to pump large sums into the coffers of other left-wing groups. New filings to the Federal Election Commission show the PAC doled out nearly $17 million last spring 2020, bringing its total cash disbursements this cycle to $48 million. Soros gave another $4 million directly to Democratic campaigns and committees without first depositing the money into his PAC. The $52 million cash influx is more than double Soros's previous high of $22 million, which came during the last presidential election in 2016.

Democratic candidates benefiting from Soros's cash have railed against the influence of money in politics. Joe Biden's government reform plan includes a promise to "reduce the corrupting influence of money in politics." The presidential candidate's website says, "We could improve our politics overnight if we flushed big money from the system and had public financing of our elections…. Democracy works best when a big bank account or a large donor list are not prerequisites for office."

Such rhetoric from Soros-backed candidates has drawn criticism from the Right. "While Democrats across the country sanctimoniously rail against the influence of dark money in politics, their party's largest donors are bankrolling a massive web of liberal organizations to get them elected," one GOP operative told the Washington Free Beacon.

Soros is one of several Democratic megadonors who opened their checkbooks in 2020 to provide large sums to outfits backing Biden and hammering Republicans. The Biden Victory Fund in particular has benefited from a windfall of cash. It pulled in a whopping $83 million thanks to the Democratic Party's wealthiest donors, including Soros, who donated $500,000.

The leftist billionaire is taking steps to obscure his election spending this cycle. In the past, he made donations to groups directly in his own name. This cycle, he has operated primarily by transferring tens of millions from the Fund for Policy Reform, a $750 million nonprofit in his sprawling Open Society Foundation (OSF) network, into Democracy PAC. The PAC then disburses it to other Democratic PACs and committees. This arrangement allows Soros to keep his name from the top of donor lists. His $50 million in contributions makes him the largest donor of the 2020 cycle, though only $8 million is coming directly from him.

Soros has said he views the 2020 elections as especially important. Earlier in 2020 during a speech at the World Economic Forum, the 89-year-old billionaire said the "fate of the world" is at stake and referred to Trump as a "con man" and "authoritarian" who is "willing to sacrifice the national interests for his personal interests."

Democracy PAC has provided financial backing to dozens of liberal PACs and state-level politicians. In the spring quarter of 2020, its donations ranged from $90,000 to $2 million. Some of the largest donations went to the Nancy Pelosi-linked House Majority PAC ($2 million), Chuck Schumer-tied Senate Majority PAC ($1.5 million), Planned Parenthood Votes ($625,000), and the dark money group Sixteen Thirty Fund ($1 million).

Soros's $4 million in direct donations includes hundreds of thousands each to the DNC-led Democratic Grassroots Victory Fund, the Nancy Pelosi Victory Fund, and the Biden Victory Fund.

The leftist billionaire has also increased his lobbying expenditures. The Open Society Policy Center, his Washington, D.C.-based lobbying shop, spent $48 million in 2019—a personal record for Soros. This amount was more than corporate giants such as Amazon, Facebook, Boeing, and Google's parent company, Alphabet spent. The group finished the year as the country's second-largest lobbying spender.

Zuckerberg's $250 Million Group Funding Voting Drives in Democratic Strongholds

Facebook's billionaire founder Mark Zuckerberg and his wife Priscilla Chan have gifted a quarter of a billion dollars to this election activist group pushing major government voting initiatives in several Democratic strongholds in the battleground state of Wisconsin per the September 2020 "Zuckerberg pours $250 million into group funding voting drives in Wisconsin Democratic strongholds" article by Daniel Payne in Just the News.

The Center for Tech and Civic Life (CTCL), a group which styles itself as "a team of civic technologists, trainers, researchers, election administration and data experts working to foster a more informed and engaged democracy, and helping to modernize U.S. elections," announced that it had received $250 million from Zuckerberg and Chan.

The Center's major outreach efforts this election year appear as of this week to target predominantly Democratic strongholds. The five Wisconsin cities of Green Bay, Kenosha, Madison, Milwaukee, and Racine and Philadelphia—all have extensive histories of voting for Democrats; five of the six municipalities voted in favor of Hillary Clinton during the 2016 election, with only Kenosha going for Trump, by a razor-thin margin.

Phill Kline, the director of the Amistad Project at the conservative Thomas More Society law firm in Chicago, said his organization, working alongside the grassroots conservative group GotFreedom, "anticipates filing our first suit on these issues next week in Wisconsin." Kline said the arrangement of a private nonprofit group influencing election policy appears unseemly and possibly illegal.

"It's the legislature, under the Constitution, that determines the time, place and manner of an election," Kline told Just the News. "It's not bad that Zuckerberg wants to increase voter turnout. That's fine. He can spend it independently of government."

But election funds "should be appropriated by the state legislature and spent consistent with state laws," he continued, "as the Constitution specifically delegates the task of determining the time, place and manner of elections to the state legislatures."

"If Mr. Zuckerberg wants that money spent appropriately, he can just give it to the state," Kline added. Though the Center for Tech and Civic Life styles itself as nonpartisan, the conservative watchdog group Influence Watch identifies it as a "center-left election reform advocacy group."

Two of its executives—Whitney May and Donny Bridges—both used to work at the progressive New Organizing Institute in Washington, D.C. Its founder, Tiana Epps-Johnson, meanwhile, was the election administration director for that group.

The group has also in the past partnered with Rock the Vote, a progressive grassroots organization, as well as the liberal group Women Donors Network.

The Impact of Illegitimate Infusion of Private Funding on the 2020 Electorate

The confusion and negative effect from illegitimate infusion of private funding in Michigan, Wisconsin, Pennsylvania, and several other states during the 2020 election can be shown to have had a disparate and inequitable impact on the electorate.

Although history is replete with examples of elite groups attempting to gain influence, the current incidence of CTCL and other private donors purposefully injecting hundreds of millions of dollars into swing states is troubling because county officials who should know better actually accepted the grants, to the exclusion of abundantly available public funding. Even the most casual of observers can understand that acceptance of any private funding for administration of public elections creates inequity, dependency, and the potential for collusion, or even fraud.

It seems odd that while CTCL promotes having nationwide expertise in elections and electoral policy, its funding of local counties and municipalities in the 2020 general election blatantly circumvented well-funded and legislatively adopted state and federal HAVA plans.

Perhaps even more troubling is the collaboration of the Michigan and Pennsylvania Secretaries of State and representatives who sit on the election commission of Wisconsin in promoting CTCL grants, granting access to databases, or otherwise promoting non-profit activities while subordinating CARES funding and HAVA state implementation plans. Several of these officials have longstanding affiliations with progressive non-profits and foundations who actively endeavor to collect voting information for purposes of affecting elections or altering electoral policies.

The presence of vast quantities of public funds for administration of the 2020 elections in Michigan, Wisconsin, and Pennsylvania raises questions as to whether CTCL and its supporting foundations understood that there was no resource deficit for administration of elections, including extra expenses due to COVID-19.

Public-Private Partnerships (Zuckerberg-Soros Effect)

For example, Wisconsin used a $6.3 million CTCL grant from Mark Zuckerberg to support the installation of drop-boxes and illegal ballot harvesting events like "Democracy in the Park." These funds were also used to help with various other election administration activities in several Democrat strongholds including Milwaukee, Madison, Green Bay, Racine, and Kenosha.

Similarly, Pennsylvania received over $12 million from CTCL. Fully $10 million of those funds poured into the Democrat-dominated Philadelphia to help boost turnout and count ballots. The strings attached to these funds required the city to open no fewer than 800 new polling places, thereby dramatically changing how Philadelphia managed its General Election processes.45 In a clear violation of its tax-exempt status, CTCL has posted anti-Republican and anti-Trump statements on social media."

Despite its claims of non-partisanship, CTCL's officials have a documented history of involvement in left-wing political movements. A complaint filed on August 28, 2020 with the Wisconsin Elections Commission (WEC) showed that the organization is comprised of Barack Obama's allies who were highly skilled in recruiting Democrat voters to the polls.

It is also worth noting here that while this report does not examine any possible interventions by the Chinese Communist Party (CCP) into our election, Mark Zuckerberg has long sought to enter the Chinese market. He speaks fluent Chinese, and his company, Facebook, has–despicably–hired Chinese Communist Party members to increase Facebook's ability to censor Trump supporters and the conservative movement.

Zuckerberg also has expressed sympathies for Chinese Communist Party ideology. In 2014, Zuckerberg met with Chinese internet Czar Lu Wei in Silicon Valley, and was caught on Chinese state-run media promoting Chairman Xi's book entitled "The Governance of China." In fact, Zuckerberg also distributed this propaganda to his colleagues, because he desired for them to understand Communist Party ideology such as "socialism with Chinese characteristics." In 2016, Zuckerberg also met with China's propaganda chief, Liu Yunshan, and praised the Communist Party for its "development of the internet."

As for George Soros and his web of progressive organizations, the Soros effort to influence the 2020 election ironically would be assisted by a key department in the Trump Administration, the Department of Homeland Security (DHS). In November 2019, DHS announced it would partner with Soros-funded VotingWorks—a left-of-center non-profit provider of voting machines and open-source election verification software—to salt key battleground states with voting machines.

Alleged Russia Hoax participant Marc Elias used tactics similar to Soros and Zuckerberg that likewise helped advance the Democrat Party's Grand Strategy. For example, Elias assisted Stacey Abrams' nonprofit, the New Georgia Project, in filing a complaint on May 8, 2020, which called for radical Election Law changes. These changes included absentee ballot receipt deadline extensions and increased ballot curing.

Elias' plan would reap major fruit in Gwinnett, Georgia, as Republicans lost major races for District Attorney, Sheriff, and County Commission Chair. The Democrat Party also flipped the 7th Congressional District seat to the blue side.

This Warrants Investigation

Based upon the information in the Stillwater Technical Solutions (STS) report and related research, STS offers the following actions and activities for consideration:

1.   The secretaries, attorneys general, and/or legislatures of states whose county governments received CTCL funds should commission a comprehensive, third-party audit of the consistency of private/public transactions with the HAVA implementation plans of their state. This should include compliance with NIST standards, and state procurement requirements.

2.   State secretaries, attorneys general and/or legislatures who have membership in the non-profit Electronic Registration Information Center (ERIC) should audit the information access, collection, storage, security and/or potential voter information sharing practices of ERIC with other states or third-party non-profit associations.

3.   In the fall of 2020, the Center for Election Innovation (CEIR) issued grants to state secretaries, local governments, and non-profit associations for election-related purposes. Secretaries, attorneys general, and/or legislators of states receiving CEIR grants should request and evaluate CEIR contracts for HAVA compliance and the fiscal and procurement requirements of their individual states.

4.   CTCL is a non-profit organization chartered in Illinois but who has negotiated grant contracts with county and municipal governments in multiple jurisdictions across many states. The public record is silent as to whether CTCL is licensed in all the states in which it continues to conduct contractual business.

5.   The claw back language in CTCL agreements with counties and municipalities who received grants represents a long-term, contingent liability and is subject to federal audit, bonding, or pension risks. County commissioners should coordinate with their respective attorneys general or legislatures to understand and mitigate potential future liabilities.

Well-Funded Campaign to Replace Judicial Elections With Liberal Special Interests

Over the past 10 years, special interests have engaged in a highly coordinated, well-funded campaign to fundamentally alter the composition of America's state courts as outlined in the September 2010 "Hijacking Justice: The Well-Funded Campaign to Replace Judicial Elections with Selection by Liberal Special Interests" article by The Heritage Foundation's Colleen Pero.

The campaign's goal: to exclude conservative, rule-of-law judges from the bench. This campaign has been bankrolled by George Soros, a hedge fund operator with a net worth of $13 billion, according to the Forbes 400 list of the world's richest people and the "funding father" of leftist movements, organizations, and causes in the United States.

A groundbreaking study released by the American Justice Partnership, Justice Hijacked: Your Right to Vote Is at Stake, reveals that Soros's Open Society Institute (OSI) has invested at least $45.4 million in earmarked funds in its campaign to reshape the judiciary. Shockingly, this is a conservative estimate that does not include the millions of additional dollars that flow to these organizations' general operating funds or through intermediary "conduit" organizations.

Merit Selection

This multi-million-dollar campaign to reshape America's courts encompasses efforts to revise state constitutions, rewrite judicial recusal rules, abolish democratic judicial elections, and impose a judicial selection system known by its proponents as "merit selection."

Under "merit selection," the power to select judges is transferred from the people to a small, unelected, unaccountable commission comprised primarily of legal elites, typically including representatives of powerful special interest groups, such as state trial lawyers associations—whose politics, not surprisingly, are more liberal than the general public.

Promoted as a method to keep "politics" out of the judicial selection process, the merit committees in many states are extremely politicized and have fueled several high-profile political controversies in the past few years. Such confrontations have prompted scholars to question whether the merit selection system serves any of its stated purposes.

Nevertheless, proponents of merit selection have continued their campaign unabated. Indeed, the campaign now uses the Supreme Court's recent decision in *Citizens United v. Federal Election Commission*—a decision that allows corporations and unions to make independent expenditures related to federal races but does not permit corporations or unions to make direct contributions to candidates—as its rallying cry, arguing that the decision will precipitate a "flood of money" into state judicial races.

Backroom Political Deals

Ironically, the same opponents of judicial elections who loudly protest about contributions negatively affecting the independence of the judiciary—a claim for which they have yet to provide any concrete evidence—are receiving and spending tens of millions of Soros dollars to not merely influence judicial elections but eliminate them and turn judicial selection over to special interests and backroom political deals. This does not remove politics from the process but rather moves politics outside of public view.

The well-funded proponents of so-called merit selection engage in a kind of political self-dealing, promoting selection by interest groups who are more closely aligned to their liberal agenda. Those who are concerned about the influence of money in judicial elections should pay more attention to the money spent by those seeking to use "merit" selection not to eliminate politics but to embed interest group politics formally into the selection process, thereby tilting judicial selection in their political favor.

Snubbing Trump, Lawyers Doling More Cash to Democrats

Contributions to Trump from legal profession continue to dwindle and Big Law's favorite candidates thus far, Biden and Harris, data show. Lawyers have long been a reliable source of campaign funds for Democratic presidential hopefuls. But the legal set's political contributions haven't been this blue since at least 2004.

Lawyers and employees of the nation's law firms have contributed nearly $17 million to presidential campaigns so far this election cycle and 95% of the total has gone to Democrats, according to the Center for Responsive Politics. President Donald Trump's campaign has raised just over $785,000 from lawyers and law firms.

Per the November 2019 Bloomberg Law "Snubbing Trump, Lawyers Doling More Cash to Democrats" article by Roy Strom: Since 2004, Republican presidential candidates have had at most 41% of law firm employees' contributions through the third quarter of the year before a presidential election, CRP data show.

Legitimacy and Effect of Private Funding in Federal and State Electoral Processes

The 2020 presidential election witnessed an unprecedented and coordinated public-private partnership to improperly influence the 2020 presidential election on behalf of one particular candidate and party—the Democratic Party. Phill Kline, Director of the Amistad Project of the Thomas More Society notes in his "The Legitimacy and Effect of Private Funding in Federal and State Electoral Processes" report, the following observations:

Using the COVID-19 flu pandemic as justification and the excuse that local elections lacked funding to facilitate safe elections, a well-funded network of foundations and non-profit organizations gave hundreds of millions of dollars of private funding directly to counties and municipalities across Michigan, Wisconsin, and Pennsylvania for electoral purposes.

The illegitimate infusion of private funding and third-party promotion of training, equipment, security, staffing and reporting programs by a network of private nonprofits at the local level bypassed state administrative processes, violated legislative prerogatives codified in state Help

America Vote Plans (HAVA), and resulted in questions about the integrity of the US electoral system.

Funded by hundreds of millions of dollars from Facebook founder Mark Zuckerberg and other high-tech interests, activist organizations created a two-tiered election system that treated voters differently depending on whether they lived in Democrat or Republican strongholds.

Private monies dictated city and county election management contrary to both federal law and state election plans endorsed and developed by state legislatures with authority granted by the United States Constitution.

Moreover, executive officials in swing states facilitated, through unique and novel contracts, the sharing of private and sensitive information about citizens within those states with private interests, some whom actively promote leftist candidates and agendas.

This data sharing allowed direct access to data of unique political value to leftist causes and created new vulnerabilities for digital manipulation of state electronic poll books and counting systems and machines.

This public-private partnership in these swing states effectively placed government's thumb on the scale to help these private interests achieve their objectives and to benefit the candidates of the Democratic Party.

The Amistad Project Began Monitoring These Activities Beginning in Spring of 2019

The Amistad Project began monitoring these activities beginning in the spring of 2019, originally focusing on the digital vulnerabilities of state election systems.

The Amistad Project became aware that states and local election officials failed to maintain the legal right to access computer logs on the machines counting ballots. The first step to engage any computer forensic examination is to gain access to machine logs, yet scores of election officials failed to maintain the right to even review such information, much less establish a method for bipartisan review.

In effect, America purchased a complex ballot box (computer) into which its votes would be deposited but didn't have the right to open the box and review the count. As a related example, the May 2021 Arizona audit of the servers was halted (temporality?) due to no one party able (or willing?) to provide the access codes to them.

As COVID escalated in March of 2020, the Amistad Project began witnessing troubling efforts to undermine the integrity of the 2020 by assaulting laws designed to protect the integrity of the absentee ballot. The use of absentee ballots is uniquely vulnerable to fraud, as detailed in a special bipartisan congressional report authored by former President Jimmy Carter and James Baker.

Accordingly, states have basic, common-sense laws protecting the integrity of the absentee, advance, or mailed ballot.

Left-Leaning Organizations Filed a Massive Number of Lawsuits to Challenge These Integrity Laws

Beginning in the spring of 2020, left-leaning organizations filed a massive number of lawsuits to challenge these integrity laws. Lawsuits sought to set aside witness requirements, identification requirements, deadlines, delivery requirements, ballot deadlines, signature requirements, application requirements, and even argued that the Constitution required all returned ballot envelopes be postage prepaid due to COVID.

Swing state governors also started issuing emergency executive orders shutting down in-person voting while pouring new state resources into encouraging persons to vote in advance. Polling data revealed this coordinated assault on in-person voting generally favored Democrat Party voters who preferred to vote in advance, while placing Republicans, who preferred to vote in person, at a disadvantage.

These actions represent the beginning of the formation of a two-tier election system favoring one demographic while disadvantaging another demographic.

Also in March 2020, David Plouffe, former campaign manager for President Barak Obama, published his book entitled *A Citizen's Guide to Defeating Donald Trump*. At the time, Plouffe was working for the charitable initiative of Mark Zuckerberg and his wife Priscilla Chan.

On page 81 of his book, Plouffe correctly identifies that the 2020 general election will come down to a "block by block street fight" to turn out the vote in the urban core, a key stronghold of Democrat Party votes. Plouffe specifically highlighted high turnouts in Milwaukee, Detroit, and Philadelphia as the key to a Democrat victory.

Zuckerberg's Center for Tech and Civic Life (CTCL)

Soon after the pandemic struck, the Thomas More Society witnessed the rumblings of a previously sleepy 501(c)(3) organization entitled the Center for Tech and Civic Life (CTCL) whose previous annual revenues never exceeded $1.2 million. CTCL began sending agents into states to recruit certain Democrat strongholds to prepare grants requesting monies from CTCL.

For example, CTCL inked a $100,000 grant to the Mayor of Racine, WI in May of 2020 directing the Mayor to recruit four other cities (Green Bay, Kenosha, Madison, and Milwaukee) to develop a joint grant request of CTCL. This effort results in these cities submitting a "Wisconsin Safe Election Plan" on June 15, 2020 to CTCL and, in turn, receiving $6.3 million to implement the plan.

This privatization of elections undermines the Help America Vote Act (HAVA), which requires state election plans to be submitted to federal officials and approved and requires respect for equal protection by making all resources available equally to all voters.

The provision of Zuckerberg-CTCL funds allowed these Democrat strongholds to spend roughly $47 per voter, compared to $4 to $7 per voter in traditionally Republican areas of the state. Moreover, this recruiting of targeted jurisdictions for specific government action and funding runs contrary to legislative election plans and invites government to play favorites in the election process.

Because the availability of adequate public funding severely contrasted the narrative by the Center for Technology and Civic Life (CTCL) that private monies were needed for safe administration of public elections.

The Amistad Project explored the background of CTCL and discovered a deep and integrated apparatus of progressive foundations and affiliated non-profits whose mission is to transition the bottom-up, electoral system of the United States to a top down, electronic system that centralizes voter information, interfaces with state registration databases, and promotes advocacy, all of which could, over time, have the capacity to exert strong local influence on the electoral processes of the United States.

The "Wisconsin Safe Election Plan" Was Not Authored by the State

The "Wisconsin Safe Election Plan" was not authored by the state and considered state election integrity laws as obstacles and nuisances to be ignored or circumvented. Moreover, CTCL retained the right, in the grant document, to, in its sole discretion, order all funds returned if the grantee cities did not conduct the election consistent with CTCL dictates.

Effectively, CTCL managed the election in these five cities. And this plan violated state law in, at least, the following fashion:

1)   The plan circumvented voter identification requirements for absentee ballots by attempting to classify all voters as "indefinitely confined" due to COVID and later, after Wisconsin Supreme Court criticism, by ordering election clerks to not question such claims.

2)   The plan initiated the use of drop boxes for ballot collection, significantly breaching the chain of custody of the ballot and failing to maintain proper logs and reviews to ensure all properly cast ballots were counted and all improperly cast ballots were not counted.

3)   Initiated the consolidation of counting centers, justifying the flow of hundreds of thousands of ballots to one location and the marginalization of Republican poll watchers such that bipartisan participation in the management, handling, and counting of the ballots was compromised.

The Disparate and Inequitable Impact of Zuckerberg's CTCL Funding in Pennsylvania

Documents obtained through court order revealed communication between the City of Philadelphia and CTCL emphasizing that CTCL paid election judges in Philadelphia and other election officials. CTCL mandated Philadelphia to increase its polling locations and to use drop boxes and eventually mobile pick-up units. Moreover, Zuckerberg monies allowed Philadelphia to "cure" absentee ballots in a manner not provided for in Republican areas of the state.

In Democrat Delaware County, Pennsylvania, one drop box was placed every four square miles and for every 4,000 voters. In the 59 counties carried by Trump in 2016, there was one drop box for every 1,100 square miles and every 72,000 voters. Government encouraging a targeted demographic to turn out the vote is the opposite side of the same coin as government targeting a demographic to suppress the vote.

These irregularities existed wherever Zuckerberg's money was granted to local election officials. In effect, Mark Zuckerberg was invited into the counting room, and the American people were kicked out.

Additionally, Amistad became alarmed at the new vulnerabilities created in our election system with "data sharing agreements" that gave left-leaning third-party organizations front door access to electronic poll books. Rock the Vote and other organizations inked agreements with blue state election officials to enter new registrations into state poll books. Such agreements are unprecedented and unwise.

Previously, voter registrations were entered solely by election clerks, who have three important checks on their authority. These checks are: 1) they must be transparent subject to FOIA and open records laws; 2) they are geographically limited rendering audits manageable; and 3) they are politically accountable. No such checks apply to Rock the Vote.

Allowing such access creates new digital vulnerabilities easily allowing nefarious actors to access poll books and alter entries. The Amistad Project's concerns were amplified by the nature of a contract offered by Michigan's health director to a subsidiary of NGP VAN, a Democrat fundraiser and data services company.

Pro-China Communists Working to Mobilize 40 Million New Voters Against Trump

Jon Liss is one of the most influential and little-known political operatives in the United States today. A longtime leader of the Freedom Road Socialist Organization (FRSO), Liss has been building political influence in Northern Virginia for over three decades. He has been active in Tenants and Workers United, the Rainbow Coalition/Jesse Jackson presidential campaign, the Fairfax County Taxi-drivers Association, and the Left Strategies Collective.

Liss' organization, FRSO, itself grew out of the Maoist "New Communist Movement" of the 1970s and has maintained ties to the People's Republic of China. The FRSO is probably about 2,000 members strong, but it works in partnership with the 5,000 members of the equally pro-China Communist Party USA (CPUSA) and the nearly 60,000-strong Democratic Socialists of America (DSA).

Working together in an alliance called the "Left Inside/Outside Project," these three groups have infiltrated the Democratic Party in every state of the union with great success as reported in the July 2019 "Pro-China Communists Working to Mobilize 40 Million New Voters Against Trump" *Epoch Times* article by Trevor Loudon.

President Donald Trump and the Republican Party were not ready for a tsunami of these new Democratic voters coming their way in 2020 and Liss' alliance deserves much of the credit. Far from the easy victory many pundits predicted, there was a strong chance the president and his party (strong economy notwithstanding) could be overwhelmed by an unexpected wave of new voters coming mainly from young, female, and diverse voters.

This is exactly what happened with these unsapient young adults—mostly Generation Z and Millennials and a strong percentage of Generation X voters that showed strong socialist and liberal tendencies and a Democratic Party preference—many voting for the first time in the 2020 election.

9 – Questionable Voting Dumps, Irregularities & Anomalies in the 2020 Election

Credit: CBS46.

A major voting processing center in Fulton, Georgia's most populous county, claimed at one point to have trouble counting ballots in the evening because of a burst pipe or even, some officials said, a water main break. It turned out it was actually a minor urinal leak that had occurred that morning and hadn't really disrupted anything. Diversion?

Documented in the March 2021 "Media's Entire Georgia Narrative Is Fraudulent, Not Just The Fabricated Trump Quotes" article by Mollie Hemingway in *The Federalist*: Things only got weirder. That night, an election official curiously announced that they were closing up shop for the evening, even though there were tons of ballots left to count. As workers closed their counting operations and many began to leave, the news media and other election observers left. The news media reported they'd been told the ballot counting would stop.

But even though Fulton publicly said they were stopping the count, they didn't stop counting ballots. Republicans who were already frustrated that they weren't near enough to properly observe the counting were outraged and cried foul when they discovered they'd been misled and encouraged to leave.

Election officials denied wrongdoing. A video came out (as shown on previous page) corroborating the claims of Republican poll watchers and the media about being told the counting would stop. The video also showed ballots being pulled out from under a table, and other suspicious actions that led many observers to question the integrity of the operation.

Fulton County and Georgia secretary of state officials pooh-poohed the concerns or claimed, without providing a report or substantive rebuttal, that they'd looked into the situation and found nothing problematic.

For Republicans concerned about the inherent lack of election integrity associated with mail-in ballots, the questionable security and chain of custody problems associated with rampant use of ballot drop-boxes, the large outside funding of vote processes by tech oligarchs, and all the other problems wrought by voting and counting ballots over a period of many weeks, if not months—the situation was deeply alarming.

Election Night and Early Morning Vote Dump 'Irregularities'

It might have been mere coincidence that Joe Biden ran behind Hillary Clinton everywhere except a handful of critical cities in the battleground states of Pennsylvania, Wisconsin, Michigan, Arizona, and Georgia.

Per "The 4 Biden vote dumps that changed the 2020 election" posted in December 2020 by Gray's Economy: That is odd, to be sure, especially when one notes that around midnight on Nov. 3, 2020, Donald Trump was running substantially ahead in those states. Then, the voting stopped. Everyone yawned and dozed off. When they woke up, what do you know, Biden had the lead everywhere!

Many statistic professionals have given sworn testimony as to the impossibility of the election results in Democratic-controlled cities like Philadelphia, Pittsburgh, Atlanta, Detroit, Milwaukee, Las Vegas, and Phoenix.

They tell how President Trump had commanding leads in all these states on the night of the election, only to wake the next day to find these cities dramatically flipped the other way and turned the state blue.

Voting Madness is going to cite some of the statistical anomalies later in this chapter that raises a number of questions concerning what took place early morning after midnight on November 3, 2020. Using a report titled a "Quantitative Analysis of Decisive Vote Updates in Michigan, Wisconsin, and Georgia on and after Election Night" by Vote Pattern Integrity: Data analytics, their statistical and probability analysis of swing state voting results is very troubling.

Early on in the report the authors point to four voter dumps in Michigan, Wisconsin, and Georgia. The reports says that it is statistically important to look at the ratios of these voter updates since they are so outside the ratios reported in 8,950 other voter updates nationally.

Four Key Vote Dumps Came Within a 5-Hour Window After Voting Was 'Allegedly' Suspended

It is also very important to note that all four of these highly questionable voter dumps came within a five hour window when these states allegedly suspended the counting.

In particular, ratios are almost never used in expressing vote counts (one typically hears of percentages or, when a race is close, numbers) and so anyone committing fraud and looking to "cover their tracks" is more likely to be "gaming" the metrics they're used to, and much more likely to leave tells in metrics they're not considering.

This "Quantitative Analysis of Decisive Vote Updates in Michigan, Wisconsin, and Georgia on and after Election Night" report studies 8,954 individual updates to the vote totals in all 50 states and finds that four individual updates—two of which were widely noticed on the internet, including by the President—are profoundly anomalous; they deviate from a pattern which is otherwise found in the vast majority of the remaining 8,950 vote updates.

The findings presented by this report suggest that four vote count updates—which collectively were decisive in Michigan, Wisconsin, and Georgia, and thus decisive of a critical forty-two electoral votes—are especially anomalous and merit further investigation.

There is also a section explaining how the Michigan ratio between President Trump and the third-party candidate was running at more than 31:1 in the state, but in Wayne County (Detroit area} the ratio collapsed to 2.5:1. This could suggest that Trump had such a commanding lead that they could not overcome it by flipping votes to Biden because that ratio would be too over to top, so they flipped Trump votes to third-party.

Americans' ability to trust an election is free and fair is one of the most important and basic things that preserves the republic, and any irregularities need to be investigated further.

Benford's Law and Statistical Anomalies in Biden Votes

With the 2020 elections marred by legal challenges and fraud allegations, some have used statistical analysis to try to determine if foul play was involved. In several states, analyses of election data indeed show statistically odd phenomena in the tallies of votes for the Democratic candidate, former Vice President Joe Biden.

As per the April 2021 "Statistical Anomalies in Biden Votes, Analyses Indicate" article by *Epoch Times'* writer Petr Svab: One of the most common arguments is that in some localities, vote counts for Biden violate Benford's Law. In simple terms, the law states that in many real-world data sets, such as demographic data, geographical data, or even sports statistics, the first digit of the numbers will more likely be 1 than 2, and 2 more likely than 3, etc. following logarithmic scale. If the first-digit distribution significantly diverges from this rule, it could be evidence of artificial manipulation of the data.

The law has been used to identify fraudulent financial records and other illegal activities. Walter Mebane, a political science professor at the University of Michigan, used the law to back ballot-stuffing allegations in the 2009 Iran election. Some researchers also used the law to check for irregularities in the 2016 election in Wisconsin.

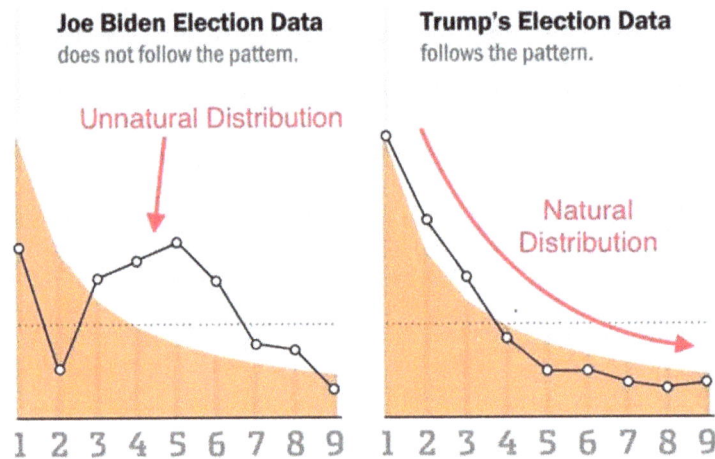

Joe Biden Election Data
does not follow the pattern.

Unnatural Distribution

1 2 3 4 5 6 7 8 9

Trump's Election Data
follows the pattern.

Natural
Distribution

1 2 3 4 5 6 7 8 9

Credit: Himalaya Australia.

Allegations About Dominion Voting Machines

Dominion machines can be altered to manipulate tallies in just a few minutes, using malicious code, according to Princeton professor of computer science and election security expert Andrew Appel.

A ballot can be spoiled or altered by the Dominion machine because "the ballot marking printer is in the same paper path as the mechanism to deposit marked ballots into an attached ballot box," a study by University of California–Berkeley said.

The voting machines are susceptible to hacking or remote tampering because they are connected to the internet, even though they're not supposed to be, according to a lawsuit. "If one laptop was connected to the internet, the entire precinct was compromised."

There is evidence of remote access and remote troubleshooting, "which presents a grave security implication," according to Finnish computer programmer and election security expert Hari Hursti. His declaration also claims the activity logs of the voting machines can be overwritten by hackers to erase their steps.

Dominion machine operators can change settings to exclude certain ballots from being counted. The ballots can be put in a separate file and deleted simply, according to Ronald Watkins, a software and cyber-security expert who reviewed the Dominion software manual. He also said final vote count involved machine operators copying and pasting the "Results" folder onto a USB drive, a process he calls "error-prone and very vulnerable to malicious administrators."

Anomalies in Vote Counts and Their Effects on Election 2020

In the early hours of November 4th, 2020, Democratic candidate Joe Biden received several major "vote spikes" that substantially—and decisively—improved his electoral position in Michigan, Wisconsin, and Georgia.

Much skepticism and uncertainty surrounds these "vote spikes." Critics point to suspicious vote counting practices, extreme differences between the two major candidates' vote counts, and the timing of the vote updates, among other factors, to cast doubt on the legitimacy of some of these spikes.

While data analysis cannot on its own demonstrate fraud or systemic issues, it can point us to statistically anomalous cases that invite further scrutiny as demonstrated in the November 2020 "Anomalies in Vote Counts and Their Effects on Election 2020 A Quantitative Analysis of Decisive Vote Updates in Michigan, Wisconsin, and Georgia on and after Election Night" report by Vote Integrity which the middle of this chapter is comprised of. A link to the full report is included in the Appendix.

This is one such case documented by Vote Pattern Analysis (VPA) and their extensive statistical analysis finds that a few key vote updates in competitive states were unusually large in size and had an unusually high Biden-to-Trump ratio. This demonstrate the results differ enough from expected results to be cause for concern.

Per VPA: With this report, we rely only on publicly available data from the *New York Times* to identify and analyze statistical anomalies in key states. Looking at 8,954 individual vote updates (differences in vote totals for each candidate between successive changes to the running vote totals, colloquially also referred to as "dumps" or "batches"), we discover a remarkably consistent mathematical property: there is a clear inverse relationship between difference in candidates' vote counts and the ratio of the vote counts.

In other words, it's not surprising to see vote updates with large margins, and it's not surprising to see vote updates with very large ratios of support between the candidates, but it is surprising to see vote updates which are both.

The significance of this property will be further explained in later sections of this report. Nearly every vote update, across states of all sizes and political leanings follow this statistical pattern. A very small number, however, are especially aberrant. Of the seven vote updates which follow the pattern the least, four individual vote updates—two in Michigan, one in Wisconsin, and one in Georgia—were particularly anomalous and influential with respect to this property and all occurred within the same five hour window.

In particular, per VPA:

We are able to quantify the extent of compliance with this property and discover that, of the 8,954 vote updates used in the analysis, these four decisive updates were the 1st, 2nd, 4th, and 7th most anomalous updates in the entire data set. Not only does each of these vote updates not follow the generally observed pattern, but the anomalous behavior of these updates is particularly extreme. That is, these vote updates are outliers of the outliers.

The four vote updates in question

Through several investigative mechanisms, we find these four vote updates to be extraordinarily anomalous. While these alone do not prove the existence of fraud or systemic issue, it invites further scrutiny.

- An update in Michigan listed as of 6:31AM Eastern Time on November 4th, 2020, which shows 141,258 votes for Joe Biden and 5,968 votes for Donald Trump.

- An update in Wisconsin listed as 3:42AM Central Time on November 4th, 2020, which shows 143,379 votes for Joe Biden and 25,163 votes for Donald Trump.

- A vote update in Georgia listed at 1:34AM Eastern Time on November 4th, 2020, which shows 136,155 votes for Joe Biden and 29,115 votes for Donald Trump.

- An update in Michigan listed as of 3:50AM Eastern Time on November 4th, 2020, which shows 54,497 votes for Joe Biden and 4,718 votes for Donald Trump.

This report predicts what these vote updates would have looked like, had they followed the same pattern as the vast majority of the 8,950 others. We find that the extents of the respective anomalies here are more than the margin of victory in all three states—Michigan, Wisconsin, and Georgia—which collectively represent forty-two electoral votes.

Extensive mathematical detail is provided and the data and the code (for the data-curation, data transformation, plotting, and modeling) are all linked and provided for in the Appendix for further research and investigation.

Background

Late on Election Night 2020, President Donald J. Trump had a lead of around 100,000 votes in Wisconsin, a lead of around 300,000 votes in Michigan, and a lead of around 700,000 votes in Pennsylvania. Back-of-the-envelope calculations showed that in order to overtake President Trump, Joe Biden would have to substantially improve his performance in the remaining precincts—many of which were in heavily blue areas like Detroit, Milwaukee, and Philadelphia.

On Election Night, conflicting news reports came in that various precincts were stopping their count for the evening, sending election officials home, or re-starting their counts. There remains a large amount of confusion to this day about the extent to which various precincts stopped counting, as well as the extent to which any state election laws, or rules were broken by sending election officials home prematurely. Whatever the case is, various precincts in Wisconsin, Michigan, and Pennsylvania continued to report numbers throughout the night.

By the early hours of the following morning, Wisconsin had flipped blue, as did Michigan soon after. A few days later, Georgia and Pennsylvania followed suit. Given the uncertain context, many American observers and commentators were immediately uncomfortable or skeptical of these trends.

In other words, given X for Biden and Y for Trump, either metric will produce a score which is the opposite of what it would produce if the update instead had Y votes for Biden and X for Trump. This property is extremely useful and will come in handy during the statistical analysis.

Readers might ask: Why are you measuring the ratio? Why not measure the difference between the vote proportions (or, equivalently, their percentages). The answer to this lies in what we are looking for, i.e. evidence of fraud or foul play which manifests in extremely unusual outcomes.

In particular, ratios are almost never used in expressing vote counts (one typically hears of percentages or, when a race is close, numbers) and so anyone committing fraud and looking to "cover their tracks" is more likely to be "gaming" the metrics they're used to (i.e., vote counts and percentages) and much more likely to leave tells in metrics they're not considering.

This obscures critical differences between the two statistics

Ratios demonstrate an important property: the farther ahead a candidate is, the harder it is to move the next 1 percent ahead. They reflect the relative difficulty of each marginal vote as the pool of remaining votes decreases. As a candidate approaches 0% or 100% of the vote, the rates at which the ratio of that candidate's votes to the other candidate's votes converge to zero or infinity are very different.

As seen in Michigan's vote dumps, we see when we weight by the number of votes in any given update, this update is particularly anomalous which means deviating from what is standard, normal, or expected. The next closest vote-weighted Other: Trump ratio is less than two-thirds of this one, and the median—137.56—is smaller by a factor of about 464.5. For such a large batch of votes to be counted while also showing such an exceptionally poor performance of Trump relative to the non-two-party vote is clearly very surprising.

Per VPA: In particular, it calls into serious question the veracity of this vote update and is perhaps some of the strongest direct evidence of fraud in this entire report. Someone looking to fraudulently improve Joe Biden's margins relative to Donald Trump is likely to be focused on covering their tracks by keeping Joe Biden's share of the update at a reasonable value. 95% might seem plausible, but 99.9% at this scale becomes prima facie implausible to any honest observer.

One effective way of achieving the desired goal of decreasing Donald Trump's lead at this point would have been to suppress the Trump vote while artificially inflating the non-two-party vote in an attempt to disguise just how Biden-favoring this update actually was.

Indeed, this is precisely the reason this report uses ratios—because they are a metric virtually never used for any practical purpose in discussing election results, someone committing fraud is far less likely to consider how unusual a ratio might look.

In particular, because the non-two-party candidates received far less media attention than in the 2016 Presidential election, and the Green Party candidate was even successfully sued off of the ballot in one or more states, it is hard to believe that this vote update only favored Trump over the non-two-party vote by less than a factor of 2.5, when the statewide ratio was over 31.

Absent a compelling explanation of why this particular update—at such a crucial time, in a crucial state, which improved Biden's standing in the state so dramatically—also had non-two-party votes performing so unusually relative to Trump votes, it seems unlikely that this vote update reflects an honest accounting of the legitimate votes.

Subsequent sections of this report quantify how extreme it is in other respects and consider the implications if it had been slightly less extreme.

Quantifying the extremity

Having demonstrated visually how anomalous the four key vote updates are per VPA, we can now proceed to attempt to quantify how unusual it is that these three points exist at once and that two of them are from the same state.

Important considerations

It is important to note one crucial indicator of why these results are bizarre. In virtually all other cases, areas which are very pro-Biden or pro-Trump have vote updates of varying size, and so a large vote update heavily favoring one candidate is almost always accompanied by even smaller updates which have a higher variance in the ratio, and at least some of them will favor the candidate who won the largest batch.

In particular, to accept the results as seen in Michigan as legitimate, one would need to believe that the one or two most possible pro-Biden areas of the state were somehow each counted their ballots entirely in one or two vote updates.

If they were counted incrementally and released in smaller batches, as is typically the case, we would expect to see smaller updates with higher variance in outcome and would almost certainly see updates with a higher Biden: Trump ratio than the two Michigan updates discussed in this report.

Indeed, if it is subsequently discovered that these did not comprise the entire count (for either mail-in votes or all votes) in these areas, then these results should be regarded with extreme suspicion.

While vote counts are by no means a random sample nationally, given a small enough sub-population at which votes are counted, they eventually are. If it can be shown by those with access to time-series county-level (or precinct-level) data that, for whichever counties or precincts reported in this update, that there were other updates (or other updates with mail-in ballots), then these results become almost impossible to believe.

This is to say, the believability of these updates relies on the premise that the one or two most Biden-favoring parts of the state (perhaps by ballot type) were counted entirely in these two batches. If it cannot be shown that the ballots counted during these spikes were qualitatively different from all other vote updates in Michigan, then the results are likely too extreme along multiple dimensions to be accepted at face value.

One would also need to believe that mail-in ballots, which have generally been understood to be more pro-Biden, sometimes substantially so, were counted in their entirety in these regions. While this data set does not provide breakdowns of how many votes in each update came from different types of votes, it is extremely surprising that we do not see smaller vote updates with mail-in votes which favor Biden more heavily.

This is also the case in Wisconsin, there the update discussed in this report, which had the largest Biden margin by far, also had the second-highest Biden: Trump ratio, by only a small amount.

Accepting this at face value requires the belief that the most pro-Biden subset of the votes–by geography and vote type–was counted entirely in one batch. It would be extremely surprising if all mail-in ballots in the two most favoring Biden counties in the state, Dane, and Milwaukee County, were entirely contained in this batch, and so it raises the question as to why we didn't see even more pro-Biden updates in smaller, higher-variance vote updates in these heavily Democratic areas.

If we are to accept that these votes were counted entirely in one batch, this raises serious questions as well. In particular, given the ambiguity—to this day—about where the vote-tabulation process was stopped and why, it makes little sense why these votes would be released in such an unusually large batch.

All of this is especially surprising when viewed in contrast to the prevailing analysis of the election, i.e. that Joe Biden's victory was the result of improved performance in suburban areas. Looking at a map of final results by county, it is highly likely that these vote updates came from more densely-populated urban counties where Biden's ratios were much higher.

The findings here call that into question, however, as we can see that he relied heavily on four extremely aberrant vote updates which were almost certainly in heavily pro-Biden urban areas to provide a much-needed boost in the early hours of November 4th.

Follow-up and Conclusions

If these vote updates were only more extreme than 99% of all updates nationally in terms of their deviation from this generally-observed pattern, that, holding all else equal, Joe Biden may very well have lost the states of Michigan, Wisconsin, and Georgia, and that he would have 42 fewer Electoral votes—putting Biden below the number required to win the Presidency. Either way, it is indisputable that his margin of victory in these three states relies on four most anomalous vote updates identified by the metric developed in this report.

Per VPA, we once again note that this analysis is largely restricted to four individual vote updates out of a sample of nearly 9,000. This report by no means suggests stopping investigations in Michigan, Wisconsin, Pennsylvania, Georgia, or elsewhere; it is merely that these four key ballot updates are both profoundly anomalous with respect to a metric which removes any component of different states having different partisan leanings or a different number of voters.

Furthermore, this analysis does not require that we regard the final vote totals in any of these states (or counties thereof) as suspicious, nor, critically, does it require that we accept that the observed data should follow any particular distribution a priori. We merely show that the data, adjusted appropriately to remove differences in size and political leaning between states, does follow a certain pattern, and that four key vote updates deviate profoundly from that pattern.

It is our belief that the extraordinarily anomalous nature of the studied vote updates here, combined with the staggering political implications, demands immediate and thorough investigation.

The Navarro Report, Vol. 3: Yes, President Trump Won

Volume 3 of The Navarro Report; *Yes, President Trump Won*, is designed to serve as a summary to what has been a comprehensive analysis of the question: Was the 2020 presidential election stolen from Donald J. Trump? In this report, Peter Navarro provides the most up-to-date statistical "receipts" with respect to the potential number of illegal votes in each battleground state.

The broader goal of this final and third installment of the Navarro Report is to provide investigators with a well-documented tally of potentially illegal votes on a state-by-state and category-by-category basis as shown in the Vote Irregularities and Illegalities by Category and State (Summary figure below). If there is one statistical summary throughout *Voting Madness* that should stand out more than any other—this is the one.

In the remainder of this report, we will simply present the statistical "receipts" on a state-by-state and subcategory-by-subcategory basis what may well be the worst theft in American political history. If the U.S. Congress and State Legislatures across the six battleground states ignore this evidence, they will do so not just at their own peril but also at the peril of America's faith in our elections and the sanctity of our Republic.

For a complete copy of The Navarro Report with all three volumes, please follow the link in the Appendix.

Arizona Battleground

The report tabulates by category a total of 254,722 potentially illegal votes. This number constitutes roughly 24 times the alleged Biden victory margin of 10,457 votes.

Vote Irregularities and Illegalities by Category and State

	ARIZONA	GEORGIA	MICHIGAN	NEVADA	PENNSYLVANIA	WISCONSIN
Absentee ballots cast without statutorily required application						170,140
Absentee ballots cast that arrived after Election Day					10,000	
Absentee ballots cast that were requested before & after statutory deadline		305,701				
Absentee ballots cast from addresses other than where voters legally reside	19,997			15,000	14,328	
Absentee ballots cast that were returned on or before the postmark date	22,903				58,221	
Absentee ballots cast without a postmark					9,005	
Absentee ballots requested under the name of a registered voter without consent			27,825			
Dead voters		10,315	482	1,506	8,021	
Double voters: In-state	157	395		42,284	742	234
Felon voters		2,560				
Ghost voters	5,790	15,700				
Illegal ballot harvesting						17,271
Indefinitely confined voter abuses						216,000
Juvenile voters (<18 years old)		66,247				
Mail-in ballots cast by voters registered after the registration deadline	150,000					
No address on file for voter	2,000	1,043	35,109	8,000		
Non-citizen voters	36,473			4,000		
No corresponding voter registration numbers			174,384			
Non-registered voters(not on voter rolls)		2,423				
Out-of-state voters who voted in-state	5,726	20,312	13,248	19,218	7,426	6,848
Over-votes	11,676				202,377	
Poll watcher & poll observer abuses					680,774	
Signature matching errors				130,000		
Voting machine irregularities (fake/manufactured ballots & spikes)		136,155	195,755			143,379
Voters over 100 years old					1,573	
Voters who vote in the wrong county		40,279				
Possible Illegal Votes	254,722	601,130	446,803	220,008	992,467	553,872
Biden "Victory" Margin	10,457	11,779	154,818	33,596	81,660	20,682

Credit: Summary – The Navarro Report.

By far the largest category is 150,000 mail-in ballots cast by voters registered after the registration deadline. Another 22,903 absentee ballots were on record as having been returned on or before the postmark date, which is highly unlikely.

In reviewing the statistics, it is worth noting that Arizona had statistically improbable high voter turnouts in Maricopa and Pima counties; widespread ballot mishandling; and 1.6 million mail-in ballots (which disproportionately leaned towards Biden) which were subjected to much lower standards of certification and ID verification than in-person votes (which leaned toward Trump).

The Copper State also accomplished the remarkable feat of exceeding 100% turnout of its registered voters. This is indeed a remarkable feat because Arizona does not allow same-day voter registration. The "over-votes" alone totaled 11,676, an amount more than the purported Biden "victory" margin of 10,457.

It should also be clear that Arizona boasts a litany of other election irregularities. For example, a total of 19,997 persons voted where they did not reside5 while 2,000 voters did not have an address at all. 5,790 voters moved out of state or registered to vote in another state, 5,726 out-of-state residents voted in Arizona, and 36,473 individuals voted without providing evidence of citizenship.

Georgia Battleground

The report tabulates by category a total of 601,130 potentially illegal votes in Georgia. This is more than 50 times the alleged Biden victory margin of 11,779 votes.

The largest category of potentially illegal votes is that of absentee ballots cast requested before or after the statutory deadline. In the state of Georgia, voters have 180 days prior to Election Day to request absentee ballots, according to state law. However, during the 2020 Presidential Election, Georgia officials counted over 305,700 ballots cast by individuals who had requested absentee ballots more than 180 days before the absentee ballot request deadline, in blatant violation of Georgia Election Code.

Per The Navarro Report, we also see that 10,000 ballots of deceased individuals were counted. 15,700 votes were counted from "ghost" voters, that is, voters who requested and submitted ballots under the names of voters who no longer reside at a particular address.13 Similarly perplexing is that over 1,000 voters without an address cast ballots.

Voting machines –which Georgia election officials were in an inexplicable rush to install leading up to the 2020 election–likewise may account for a substantial number potentially illegal ballots. There were also over 40,000 cases of voters voting in counties in which they did not legally reside, as well as over 66,00017 voters who had successfully cast ballots even though they were under the legal voting age of 18.

Michigan Battleground

The report tabulates by category a total of 446,803 potentially illegal votes in Michigan. This is almost three times the alleged Biden victory margin of 154,818 votes.

The largest amount of ballots in question in Michigan stems from inexplicable vote tabulation surges along with alleged voting machine irregularities18 and ballots counted despite lacking voter-registration numbers.

There were also two major questionable "Biden vote spikes" in the early hours of November 4th. At 3:50 AM EST, Michigan added 54,497 additional ballots cast for Joe Biden and just 4,718 votes cast for President Trump. At 6:31 AM EST, an update showed an additional 141,258 votes cast for Biden, while President Trump received just 5,968 additional ballots.

Additionally, it is illegal in Michigan to count absentee ballots without having corresponding voter registration numbers for corresponding precincts, according to state law. Despite this, election officials allowed over 174,000 of these ballots to be counted anyway.

Michigan also processed ballots of over 35,000 voters without addresses on state records, at least over 480 confirmed dead voters,22 and over 13,200 voters registered to vote in other states—in blatant violation of state election law. 23 Lastly, over 27,800 ballots were requested under the name of a registered voter without their knowledge and/or consent.

Nevada Battleground

The report tabulates by category a total of 220,008 potentially illegal votes in Nevada. This is roughly six times the alleged Biden victory margin of 33,596 votes.

Nevada's largest irregularities stemmed from the use of the Agilis signature-matching machines installed in Clark County to verify signatures on ballots. Using machines instead of people for signature match verification is in blatant violation of state law and calls into question the 130,000 ballots verified by these Agilis machines.

The Agilis machines were also alleged to have not been operated "in conformance with the manufacturer's recommendations" on Election Day. First, the images on file used by the Agilis machine to compare to the signatures on the outside of the mail-in ballots were of lower image quality than "suggested by the manufacturer" for the machine to operate properly, and the machine was altered or adjusted by election officials to a setting "lower than the manufacturer's recommendations," making the machine unreliable.

Nevada also registered 42,284 double voters, ascertained by reviewing the list of voters and comparing voters with the same name, address, and date of birth—a method shown in peer reviewed papers to have over 99% accuracy. That category alone exceeds the alleged Biden victory margin of 33,596 votes.

In addition, 19,218 out-of-state voters cast ballots in Nevada. This was ascertained by lining up voter lists from all counties against publicly available USPS records on permanent change of addresses with other states and correcting for military and student voters.

Finally, 1,506 votes were cast in the name of deceased persons—verified by comparing mail voters with social security death records.30 Over 8,000 ballots were cast by persons without addresses—found by referencing voters with the Coding Accuracy Support System and finding undeliverable addresses.31 4,000 non-U.S. citizens also appear to have voted—found by comparing non-citizen DMV records to the list of voters.

Pennsylvania Battleground

The report tabulates by category a total of almost a million potentially illegal votes in Pennsylvania. This is roughly twelve times the alleged Biden victory margin of 81,660 votes.

By far the largest category of potentially illegal ballots—over 680,000—is associated with poll observer abuses. Certified Republican poll observers were kept at distances the length of a football field. They were prevented from accessing back rooms where tens of thousands of ballots were being processed, and they were rounded up into restricted areas when trying to fulfill their legal duty to observe the ballot counting process. Without meaningful observation of the ballot counting process, it is impossible to verify the legality of absentee and mail-in ballots.

State Representative Frank Ryan, along with several other members of the State Legislature, found that over 202,000 more ballots were cast than actual registered voters in the state. In addition, there were 58,221 absentee ballots counted that were returned on or before the postmarked date on the envelope.37 9,005 additional ballots were counted without a postmark on the envelope, in clear violation of state election law.

There were also over 14,300 absentee ballots cast from addresses in which registered voters did not legally reside, over 7,400 registered voters from other states that successfully cast ballots in the state of Pennsylvania, over 8,000 likely dead voters according to an analysis of state records and publicly available obituaries, and over 1,500 suspect votes in the names of persons over 100 years old.

Pennsylvania was not exempt from the double-voter problem either, with 742 voters on record as having voted twice, adding several hundred fraudulent ballots into the mix.

Wisconsin Battleground

The report tabulates by category a total of over half a million potentially illegal votes in Wisconsin. This is more than 25 times the alleged Biden victory margin of 20,682 votes.

By far the largest category of potentially illegal votes is associated with alleged "bad-faith voters" who registered as "indefinitely confined" and thereby broke "Wisconsin election law to circumvent election integrity photo identification requirements." These persons voted without showing a voter identification photo and therefore underwent a far less rigorous I.D. check than would otherwise have been conducted. (Wisconsin voters who had registered under "indefinitely confined" status were also seen attending weddings, riding their bikes, going on vacation, and otherwise not confined.)

In the wake of the expanded definition of indefinitely confined voters—a definition ruled legally incorrect by the Wisconsin Supreme Court—the number of indefinitely confined voters surged from just under 70,000 voters in 2019 to over 200,000 in 2020. Through this one problematic dimension, the integrity of 216,000 Wisconsin votes were compromised in the 2020 General Election.

In addition, as previously illustrated in The Navarro Report, 17,271 ballots were cast at 200 illegal polling places through "Democracy in the Park" events, in direct violation of Wisconsin state law. These polling locations provided witnesses for absentee ballots and acted in every way like legal polling places. Moreover, many received ballots outside of the limited 14-day period preceding an election that is authorized by statute for in-person or absentee balloting. These were clear violations of state law. City of Madison officials facilitated the event which was broadcasted by Biden radio advertisements.

Finally, as noted in the figure, there were 6,848 voters registered in other states who voted in the state of Wisconsin—ascertained by comparing all states' voter databases with the National Change of Address (NCOA) database. Also, 234 individuals were documented as having voted twice in Wisconsin. Moreover, a whopping 170,000 in-person absentee ballots were cast without the submission of a legally required absentee ballot application.

Concluding Remarks

Based on this third and final volume of The Navarro Report, it should be clear that there are far more questions raised about the potential illegality of the 2020 presidential election than have been answered. Clearly, the case, evidence, and statistical receipts presented in this report provide a strong case that the 2020 election may well have been stolen not just from President Trump but also from the 74 million Americans who went to the ballot box in good faith in support of President Trump.

In light of this evidence, it is impossible for anyone to claim that President Trump was in any way wrong in stoutly raising the question of election fraud and irregularities in the weeks following the November 3 election and in calling for his supporters to peacefully protest. Indeed, for the president not to rise to defend the integrity of the ballot box would have been a betrayal of the 74 million Americans who voted for the president thinking they were participating in what may well not have been a free and fair election.

In light of this evidence, it is also irresponsible—in the extreme—for the Democrat Party and its leadership, or journalists in the mainstream media, or RINO Republicans to claim there is no evidence of election irregularities. That's absurd on its face. As this report shows, there is an abundance of evidence—a virtual cornucopia of potentially poisonous election irregularities.

In light of this evidence, this must also be said: Those American citizens who are now questioning the potential illegality of votes cast in the 2020 election should not be subjected by cable news networks, social media platforms, or the print media to the kind of abhorrent behaviors that we are now observing—social and political behaviors that are far more worthy of Communist China authoritarianism than American democracy.

From public shaming to de-platforming, doxing, and public calls to punish and shun all those who have supported the president or worked in his administration, these types of behaviors are not the American way. Rather, this is Orwell, Kafka, and Xi Jinping all rolled up into the death of the First Amendment and the death knell of our democracy.

Based on the analysis and the granular, documented quantities of illegal votes in this report, the only thing that must happen now as we engage in a peaceful transition of power is a full investigation of this matter.

• The Department of Justice should immediately appoint a Special Counsel before the Biden administration begins.

• State legislators and Attorneys Generals in the battleground states, particularly Republican states, must launch similar investigations.

Absent a full investigation, we as a nation run the risk of institutionalizing a rigged electoral system in which a large segment of America will no longer have faith in. That's why clearing the air about the 2020 presidential election is not just about Donald J. Trump but rather about something much larger and of far more import—the future of our election system, the public perception of that system, and ultimately the future of our free and democratic Republic.

10 – Six Dimensions of 'Alleged' Election Irregularities in Six Battleground States

Credit: Figure One – The Navarro Report.

While Democrat Party government officials cheated and gamed the electoral process across all six battleground states, many Republican government officials–from governors and state legislators to judges–did little or nothing to stand in their way.

Consider that the Republican Party controls both chambers of the State Legislatures in five of the six battleground states–Arizona, Georgia, Michigan, Pennsylvania, and Wisconsin. These State Legislatures clearly have both the power and the opportunity to investigate the six dimensions of election irregularities presented in this report and summarized in Figure One above.

Yet, wilting under intense political pressure, these politicians failed in their Constitutional duties and responsibilities to do so–and thereby failed both their states and this nation as well as their party.

The same can be said for the Republican governors in two of the six battleground states–Arizona and Georgia. Both Arizona's Doug Ducey and Georgia's Brian Kemp have cowered in their Governor's mansions and effectively sat on their hands while their states have wallowed in election irregularities.

143

The judicial branch of the American government should be the final backstop for the kind of issues examined in this report. Yet both our State courts and Federal courts, including the Supreme Court, have failed the American people in refusing to properly adjudicate the election irregularities that have come before them. Their failures likewise pose a great risk to the American Republic.

A Flood of Mail-in and Absentee Ballots Began Entering the Count

At the stroke of midnight on Election Day, President Donald J. Trump appeared well on his way to winning a second term. He was already a lock to win both Florida and Ohio; and no Republican has ever won a presidential election without winning Ohio while only two Democrats have won the presidency without winning Florida.

At the same time, the Trump-Pence ticket had substantial and seemingly insurmountable leads in Georgia, Pennsylvania, Michigan, and Wisconsin. If these leads held, these four key battleground states would propel President Trump to a decisive 294 to 244 victory in the Electoral College.

Shortly after midnight, however, as a flood of mail-in and absentee ballots began entering the count, the Trump red tide of victory began turning Joe Biden blue. As these mail-in and absentee ballots were tabulated, the President's large leads in Georgia, Pennsylvania, Michigan, and Wisconsin simply vanished into thin Biden leads.

At midnight on the evening of November 3, President Trump was ahead by more than 110,000 votes in Wisconsin and more than 290,000 votes in Michigan. In Georgia, his lead was a whopping 356,945; and he led in Pennsylvania by more than half a million votes. By December 7, however, these wide Trump leads would turn into razor thin Biden leads—11,779 votes in Georgia, 20,682 votes in Wisconsin, 81,660 votes in Pennsylvania, and 154,188 votes in Michigan.

There was an equally interesting story unfolding in Arizona and Nevada. While Joe Biden was ahead in these two additional battleground states on election night—by just over 30,000 votes in Nevada and less than 150,000 votes in Arizona—internal Trump Campaign polls predicted the President would close these gaps once all the votes were counted. Of course, this never happened.

The Navarro Report, Vol. 2: The Immaculate Deception

Per The Navarro Report; The Immaculate Deception assessed the fairness and integrity of the 2020 Presidential Election by examining six dimensions of alleged election irregularities across six key battleground states. Evidence used to conduct this assessment includes more than 50 lawsuits and judicial rulings, thousands of affidavits and declarations, testimony in a variety of state venues, published analyses by think tanks and legal centers, videos and photos, public comments, and extensive press coverage.

The Summary figure indicates that significant irregularities occurred across all six battleground states and across all six dimensions of election irregularities that lends credence to the claim that the election may well have been stolen from President Donald J. Trump.

From the findings of this report, it is possible to infer what may well have been a coordinated strategy to effectively stack the election deck against the Trump-Pence ticket. Indeed, the observed patterns of election irregularities are so consistent across the six battleground states that they suggest a coordinated strategy to, if not steal the election outright, strategically game the election process in such a way as to "stuff the ballot box" and unfairly tilt the playing field in favor of the Biden-Harris ticket.

Topline findings of this report include:

- The weight of evidence and patterns of irregularities are such that it is irresponsible for anyone—especially the mainstream media—to claim there is "no evidence" of fraud or irregularities.

- The ballots in question because of the identified election irregularities are more than sufficient to swing the outcome in favor of President Trump should even a relatively small portion of these ballots be ruled illegal.

- All six battleground states exhibit most, or all, six dimensions of election irregularities. However, each state has a unique mix of issues that might be considered "most important." To put this another way, all battleground states are characterized by the same or similar election irregularities; but, like Tolstoy's unhappy families, each battleground state is different in its own election irregularity way.

- This was theft by a thousand cuts across six dimensions and six battleground states rather than any one single "silver bullet" election irregularity.

- The failure to aggressively and fully investigate the six dimensions of election irregularities assessed in this report is a signal failure not just of our anti-Trump mainstream media and censoring social media but also of both our legislative and judicial branches.

Republican governors in Arizona and Georgia together with Republican majorities in both chambers of the State Legislatures of five of the six battleground states—Arizona, Georgia, Michigan, Pennsylvania, and Wisconsin2—have had both the power and the opportunity to investigate the six dimensions of election irregularities presented in this report. Yet, wilting under intense political pressure, these politicians have failed in their Constitutional duties and responsibilities to do so—and thereby failed both their states and this nation as well as their party.

Both State courts and Federal courts, including the Supreme Court, have failed the American people in refusing to appropriately adjudicate the election irregularities that have come before them. Their failures pose a great risk to the American Republic.

- If these election irregularities are not fully investigated prior to Inauguration Day and thereby effectively allowed to stand, this nation runs the very real risk of never being able to have a fair presidential election again—with the down-ballot Senate races scheduled for January 5 in Georgia an initial test case of this looming risk.

For a complete copy of The Navarro Report with all three volumes, please follow the link in the Appendix.

1 – Outright Voter Fraud

Outright voter fraud ranges from the large-scale manufacturing of fake ballots, bribery, and dead voters to ballots cast by ineligible voters such as felons and illegal aliens, ballots counted multiple times, and illegal out-of-state voters.

	ARIZONA	GEORGIA	MICHIGAN	NEVADA	PENNSYLVANIA	WISCONSIN
Bribery	✓			✓		
Fake Ballot Manufacturing & Destruction of Legally Cast Real Ballots	✓	✓		*	*	
Indefinitely Confined Voter Abuses		*			*	✓
Ineligible Voters & Voters Who Voted in Multiple States	✓	✓		✓		
Dead Voters & Ghost Voters	✓	✓	*	✓	*	
Counting Ballots Multiple Times			*	*	*	✓
Illegal Out-of-State Voters	✓	✓		✓	*	

✓ = Wide-Spread Evidence   * = Some Evidence

Table Three: Outright Voter Fraud in the 2020 Presidential Election – The Navarro Report.

Let's more precisely define each of these different types of fraud shown in Table Three above using examples that are designed to be illustrative rather than exhaustive.

Bribery

In a voter fraud context, bribery refers to the corrupt solicitation, acceptance, or transfer of value in exchange for official action, such as voter registration or voting for a preferred candidate. At least in Nevada, there is a slam dunk case that such bribery occurred.

Fake Ballot Manufacturing and Destruction of Legally Cast Real Ballots

Fake ballot manufacturing involves the fraudulent production of ballots on behalf of a candidate; and one of the most disturbing examples of possible fake ballot manufacturing involves a truck driver who has alleged in a sworn affidavit that he picked up large crates of ballots in New York and delivered them to a polling location in Pennsylvania. There may be well over 100,000 ballots involved, enough fake ballots alone to have swung the election to Biden in the Keystone State.

Likewise in Pennsylvania, there is both a Declaration and a photo that suggests a poll worker used an unsecured USB flash drive to dump an unusually large cache of votes onto vote tabulation machines. The resultant tabulations did not correlate with the mail-in ballots scanned into the machines.

Arguably the most flagrant example of possible fake ballot manufacturing on behalf of Joe Biden may have occurred at the State Farm Arena in Atlanta, Georgia. The possible perpetrators were caught in flagrante delicto on surveillance video.

Finally, as an example of the possible destruction of legally cast real ballots there is this allegation from a court case filed in the United States District Court for the District of Arizona: Plaintiffs claim that over 75,000 absentee ballots were reported as unreturned when they were actually returned. These absentee ballots were then either lost or destroyed (consistent with allegations of Trump ballot destruction) and/or were replaced with blank ballots filled out by election workers or other third parties.

Indefinitely Confined Voter Abuses

Indefinitely confined voters are those voters unable to vote in person because of old age or some disability. There are two types of possible abuses associated with such indefinitely confined voters.

The first kind of abuse involves exploiting the elderly or the infirm by effectively hijacking their identities and votes.

The second kind of indefinitely confined voter abuse is being able to vote without showing a voter identification photo and therefore underwent a far less rigorous I.D. check than would otherwise have been conducted.

Here is what is most important about this particular type of election fraud: In the wake of the expanded definition of indefinitely confined voters—a definition ruled legally incorrect by the Wisconsin Supreme Court25—the number of indefinitely confined voters surged from just under 70,000 voters in 2019 to over 200,000 in 2020.26 This 130,000 vote increment of new indefinitely confined voters is more than five times the Biden victory margin in Wisconsin.

Ineligible Voters and Voters Who Voted in Multiple States

Ineligible voters include felons deemed ineligible, underage citizens, nonregistered voters, illegal aliens, illegal out-of-state voters, and voters illegally using a post office box as an address.

In a court filing by the Trump campaign legal team, lead counsel Ray Smith provided a list of more than 70,000 allegedly ineligible voters casting ballots in Georgia in the 2020 election.28

Also in Georgia, over 20,000 people appear to have filed a Notice of Changed Address form to the Georgia state government or had other indications of moving out of state. Yet, these clearly ineligible out-of-state voters appeared to have remained on the voter rolls and voted in the 2020 election.

Dead Voters and Ghost Voters

In Pennsylvania, for example, a statistical analysis conducted by the Trump Campaign matching voter rolls to public obituaries found what appears to be over 8,000 confirmed dead voters successfully casting mail-in ballots.33 In Georgia—underscoring the critical role any given category of election irregularities might play in determining the outcome—the estimated number of alleged deceased individuals casting votes almost exactly equals the Biden victory margin.

In Michigan, according to one first-hand account offered in a declaration, computer operators at a polling location in Detroit were manually adding the names and addresses of thousands of ballots to vote tabulation systems with voters who had birth dates in 1900.

On the Ghost Voter front, a "Ghost Voter" is a voter who requests and submits a ballot under the name of a voter who no longer resides at the address where that voter was registered. In Georgia for example, it is alleged that over 20,000 absentee or early voters—almost twice the Biden victory margin—cast their ballots after having moved out of state.36 In Nevada, a poll worker reported that there were as many as 50 ballots per day being delivered to homes vacated by their former residents.

Counting Ballots Multiple Times

Counting ballots multiple times occurs most egregiously when batches of ballots are repeatedly rescanned and re-tabulated in electronic voting machines. It can also happen when the same person votes multiple times within the same day. Evidence of these particular kinds of "ballot stuffing" are present across all six battleground states.

2 – Ballot Mishandling

Ballot mishandling represents the second major dimension of alleged election irregularities in the 2020 presidential election. This is a multifaceted problem across the battleground states. Let's work our way through with the failure to properly check the identification of voters.

No Voter I.D. Check

It is critical for the integrity of any election for poll workers to properly verify a voter's identity and registration when that voter comes in to cast an in-person ballot. However, there is at least some evidence of a lack of adequate voter ID check across several of the battleground states.

Signature Matching Abuse

It is equally critical that ballot counters legally verify mail-in and absentee ballots by checking if the signatures on the outer envelopes match the voters' registration records. Note, however, that a variety of signature matching abuses represent a major issue in Nevada, Pennsylvania, and especially in Georgia.

"Naked Ballots" Lacking Outer Envelope

A naked ballot is a mail-in or absentee ballot lacking an outer envelope with the voter's signature on it. It is illegal to accept the naked ballot as the outer envelope provides the only way to verify a voter's identity.

The illegal acceptance of naked ballots appears to be particularly acute in Pennsylvania as a result of ill-advised "guidance" issued by the Secretary of State–a registered Democrat–that such naked ballots be counted.

Broken Chain of Custody & Unauthorized Ballot Handling or Movements

The maintenance of a proper chain of custody for ballots cast is the linchpin of fair elections. Chain of custody is broken when a ballot is fraudulently transferred, controlled, or moved without adequate supervision or oversight.

While chain of custody issues can apply to all ballots, the risk of a broken chain of custody is obviously higher for mail-in and absentee ballots. This is because the ballots have to go through more hands.

In the 2020 presidential election, the increased use–often illegal use–of unsupervised drop boxes arguably has enhanced the risk of a broken chain of custody. So, too, has the increased practice of so-called "ballot harvesting" whereby third parties pick up ballots from voters and deliver them to drop boxes or directly to election officials.

Both drop boxes and ballot harvesting provide opportunities for bad actors to insert fraudulent ballots into the election process.

That this is a very serious matter is evident in this observation by BlackBoxVoting.org: "In court cases, chain of custody violations can result in refusal to admit evidence or even throwing a case out. In elections, chain of custody violations can result in 'incurable uncertainty' and court orders to redo elections" (emphasis added).

As an example of the drop box problem, in Pennsylvania, ballots were illegally dumped into drop boxes at the Nazareth ballot drop center in violation of state law. Likewise in Pennsylvania, a man caught on videotape and photos came out of an unmarked Jeep extracting ballots from an unsupervised ballot drop-box to bring them into a ballot counting center. That same man was observed to come back with an empty ballot container to place in the unsupervised drop box.

In Wisconsin, the state's Election Committee illegally positioned five hundred drop boxes for collection of absentee ballots across the state. However, these drop boxes were disproportionately located in urban areas which tend to have much higher Democrat registration, thereby favoring the candidacy of Joe Biden. Note: Any use of a drop box in

Wisconsin is illegal by statute. Therefore, the votes cast through them cannot be legally counted in any certified election result.

As an example of ballot harvesting–in this case at the front end of the process–25,000 ballots were requested from nursing home residents in Pennsylvania at the same time.

As additional examples of a possible broken chain of custody, there are these: Large bins of absentee ballots arrived at the Central Counting Location in Wisconsin with already opened envelopes, meaning that ballots could have been tampered with. They were nonetheless counted.

Ballots Accepted Without Postmarks and Backdating of Ballots

Across all of the battleground states, it is against state law for poll workers to count either mail-in or absentee ballots that lack postmarks. It is also illegal to backdate ballots so that they may be considered as having met the election deadline for the receipt and counting of such ballots. There is some evidence of these irregularities in several of the battleground states.

For example, in Wisconsin, according to one Declaration, employees of the United States Postal Service (USPS) in Milwaukee were repeatedly instructed by two managers to backdate late-arriving ballots so they could still be counted. In addition, the USPS was alleged to have backdated as many as 100,000 ballots in Wisconsin.

3 – Contestable Process Fouls

Contestable process fouls represent the third dimension of election irregularities in the 2020 presidential election. The various forms such process fouls can take across the six battleground states.

Abuses of Poll Watchers and Observers

Central to the fairness and integrity of any election is the processes by which observers monitor the receipt, opening, and counting of the ballots.

In Georgia, Michigan, and Pennsylvania, poll watchers and observers were denied entry to ballot counting centers by Judges of Elections and other poll workers. This was despite presenting proper certification and identification.

In Georgia, Michigan, Nevada, and Pennsylvania, Republican poll watchers were also forced inside confined areas, thereby limiting their view. In some cases, this confinement was enforced by local law enforcement.

Across these four battleground states, Republican poll watchers were also directed to stand at unreasonably lengthy distances from ballot counters. In Michigan–arguably the "first among equals" when it comes to observer abuses–poll workers put up poster boards on the windows of the room where ballots were being processed and counted so as to block the view. In Pennsylvania, tens of thousands of ballots were processed in back rooms where poll observers were prohibited from being able to observe at all.

Mail-In Ballot and Absentee Ballot Rules Violated Contrary to State Law

In Georgia, more than 300,000 individuals were permitted to vote who had applied for an absentee ballot more than 180 days prior to the Election Day. This is a clear violation of state law.

In both Pennsylvania and Wisconsin, Democrat election officials acted unilaterally to accept both mail-in and absentee ballots after Election Day. State Republicans have argued this is contrary to state law.

In Pennsylvania, absentee and mail-in ballots were accepted up to three days after Election Day.

Wisconsin state law does not permit early voting. Nonetheless, city officials in the Democrat stronghold of Madison, Wisconsin assisted in the creation of more than 200 "Democracy in the Park" illegal polling places.

These faux polling places were promoted and supported by the Biden campaign. They provided witnesses for absentee ballots and acted in every way like legal polling places. Moreover, they received ballots outside of the limited 14-day period preceding an election that is authorized by statute for in-person or absentee balloting. These were clear violations of state law.

Voters Not Properly Registered Allowed to Vote

One of the jobs of poll workers is to ensure that in-person voters are legally registered and are who they say they are. Across at least three of the six battleground states–Georgia, Nevada, and Wisconsin–this job may not have been effectively done.

Illegal Campaigning at Poll Locations

Poll workers are supposed to remain politically neutral. When a poll worker displays bias for one political candidate over another at a polling location, this is contrary to state law. Unfortunately, this law appears to have been repeatedly violated in Michigan, Pennsylvania, and Wisconsin.

In a similar type of illegal campaigning in Michigan, poll workers were allowed to wear Black Lives Matter shirts and were seen carrying tote bags of President Obama paraphernalia. In addition, poll workers with Biden and Obama campaign shirts on were allowed on the ballot counting floor.

Ballots Cured by Poll Workers or Voters Contrary to Law

Under prescribed circumstances, both poll workers and voters may fix ballots with mistakes or discrepancies. This process is known as "ballot curing."

In nineteen states, poll workers must notify voters if there are errors or discrepancies on their ballots and allow them to "cure" or correct any errors so their votes will count. However, in states that do not allow curing, ballots with discrepancies such as missing or mismatched signatures must be discarded.

In Pennsylvania, and contrary to state law, poll workers were trained to allow voters to cure or "correct" their ballots. According to one court filing, Democrat-controlled counties in Pennsylvania participated in pre-canvass activities prior to Election Day "by reviewing received mail-in ballots for deficiencies." Such discrepancies included "lacking the inner secrecy envelope or lacking a signature of the elector on the outer declaration envelope." Voters were then notified so that they could cure their ballots–a clear violation of state law.

Numerous other examples of illegally cured ballots abound. For example, in Wisconsin, tens of thousands of ballots were observed to be corrected or cured despite election observer objections.

In Pennsylvania, poll workers sorted approximately 4,500 ballots with various errors into bins. Poll workers then re-filled out the 4,500 ballots so that they could be read by tabulation machines, an action contrary to state law.

In Michigan, poll workers altered the dates on the outer envelopes of the ballots so that they would be able to count them. Michigan poll workers also filled out blank ballots to "correct" mail-in and absentee ballots according to what they believed the "voter had intended."

4 – Equal Protection Clause Violations

The Equal Protection Clause is part of the 14th Amendment of the U.S. Constitution and a fundamental pillar of the American Republic. This Equal Protection Clause mandates that no State may deny its citizens equal protection of its governing laws.

Three major alleged violations of the Equal Protection Clause in the 2020 presidential election and each violation was observed to occur across all six battleground states.

Higher Standards of Certification & I.D. Verification Applied to In-Person Voters

The first alleged violation focuses on the application of higher standards of certification and voter identification for in-person voters than mail-in and absentee ballot voters. In effect, these higher standards disproportionately benefited the candidacy of Joe Biden because President Trump had a much higher percentage of in-person voters than mail-in and absentee voters. Indeed, mail-in and absentee ballots were largely skewed for Joe Biden across the country by ratios as high as 3 out of 4 votes in some states.

Note here that much of the alleged fraud and ballot mishandling focused on mail-in voters and absentee ballots. Therefore, the lower the level of scrutiny of these voters, the more illegal votes for Joe Biden relative to Donald Trump could slip in. It should likewise be noted here that this particular violation of the Equal Protection Clause was further enabled by poll watchers being denied meaningful observation.

Different Standards of Ballot Curing

As a second major violation of the Equal Protection Clause, likewise, observed across all six battleground states, different standards for correcting mistakes on ballots (ballot curing) were applied across different jurisdictions within the states. Often, jurisdictions with predominantly Democrat registration were more expansive about allowing the curing of ballots than jurisdictions with predominantly Republican registration.

Differential and Partisan Poll Watcher Treatment

In most states, political party candidates and ballot issue committees are able to appoint poll watchers and observers to oversee the ballot counting process. Such poll watchers and observers must be registered voters and present certification to the Judge of Elections in order to be able to fulfill their duties at a polling location.

Such certified poll watchers should be free to observe at appropriate distances regardless of their party affiliation. Yet in key Democrat strongholds, e.g., Dane County in Wisconsin and Wayne County in Michigan, which yielded high Biden vote counts, Republican poll watchers and observers were frequently subject to different treatment ranging from denial of entry to polling places to harassment and intimidation.

5 – 2020 Election Voting Machine Irregularities

Perhaps no device illustrates that technology is a double-edged sword than the machines and associated software that have come to be used to tabulate votes across all 50 states.108 Types of voting equipment include optical scanners used to process paper ballots, direct recording electronic systems which voters can use to directly input their choices, and various marking devices to produce human-readable ballots.

Two main types of voting machine irregularities have been alleged in the 2020 presidential election. These types of irregularities include large-scale voting machine inaccuracies together with inexplicable vote switching and vote surges, often in favor Joe Biden.

Large-Scale Voting Machine Inaccuracies

The controversy swirling over Dominion and Smartmatic notwithstanding, one of the biggest problems with machine inaccuracies may be traced to a company called Agilis. Nevada election officials in Clark County, a Democrat stronghold in Nevada, used Agilis signature verification machines to check over 130,000 mail-in ballot signatures.

According to a court case filed in the First Judicial District Court in Carson City, the Agilis machines used a "lower image quality than suggested by the manufacturer." Clark County Election Department officials also lowered the accuracy rate below the manufacturer's recommendations, making the whole verification process unreliable.

In a test run, it was proven that, at the manufacturer's setting, the Agilis machine already had a high tolerance for inaccuracies—as high as 50% non-matching. In other words, half of the ballots that might be moved through the machine would be impossible to verify; and Clark County officials lowered that threshold even further.

As a final comment on this case, there is also the broader legal matter that the Agilis machines were used to "entirely replace signature verification by election personnel." This is contrary to Nevada state law.

As noted in a court case: "In violation of Nevada law, the Clark County Election Department allows the Agilis machine to solely verify 30% of the signatures accompanying the mail-in ballots without ever having humans inspect those signatures."

A similar problem has been alleged in a court filing in Arizona with a software known as the Novus 6.0.0.0. In cases where ballots were too damaged or illegible to be read by vote tabulation machines, Novus was used in an attempt to cure or restore the ballots. The system would do so by trying to read the applicable scans of the original rejected ballots. However, as noted in a court case filed by Kelli Ward, Chairwoman of the Arizona Republican Party: "the software was highly inaccurate, and it often flipped the vote."

Inexplicable Vote Switching and Vote Surges In Favor of Biden

As a further complication to the Novus software problem in Arizona referenced above, the software was not only highly inaccurate. According to observers, and as an example of inexplicable vote switching, "the software would erroneously prefill 'Biden' twice as often as it did 'Trump.'"

At least one instance of a large and inexplicable vote switching and vote surge in favor of Joe Biden took place in Antrim County, Michigan–and it is associated with the controversial aforementioned Dominion-Smartmatic voting machine hardware-software combo. In this Republican stronghold, 6,000 votes were initially, and incorrectly, counted for Joe Biden. The resulting vote totals were contrary to voter registration and historical patterns and therefore raised eyebrows. When a check was done, it was discovered that the 6,000 votes were actually for Donald J. Trump.

A subsequent forensic audit of the Antrim County vote tabulation found that the Dominion system had an astonishing error rate of 68 percent.120 By way of comparison, the Federal Election Committee requires that election systems must have an error rate no larger than 0.0008 percent.

In Georgia, there were numerous "glitches" with the Dominion machines where the results would change. The most notable of these changes was a 20,000 vote surge for Biden and 1,000 vote decrease for Trump.

6 – Statistical Anomalies in the Six Battleground States

The 2020 presidential election appears to feature at least four types of statistical anomalies that raise troubling questions. Table Eight illustrates the incidence of these statistical anomalies across the six battleground states. As you can see from the table, Wisconsin and Georgia are characterized by the highest degree of statistical anomalies, with three of the four anomalies present. Nevada and Arizona show two anomalies present while Michigan has at least one. Let's take a more granular look now at each of these types of statistical anomalies.

	ARIZONA	GEORGIA	MICHIGAN	NEVADA	PENNSYLVANIA	WISCONSIN
Significant Changes In Absentee Ballot Rejection Rates From Previous Elections		✓		✓	✓	
Excessively High Voter Turnout (at times exceeding 100%)	✓	✓	✓	✓		✓
Statistically Improbable Vote Totals Based on Party Registration & Historical Patterns	✓					✓
Unusual Vote Surges		✓	*			✓

✓ = Wide-Spread Evidence   * = Some Evidence

Table Eight: Statistical Anomalies in the Battleground States – The Navarro Report.

Dramatic Changes in Mail-in and Absentee Ballot Rejection Rates from Previous Elections

It is routine across the 50 states for mail-in-and absentee ballots to be rejected for any number of reasons. These reasons may include: the lack of a signature or adequate signature match, a late arrival past a deadline,124 the lack of an external envelope that verifies voter-identification (a naked ballot), or if voters provide inaccurate or incomplete information on the ballots.

In the 2020 presidential race, Joe Biden received a disproportionately high percentage of the mail-in and absentee ballots. Perhaps not coincidentally, we saw a dramatic fall in rejection rates in Pennsylvania, Nevada, and especially Georgia.

For example, in Nevada, the overall rejection rate dropped from 1.6%127 in 2016 to 0.58% in 2020.128 In Pennsylvania, the 2016 rejection rate of 1.0%129 dropped to virtually nothing at 0.28%.130 The biggest fall in the overall absentee ballot rejection rate came, however, in Georgia. Its rejection rate fell from 6.8%131 in 2016 to a mere 0.34%132 in 2020.

These dramatically lower rejection rates point to a conscious effort by Democrat election officials across these key battleground states to subject mail-in and absentee ballots to a lower level of scrutiny. That this kind of government conduct and gaming of our election system may have contributed to tipping the scales in favor of Joe Biden can be illustrated in this simple calculation:

In the 2020 race, Georgia election officials received 1,320,154 mail-in and absentee ballots. If these ballots had been rejected at the 2016 rate of 6.8% instead of the 2020 rate of 0.34%, there would have been 81,321 ballots rejected instead of the 4,489 ballots that were actually rejected.

Under the conservative assumption that 60% of these mail-in and absentee ballots went to Joe Biden,133 this dramatic fall in the rejection rate provided Joe Biden with an additional 16,264 votes. That's more than the margin of the alleged Biden victory in Georgia.

Excessively High Voter Turnout (At Times Exceeding 100%)

When there are more ballots cast than registered or eligible voters, fraud has likely taken place. During the 2020 presidential election, excessively high voter turnout occurred across all six swing states.

In analyzing this problem, it is important to distinguish between states that have same-day registration and those that don't. States with same-day registration can plausibly have voter turnout that is higher than 100%. However, is impossible for that to happen in states without same-day registration without fraud having taken place.

Consider, then, Arizona which does not allow same-day voter registration. According to testimony from an MIT-trained mathematician, candidate Biden may have received a weighted 130% total of Democrat votes in Maricopa County to help him win the state due to an algorithm programmed into the Dominion voting machines used there.

Although Michigan does allow same-voter registration, voter turnout was still abnormally high. Here again, the Dominion voting system has been implicated. To wit:

Cybersecurity executive and former NASA analyst, Russ Ramsland, testified that in Wayne County, Michigan, where Dominion Voting Systems equipment was used, 46 out of 47 precincts in the county displayed greater than a 96% voter turnout and 25 out of those precincts showed a 100% voter turnout.

Wisconsin, which also allows same-day voter registration, also reported abnormally high voter turnout when compared to 2016 numbers. For example, Milwaukee reported a record 84% voter turnout during the 2020 presidential election versus 75% in 2016. Of the city's 327 voting wards, 90 reported a turnout of greater than 90%.

Statistically Improbable Vote Totals Based on Party Registration and Historical Patterns

The 2020 presidential election was characterized by strong partisan voting patterns consistent with historical patterns. As a rule, heavily Republican jurisdictions voted heavily for President Trump and heavily Democrat jurisdictions voted heavily for Joe Biden.

In some cases, however, there were instances where these partisan and historical patterns were violated. It is precisely in such instances where either outright fraud or machine inaccuracies or manipulations are most likely to be operative.

As one example of such statistically improbable vote totals, there are the results in Arizona's Fifth Congressional District. In one precinct in the suburb of Queen Creek, the vote percent for President Trump dropped dramatically relative to 2016, from 67.4 to 58.5 percent.138 This was attributed to an "unusually high" number of duplicate ballots.

Unusual Vote Surges

Several unusual vote surges took place in the very early hours of the morning of November 4th in Georgia, Michigan, and Wisconsin. An analysis conducted by the Voter Integrity Project of *The New York Times* publicly reported data on Election Day that showed several vote "spikes" that were unusually large in size with unusually high Biden-to-Trump ratios. Such spikes or surges could well indicate that fraudulent ballots had been counted.

In Georgia, for example, an update at 1:34 AM on November 4th showed 136,155 additional ballots cast for Joe Biden, and 29,115 additional votes cast for President Trump.140 An update in Michigan at 3:50 AM on November 4th showed an update of 54,497 additional votes cast for Joe Biden, and 4,718 votes cast for President Trump.141 And an update in Wisconsin at 3:42 AM on November 4th showed 143,379 additional ballots cast for Joe Biden, and 25,163 votes cast for President Trump.

11 – How Mainstream Media & Big Tech Bias Threatens Free and Fair Elections

Majorities across parties believe social media companies have too much power and influence in politics; Republicans are especially likely to say this

% of U.S. adults who say social media companies have ___ (of) power and influence in politics today

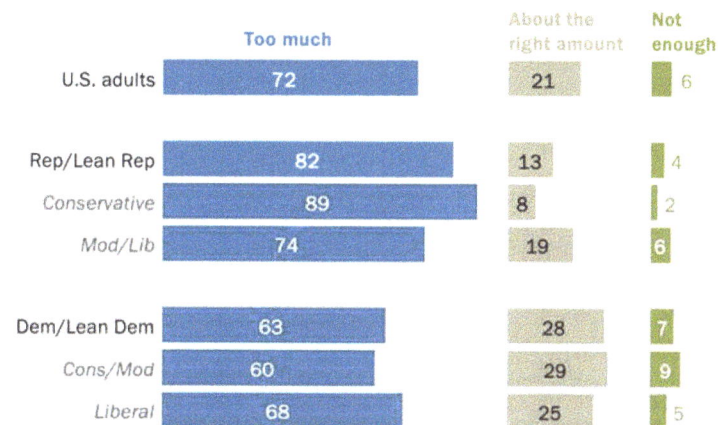

	Too much	About the right amount	Not enough
U.S. adults	72	21	6
Rep/Lean Rep	82	13	4
Conservative	89	8	2
Mod/Lib	74	19	6
Dem/Lean Dem	63	28	7
Cons/Mod	60	29	9
Liberal	68	25	5

Note: Those who did not give an answer are not shown.
Source: Survey of U.S. adults conducted June 16-22, 2020.
PEW RESEARCH CENTER

The incentives in politics and media favor propaganda over facts. Original research is complicated, and the results are often ambiguous. The easier path to widespread popularity (article placement, TV appearances, Twitter retweets) is to come up with some false but too-good-to-check bombshell factoid or statistic that precisely confirms the biases of a target audience.

Because it fits the popular narrative, the false fact will be amplified by other reporters and opinion leaders until it becomes conventional wisdom. The few skeptical fact-checkers have little chance of holding back this tsunami of misinformation. It is cited everywhere, so it must be true.

Per the January 2021 "The 'Facts' We Take on Faith: How do we know our political convictions are based in reality?" article by Brian Riedl for the *City Journal*: Verification has nearly disappeared. Partisan columnists, late-night talk shows, and even top news programs often broadcast or tweet "gotcha" videos so heavily edited as to be fraudulent. And yet they are circulated with no due diligence by top reporters and opinion leaders.

Partisanship creates blind spots. Several prominent newspaper opinion pages and political websites are known in policy circles for spending weeks fact-checking every sentence of op-ed submissions that argue against the in-house editorial slant, while giving barely a cursory fact-check to op-eds that confirm their general policy views. Even "trustworthy" columnists often slant the data or misleadingly string together disparate facts and data to present a compelling narrative that plays to their readership's partisan leanings.

Per Riedl, a research fellow once promised him more than a dozen sources for a controversial statistic he was hyping. In reality, he had a dozen blogs all linking the statistic back to one another, with no clear origin point. Conventional wisdom is often a house of cards.

The solution, for consumers of information, requires recognizing one's own biases. Most people develop their political views early in adulthood (or before), at a time of limited information and life experience and exposure to mainstream media, big tech, and the academy's biases. For most of us, those political views quickly harden, and as we get older our political engagement becomes an exercise in tribalism.

We no longer seek news or information, but rather confirmation of our own biases. Dr. Jonathan Haidt and others at the Heterodox Academy have shown that the typical response to data and information contradicting our beliefs is to double down on those beliefs.

How Big Tech Bias Threatens Free and Fair Elections

Big Tech companies have drawn intense scrutiny for perceived political bias and alleged unbalanced moderation of users' content. Critics say much of the companies' moderation in the 2020 election and during all of President Trump's term, unfairly targeted conservative speech and free speech from individuals deemed to be supporters of former President Donald Trump.

Meanwhile, groups on the other side of the aisle have been taking issue with how social media companies are operating, claiming that the Silicon Valley companies have failed to adequately address misinformation that is being proliferated online by conservatives and far right groups, particular those in connection with the Capitol Riot.

Google announced it has awarded its first round of grants to media outlets throughout North America from a pool of $300 million the internet giant has set aside to bolster largely left-leaning mainstream and legacy media organizations per the October 2019 "Google Awards Grants to Left-Wing Media Outlets, Critics Say" by *Epoch Times* writer Matthew Vadum:

Google LLC says it wishes only to index objective facts and link to media outlets without putting its thumb on the scale, but conservative critics say the company is trying to shape the news. Left-of-center media receive prime placement in search results, while right-of-center media receive less favorable placement or are banned outright, critics say.

Google, Facebook, and Twitter in particular has been put under the microscope in recent years as critics accuse the private companies of playing political favorites, engaging in censorship, and manipulating search users through algorithm abuse, cancel culture, and censorship. All three companies strenuously deny the claims.

Conservatives have long decried what they described as unfair treatment from major technology companies. "Shadowbanning"—the surreptitious suppression of a user's content by social media platforms, is also often pointed to per the October 2019 "Robert Epstein: How Big Tech Bias Threatens Free and Fair Elections" article by Irene Luo and Jan Jekielek for the *Epoch Times*.

Then President Donald Trump tweeted that "Google & others are suppressing voices of Conservatives and hiding information and news that is good. They are controlling what we can & cannot see. This is a very serious situation-will be addressed!"

Google Will 'Actively Interfere' in 2020 Elections

Robert Epstein, a senior research psychologist at the American Institute for Behavioral Research and Technology and former editor-in-chief of *Psychology Today*, has devoted the past 6 1/2 years to researching tech giant bias, especially with Google, which dominates the search engine market. He told *The Epoch Times* that Google has access to a number of powerful manipulation methods mostly through "ephemeral experiences" that can shift votes.

As exposed in the August 2019 "Google Will 'Actively Interfere' in 2020 Elections, Researcher Says" by *Epoch Times* writer Bowen Xiao, the researcher is Robert Epstein, and he warns: "Google will actively interfere in the 2020 elections. They'll actively interfere in their lobbying efforts, they'll actively interfere with their political donations, and they'll actively interfere using the online methods of manipulation that I've studied and probably other methods that I haven't yet discovered."

Per Epstein: Online ephemeral experiences are brief moments where information is generated instantaneously, such as search suggestions. They are not stored anywhere and can't be tracked. Leaked internal emails from Google in 2018 found employees specifically discussing launching "ephemeral experiences" to counter Trump's then-travel ban, the *Wall Street Journal* reported.

In his congressional testimony in July 2019, Epstein noted that if all major technology companies came together to support the same candidate in 2020—which he said was likely—they could shift 15 million votes without leaving a paper trail. Epstein has discovered a dozen methods Google uses to manipulate public opinion or votes, including search engine manipulation effect and search suggestion effects.

In 2016, Epstein conducted a secret monitoring project that showed Google hid negative auto-complete search results for Hillary Clinton months before the election. His peer-reviewed research found Google's algorithms can easily shift 20 percent or more of votes among voters and up to 80 percent in some demographic groups, the latter being Zillennials, Millennial and Generation X.

In a more recent study, Epstein analyzed Google's "Go Vote" reminder on Election Day 2018 and found it gave the Democratic party between 800,000 and 4.6 million more votes than it gave Republicans. He used the same calculations Google's data analysts performed before they added the prompt. Epstein characterized it as "vote manipulation," not a public service.

"These two processes put in the hands of a very small number of business executives are extremely dangerous to humanity," he said. "They are a danger to democracy, they undermine a fair and free election." Google's manipulation tactics, Epstein said, are legal and save the company money when compared to using other methods of influence, such as donations.

"Google can do whatever they want," he said. "In the U.S., there are no regulations, no laws restricting their ability to manipulate opinions or votes. By favoring one candidate or cause in search results or search suggestions, it costs Google—nothing."

Google can still be fined. In March 2019, the company was hit with its third antitrust penalty, a $1.7 billion fine by the European Union. In 2017, it was fined $2.7 billion for giving its own shopping service a more prominent placement than others.

What Google does with these methods is new and not like billboards or television advertisements, Epstein said. "There's no way to fight them, there's no way to counteract them. They are not competitive. That's a kind of power that has never existed before in human history. It's perfectly legal for these companies to use these techniques," he said. "It costs them little to nothing to use them, so of course they will."

To prevent Google from interfering in the 2020 elections, Epstein said one solution would be to set up a large-scale monitoring system utilizing artificial intelligence to "catch these companies in the act." He described Google as a "mind-control machine."

U.S. authorities are considering the idea that the company has an antitrust issue. Google controls about 92 percent of the internet search market.

A Google spokesman, in response to reports of election interference, told *The Epoch Times* in a previous email that they "go to great lengths to build our products and enforce our policies in ways that don't take political leanings into account."

Shifting Opinions, Thinking, Attitudes, Beliefs, Purchases, and Votes Without People Knowing

"Americans see Google search results about 500 million times a day. Google controls roughly 90 percent of search. The next largest search engine, Bing, controls about 2 percent of search," Epstein said.

Robert Epstein's peer-reviewed research found that research participants were remarkably susceptible to bias: search engine bias could easily shift 20 percent or more of the votes of undecided voters in an election. He also found that while results on Google leaned left substantially, results on Bing and Yahoo did not.

On Sept. 9, 2019, it was announced that 48 U.S. states, the District of Columbia, and Puerto Rico have opened a bipartisan antitrust probe into Google. The new investigation follows existing investigations by the Justice Department and the Federal Trade Commission into Facebook, Google, Apple, and Amazon.

One major form of bias featured in Epstein's research is the search engine manipulation effect, something he began exploring after finding research in 2012 on how search result rankings affected purchases and clicks. It said that users tended to trust the highest-ranked search results the most, so much so that 50 percent of clicks went to the top two items.

To study how search engine rankings could shift voting preferences, he conducted a series of experiments in which he showed groups of randomly assigned people biased search results. They used a Google-like search engine, Kadoodle, that featured real search results and web pages taken from Google. The only difference was the ranking of the results.

One group was shown results biased to one candidate, one saw results biased to the other candidate, and the control group was shown mixed results, with bias in both directions. Before and after looking at the search results, participants were asked about their thoughts on the candidates, and who they'd vote for if they had to decide at that moment.

"I thought I could produce a shift in voting preferences and opinions of maybe 2 or 3 percent," Epstein said. "The first experiment I ran, the shift I got was 48 percent."

Epstein conducted more than a dozen different experiments, in which he found substantial shifts every time. In one large-scale national study across all 50 states with more than 2,000 participants, Epstein found that among different demographic groups, some were especially susceptible to manipulation (such as Generations X Y Z), with shifts in preferences as high as 80 percent.

These shifts are reflective of actual behavior in the ballot box, Epstein said. Survey research has shown that "if you ask people who they're going to vote for, it turns out that's a very good predictor of who they actually vote for," he said. "Generally speaking, we're talking about 90, 95 percent accuracy in predictions."

And according to Epstein, what they found in their experiments likely underestimated the real impact that Google has since most of his experiments had participants conducting only one online search.

"In real life, people are conducting many searches over a period of weeks or months that are election-related. If they're undecided, that means they're being hit over and over and over again with biased search results, taking them to web pages that favor one candidate," he said.

So far, Epstein has identified 12 major techniques of tech giants that can shift perceptions and opinions.

No Paper Trail

"Most of these types of influence have never existed before in human history. They're made possible by the Internet. They're made possible by these huge tech monopolies, and they're entirely in the hands of these tech monopolies.

"In elections, we're influenced by billboards, by radio shows, and TV shows, and advertisements, and so on. All of that is competitive. And in that sense, it's probably a good thing. It's a good thing for democracy that there is so much competition out there vying for your attention and trying to convince you of this or that. But if there's bias in search results, that's controlled by the platform, in this case, Google. That's not competitive."

Even if you found and could measure such bias, "you cannot counteract it," he said.

2016 Election

In 2016, Robert Epstein set up a secret monitoring system that showed that Google results were significantly skewed toward Clinton in the months leading up to the presidential election. Epstein had 95 field agents in 24 states conduct election-related searches with neutral search terms on Google, Bing, and Yahoo. The results from all these searches were then saved.

"We were able to preserve 13,207 election-related searches as well as the 98,044 webpages to which the search results linked," Epstein said. In effect, they were able to permanently preserve snapshots of what are normally "ephemeral" experiences.

Epstein decided only to collect the data, but not to analyze it prior to the 2016 election, because if he found bias, he would face an impossible dilemma. "What would I do? I mean, if I announced it, there would have been absolute chaos, especially, I think, if there was bias against Donald Trump. And if I didn't announce it, then I would be complicit in the rigging of an election," he said.

In the analysis, "we found substantial bias favoring Hillary Clinton in all 10 search positions on the first page of search results on Google (but not Bing or Yahoo)," he said, adding that the probability that the bias was solely due to chance was less than 1 in 1000.

Through a series of calculations, Epstein concluded that if this level of bias was present nationwide, it would've shifted somewhere between 2.6 million and 10.4 million votes to Clinton.

Epstein describes himself as a moderate who leans liberal. And he had been a longtime supporter of the Clintons. "But I felt very strongly that since our results were so clear that I had a responsibility to report the findings," he said.

Clinton won the popular vote by more than 2.8 million votes, but the popular vote "might have been very different," Epstein said, if there had been no bias in Google's search results.

"It was uncomfortable for me to have to acknowledge that, to have to announce that. But that's what I concluded from the research."

People trust in Google's search rankings, he said, because they believe it's generated by a computer algorithm, and thus must be impartial. What was especially disturbing was the subliminal manipulation; in most cases, "people can't see the bias in search results."

For the 2018 midterm elections, Epstein set up a larger monitoring system focusing on three Republican districts in Orange County, California, which all ended up flipping Democrat. He found that on Google (but not Bing or Yahoo), search results were strongly biased in favor of Democratic candidates.

Based on Epstein's worst case scenario calculations, if that same level of bias was present nationwide in 2018, it would have shifted more than 78.2 million votes across the different elections at the state, regional, and local levels.

Is Tech Giant Bias Intentional?

Google has insisted that their algorithms for search ranking evolve according to the "organic" activity of users interacting with the algorithm.

Per Robert Epstein, "In my mind, that's complete nonsense. I've been a programmer since I was a teenager," Epstein said. "The fact is Google has total control over what happens. "So what I realized was it's very possible that a lot of important events right now in human history are being determined not by plans and goals and strategies of human beings at a company like Google, but by computer programs that are just being left to do their own thing. To me, that's far more frightening than thinking that a Google executive is out to rule the world.

"The fact is, we have let loose upon humanity powerful computer algorithms, which are impacting humanity."

Combating Bias in 2020

For the 2020 elections, Epstein plans to launch a much more ambitious monitoring system to track tech-giant bias. It will be interesting to see those results once published.

"I think that the tech companies are going to go all out" in 2020, he said. "I think they were very cautious and underconfident in 2016. I think there's a lot of crazy things they could have done to shift votes that they just didn't do."

He believes that Google could easily remove political bias in its search results using techniques it's already developed to deal with what they describe as "algorithmic unfairness."

Such techniques were thrust into the spotlight by the massive trove of documents recently leaked by former senior Google software engineer Zachary Vorhies. A simple example is the search term "American inventors." Whereas the original results might have shown a majority of white males, more black Americans can be boosted to the top of search results to make the results more "fair."

If machine learning fairness techniques can correct for what Google engineers see as racial unfairness, the same could easily be done for political bias, in Epstein's view.

"And I think we have to think beyond the United States because a company like Google is impacting more than 2 billion people around the world. Within three years, that number will swell to over 4 billion people," he said.

"They can literally impact thinking behavior, attitudes, beliefs, elections in almost every country in the world.

"In my mind, that means building larger, better-monitoring systems to keep an eye on companies like Google. I think that's necessary, not only to protect democracy around the world but to protect human autonomy."

Google Engineer Leaks Nearly 1,000 Internal Documents, Proving Conservative Bias & Censorship

In August 2019, whistleblower Zachary Vorhies, a former computer scientist at Google, shared nearly 1,000 documents with Project Veritas internal documents that purportedly evidenced Google's left-wing political bias. Among the documents was a list of popular conservative media outlets blacklisted by Google, including NewsBusters, American Thinker, Legal Insurrection, Twitchy, FrontPageMag, and GlennBeck.com.

The software engineer, Zach Vorhies, first provided the documents to Project Veritas, a right-leaning investigative journalism nonprofit, as well as the Justice Department's antitrust division, which has been investigating Google for potentially anti-competitive behavior as reported in the August 2019 "Google Engineer Leaks Nearly 1,000 Internal Documents, Alleging Bias, Censorship" from *Epoch Times* writer Petr Svab.

"The reason why I collected these documents was because I saw something dark and nefarious going on with the company, and I realized that they were going to not only tamper with the elections but use that tampering with the elections to essentially overthrow the United States," Vorhies said at the time.

Going Public

Vorhies said he worked for Google for eight years, making $260,000 a year, when counting in the gains from the Google stock he owns. Changes at the company that worried him started in 2016, he said.

"I had every incentive in the world to stay at the company and just collect the paycheck," he said, noting that most others would do that. "But I could never live with myself knowing that, if Google was able to implement the plans that they were planning, that I, at the moment of choice, backed out because I was selfish."

After Vorhies first came to Project Veritas more than a month ago, disclosing some documents and answering questions with his face hidden and his voice disguised. When he returned to work, however, Google sent him a letter demanding, among other things, that he turn over his employee badge and work laptop, which he did, and "cease and desist" from disclosing "any non-public Google files." Afraid for his safety, he posted on Twitter that if something would happen to him, all the documents he took would be released to the public.

Google then did a "wellness check" on him, he said. The San Francisco police received a call that Vorhies may be mentally ill. A group of officers waited for him outside his house and put him in handcuffs. "This is a large way in which they intimidate their employees that go rogue on the company," he said.

Vorhies then decided that it would be safer for him to go public.

Vorhies called Google a "political machine" bent on preventing anybody like President Donald Trump from getting elected again. He said there are other Google employees who "see what's going on and they are really scared."

Conservative, Republican and Trump Bias

The documents Vorhies provided previously, together with his explanations and hidden camera recordings by Project Veritas of other Google employees, indicate that the company has created a concept of "fairness" through which it infuses the political preferences of its mostly left-leaning workforce into its products.

Several studies have shown that Google News, in particular, is biased to the left.

Google has repeatedly denied political bias in its products. Vorhies suggested, though, that Google tries to present itself as a neutral platform to preserve legal protection under Section 230, which shields internet services from liability for user-generated content.

The Unsapient Ways and Means of Mediacrat Bias & Propaganda

Many in the mainstream media, big tech, and academia would rather look the other way when it comes to covering, sharing, and documenting voter fraud, gaming of election laws, and electoral abuses in all of American elections—from the presidential to municipal elections.

Worse yet, they try to dismiss or explain away the overwhelming evidence that doesn't fit the pre-approved "move along, nothing to see here" narrative. They falsely insist that there are no vulnerabilities in the electoral process as reported by Jeff Carlson for the *Epoch Times* commentary "*Time* Magazine Details the 'Shadow Campaign' Against Trump" in March 2021.

In refusing to investigate a growing number of legitimate grievances (which we have covered so far in this textbook), the anti-Trump media and censoring social media are complicit in shielding the American public from the truth, particularly internet junkies like Generation Z, Millennials and Generation X. This is a dangerous game that simultaneously undermines the credibility of the media and the stability of our political system and Republic.

In a perfect world, an ongoing debate by those journalists, pundits, and political leaders regarding many serious issues covered in *Voting Madness* should have taken place. However, as an outcome of the current Mediacrat alliance between mainstream media, big tech social media, and Democratic forces—many of you reading this textbook were not aware of the many and legitimate issues covered and discussed so far in this textbook. And the ones that you may have heard about, you read, saw, or listened to it from unsapient perspective, in some cases, and idiotic ones.

Time Magazine Glorifies the 'Shadow Campaign' Against Trump

In a surprisingly brazen article, "The Secret History of the Shadow Campaign That Saved the 2020 Election," *Time* magazine chronicles a myriad of pre-and post-election actions taken by a loose coalition of Democratic operatives, grassroots activists, mainstream media, tech companies, and corporate CEOs before and after the 2020 presidential election.

According to the Molly Ball article, the effort consisted of "a well-funded cabal of powerful people, ranging across industries and ideologies, working together behind the scenes to influence perceptions, change rules and laws, steer media coverage and control the flow of information."

In the post-election days, the author refers to this disparate grouping of players as a "conspiracy unfolding behind the scenes, one that both curtailed the protests and coordinated the resistance from CEOs" resulting in an "informal alliance between left-wing activists and business titans."

No doubt Ball is a gifted writer, but not an unbiased one—and the underlying theme and narrative almost reads in some parts like a heroic Hollywood screenplay thriller with perhaps (if I may be so bold as having written a screenplay myself) a title of "All the 'New' President's Henchmen."

Can you picture in your mind the movie marquee graphics painted like a Chinese Communist Party (CCP) propaganda poster? "Shadow Campaign 2020. They were not rigging the election; they were fortifying it for the good of America." Kind of like a leftist version of the 2004 rightist animated classic "Team America" by South Park creators Trey Parker and Matt Stone—but in this movie the Mediacrats get to "blow up" the election.

Mainstream Media (MSM) Trashes Trump 2020 Election and the Republican Party

Another Media Research Center (MRC) analysis by Rich Noyes in August 2020, shows of all evening news coverage of President Donald Trump and former Vice President Joe Biden in June and July, the networks chose to aim most of their attention and nearly all of their negative coverage on Trump, so Biden escaped any scrutiny of his left-wing policy positions, past job performance or character, etc.

From June 1 through July 31, 2020, the ABC, CBS and NBC evening newscasts focused 512 minutes of airtime on the President, or nine times more than the 58 minutes allotted to Biden. (This excludes coverage of the Trump administration in general when not associated with the President himself.) This is an even wider gap than the spring when Trump received seven times more coverage than Biden (523 minutes vs. 75 minutes).

The extra airtime devoted to Trump consisted almost entirely of anchors and reporters criticizing the President. During these two months, their analysts documented 668 evaluative statements about the President, 95 percent of which (634) were negative, vs. a mere five percent (34) that were positive. Using the same methodology, MRC found very few evaluative statements about Joe Biden—just a dozen, two-thirds of which (67%) were positive.

Do the math, and viewers heard *150 times* more negative comments about Trump than Biden. That's not news reporting—that's a negative advertising campaign in action.

If you consider the evening newscasts a reliable gauge of the liberal media at large (cable news, big newspapers, etc.), it means Biden has enjoyed an army of so-called journalists conducting a massive negative information campaign against his opponent, while he is sheltered from any scrutiny. Controversies from the spring, such as allegations from former staffer Tara Reade that he sexually assaulted her in the 1990s, completely disappeared from his evening news coverage in June and July.

Biden's various policy proposals—which by his own admission would take his administration farther to the Left than the very liberal Obama administration—received a meager 5 minutes, 22 seconds of airtime, not one second of which included any critical analysis from any journalist.

There were no labels of Biden as "progressive," "left-wing," or even "liberal" on any of these newscasts, either; reporters also neglected to tell viewers how much the Democrat would raise taxes if he were elected (spoiler: more than $4 trillion).

Biden's plan for $700 billion more federal spending (what he called "investments"), announced July 9, 2020, received a scant 40 seconds of evening news airtime (25 seconds on ABC, 15 seconds on CBS, nothing on NBC). When he outlined his massively expensive ($2 trillion) plan to combat climate change on July 14, it received six seconds, all of it on CBS.

No presidential candidate (i.e., Biden)—not even Barack Obama in 2008—has ever been on the receiving end of such a wide array of media favors. (While Obama received highly positive coverage, there was no massive media effort to destroy his GOP opponent, Senator John McCain.) While the former Vice President sat snugly in his basement before his nomination, the entire liberal "news" media complex has spent the summer on the attack against his opponent, even as they refuse to report anything negative about Biden himself.

Media Lockdown on the Hunter Biden Scandal

This same corporate media that spent more than four years claiming SpyGate was a right-wing conspiracy theory while enthusiastically pursuing the Trump–Russia collusion hoax turned around and babbled to the country that the Hunter Biden laptop was a Russian disinformation campaign.

Media Research Center (MRC) Founder and President Brent Bozell laid out on the Mark Levin Show on November 10, 2020 survey data indicating that the media's bias by omission of the Hunter Biden scandal, resulted in the defeat of President Donald Trump. Enough of Joe Biden's voters would have switched their selection had they known about his son Hunter's money scandal, enough to give President Trump a clear victory.

Bozell explained that it is well-known how the mainstream media dedicates over 90% of its Trump airtime to negative coverage of the president, but the MRC president argues that their omission of Trump's successes and Joe Biden's failures is much more dangerous.

"We took a survey after the elections, on the night of the elections, and asked Democrats if they knew about the Hunter Biden story. A full 36% of Democrats knew nothing about the Hunter Biden story," Bozell said. "Further, 4.6% of Democrats said they would not have voted for Joe Biden had they known this story. We then took that 4.6% and we spread it across the electoral landscape."

If 4.6% of the 81 million Biden votes are figured to have decided otherwise about voting for him based on the latest revelations, that could have amounted to deducting roughly 3.7 million votes from the Biden total now cutting his 7 million lead in votes in half.

"Guess what? Had they known this story, Joe Biden would not have carried Arizona, Georgia, Pennsylvania, Wisconsin, and the Trump lead would have been definitive in North Carolina. Meaning what? Meaning that Donald Trump would have won 289 electoral votes and would be the re-elect president of the United States."

A November 2020 poll by Paul Bedard, *Washington Examiner* reporter led to this conclusion per his article titled "Media's hiding of Hunter Biden scandal robbed Trump of clear win: Poll."

The story was not covered much in non-conservative media, and Twitter and other social media platforms that banned many of the reports on their sites. On the contrary, *Newsmax* and the *Epoch Times* covered it closely as they did SpyGate where other fake-news media feared to tread and held off declaring a winner until the courts and Congress had fully investigated the numerous claims of voter fraud.

"Now we know the impact of that cover-up," said MRC President Brent Bozell, adding, "4.6% of Biden voters say they would not have voted for him had they been aware of evidence of this scandal. This story would have potentially changed the outcome of this election. The media and Silicon Valley were fully aware of this, so they actively tried to prevent it from reaching the American public. The American people deserved to know the truth; now it's too late."

Twitter Goes After Trump and Campaign 325+ Times

MRC NewsBusters Corinne Weaver documented up to November 30, 2020 how Twitter has gone off the rails when it comes to censoring President Donald Trump and his campaign account. But meanwhile, Joe Biden and his campaign accounts remain untouched.

Twitter slapped labels on 63 Trump tweets since Nov. 23, 2020. When Trump tweeted: "Big Tech and the Fake News Media have partnered to Suppress. Freedom of the Press is gone, a thing of the past. That's why they refuse to report the real facts and figures of the 2020 Election or even, where's Hunter!" Twitter placed a label on the tweet, saying, "This claim about election fraud is disputed." However, nowhere in the tweet or in the accompanying video was election fraud mentioned. This tweet seemed more of a criticism of Big Tech rather than a statement implying electoral fraud.

Overall, since May 31, 2018, Trump and his campaign have been censored by Twitter 325 times. By comparison, neither former Vice President Joe Biden nor his campaign have been censored on the platform.

Twitter announced in an Oct. 9, 2020 blog, "Tweets with labels are already de-amplified through our own recommendation systems and these new prompts will give individuals more context on labeled Tweets so they can make more informed decisions on whether or not they want to amplify them to their followers." The company also stated that users who choose to retweet labeled tweets would receive a prompt "pointing them to credible information."

Labels varied based on the content of the tweet. Trump tweeted, "There is tremendous evidence of widespread voter fraud in that there is irrefutable proof that our Republican poll watchers and observers were not allowed to be present in poll counting rooms. Michigan, Pennsylvania, Georgia and others. Unconstitutional!" This tweet was marked with a label saying, "This claim about election fraud is disputed." In another tweet he said, "I won the Election!" The label under this tweet contested, "Official sources called this election differently."

A label was also placed on a tweet that mentioned the suspension of People's Pundit Daily editor Richard Baris. "Top US Pollster and Statistician Richard Baris—People's Pundit—SUSPENDED from Twitter for Reporting on Disputed Election—Political 'WrongThink' Not Allowed," tweeted Trump. The label said, "This claim about election fraud is disputed."

Some of the labels seemed arbitrarily applied. A video featuring White House Press Secretary Kayleigh McEnaney simply had the statement, "We want every *legal* vote to be counted." This tweet was given the label: "This claim about election fraud is disputed."

In a previous study, the president's Twitter account and the campaign account were found to have been censored 111 times. Tweets about the president's concern over mail-in voting, COVID-19, and the Black Lives Matter protests have been given "public interest notices."

12 – America's 21st Century Electorate: Demographics, Ideologies & Census Data

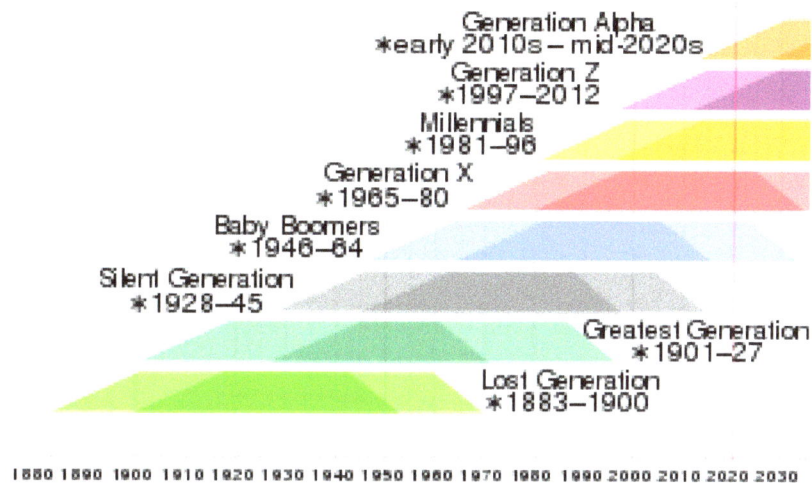

Credit: Wikipedia.

The United States holds a presidential election every four years, but it's not just the candidates and issues that change from one campaign cycle to the next. The electorate itself is in a slow but constant state of flux, too as reported in the October 2020 "Election night marks the end of one phase of campaign 2020–and the start of another" report by Pew Research Center researcher Drew DeSilver.

The profile of the U.S. electorate can change for a variety of reasons. Consider the millions of Americans who have turned 18 and can vote for president for the first time this year, the immigrants who have become naturalized citizens and can cast ballots of their own, or the longer-term shifts in the country's racial and ethnic makeup. These and other factors ensure that no two presidential electorates look exactly the same.

On or before the first Tuesday of November, millions of Americans will mail their ballots or trek to their local polling places to cast their ballots for the next president. The evening of the election after the polls close, they'll settle down in front of their televisions to watch the returns roll in from across the country. Sometime that night or early the next morning, the networks and wire services will call the race, and Americans will know the results.

Over the years, Americans have gotten used to their election nights coming off like a well-produced game show, with the big reveal coming before bedtime (a few exceptions like the early morning 2016 results and the 2000 election notwithstanding). In truth, they've never been quite as simple or straightforward as they appeared and throughout America's election history, there have been four contested elections to 2020's in 2000, 1960, 1888 and 1876.

Election Night Marks the End of One Phase of Campaign 2020 and Start of Another

Even before the COVID-19 pandemic struck, Americans had been shifting away from lining up at the polls on Election Day. In 2016, only 54.5% of all ballots nationwide were actually cast in person on Election Day, according to data from the U.S. Election Assistance Commission. The share was roughly the same (55.4%) in the 2018 midterms.

More people than ever before are likely to vote in person before Election Day, by absentee or mail ballot, or by taking ballots they've filled out at home to a drop box or other secure location. Close to half (47.3%) of the ballots cast in this year's primary season (among the 37 states, plus the District of Columbia, for which data was available) were by absentee or mail ballot or by voting early in person. As of Oct. 28, more than 75 million voters already had cast ballots.

Mail ballots pose a challenge to election workers because they must be manually removed from their envelopes and verified as valid before they can be fed into the tabulating machines. Although election workers in at least 33 states can start processing ballots (but not, in most cases, counting them) a week or more before Election Day, these counts may not be finished by election night depending on how many come in. In a half-dozen states, including the battlegrounds of Pennsylvania and Wisconsin, processing can't start until Election Day itself.

Also, in 22 states (plus Washington, D.C.), mail ballots postmarked by Election Day (or in a few cases the day before) can still be counted even if they arrive days later–further lengthening the counting process. Bottom line: Any vote totals reported on election night will be even more unofficial than they typically are.

It's all about the electors and there are 538 in total with 270 votes needed to win

Unlike other U.S. elections, in which voters pick the winners directly, those millions of presidential votes won't actually be cast for Trump or Biden. Instead, they'll count toward a statewide tally to select the electors–the mostly little-known men and women who will actually elect the president.

Each state has as many electoral votes as it has senators and representatives combined (or, in the case of the District of Columbia, as many as it would have if it were a state). There are 538 in total, with 270 votes needed to win. As the Congressional Research Service puts it, the electors "tend to be a mixture of state and local elected officials, party activists, local and state celebrities, and ordinary citizens."

In 32 states and D.C., members of the Electoral College must back the winner of the statewide popular vote In all but two states, the candidate with the most popular votes statewide (regardless of whether it's a majority or a plurality) gets all that state's electoral votes.

Maine and Nebraska do it differently: The statewide popular-vote winner gets two of the electoral votes, and the winner in each House district gets an electoral vote. That's why Democrats this year are targeting Nebraska's 2nd District and Republicans have their eyes on Maine's 2nd District. Both parties hope to squeeze a precious electoral vote out of a state that's otherwise likely to go against them.

A key date in making this year's election outcome final: Dec. 14

According to federal law, each state will have until Dec. 8 this year to resolve any "controversy or contest" concerning the appointment of its slate of electors under its own state laws. That effectively gives states more than a month after Election Day to settle any challenges to their popular votes, certify a result and award their electoral votes. If they do so by this "safe harbor" date, Congress is bound to respect the result. (The U.S. Supreme Court's 2000 ruling in *Bush v. Gore* involved whether Florida was properly applying its own recount rules, and whether those rules ran afoul of the Constitution's equal-protection guarantee.)

The electors will meet in their respective states on Dec. 14–officially, the Monday after the second Wednesday in December–and formally cast their votes for president and vice president. The Constitution expressly forbids them from meeting as a single nationwide group, a provision the Framers put in to reduce the chances of mischief. The electors are supposed to vote for the candidates whose name they were elected under–in fact, 32 states (plus D.C.) have laws intended to bind the electors to their candidates. The Supreme Court this summer unanimously upheld such laws.

So-called "faithless electors" have on occasion broken their pledges, though never enough to actually swing the outcome. In 2016, for instance, five Democratic electors voted for people other than Hillary Clinton and two Republican electors voted for people other than Donald Trump.

In any event, the electors' votes are supposed to be delivered to the vice president (in his capacity as president of the Senate) and a handful of other officials by Dec. 23 (the fourth Wednesday in December).

Wait–Congress has a role in this too?

Indeed it does. The newly elected 117th Congress will be sworn in on Jan. 3, 2021. Three days later, it is supposed to assemble in joint session to formally open the electors' ballots, count them and declare a winner. Only then is the president officially "elected."

Any pair of one senator and one representative can object to any of those votes as "not having been regularly given" (that is, not cast according to law). Following the 2004 election, for instance, Rep. Stephanie Tubbs Jones, D-Ohio, and Sen. Barbara Boxer, D-California, filed an objection against Ohio's 20 electoral votes, alleging "numerous, serious election irregularities" in that state. But to sustain such an objection, both chambers must vote (separately) to do so. In the Ohio case, they both overwhelmingly rejected the challenge.

Each state is supposed to submit one set of electoral votes to Congress, and that's what usually happens. Following the disputed Hayes-Tilden election of 1876, in which three states submitted two conflicting sets of returns, Congress passed the Electoral Count Act to try to set rules in case such a thing ever happened again. Under that law, if two conflicting sets are submitted—say, one by a Republican-run legislature and one by a Democratic governor—and the House and Senate cannot agree on which set is the legitimate one, then the electoral votes certified by the state's governor are supposed to prevail.

What the 2020 Electorate Looks Like by Various Demographics

So what does the 2020 electorate look like politically, demographically, and religiously as the race between Republican President Donald Trump and Democrat Joe Biden enters its final days? To answer that question, here's a roundup of recent Pew Research Center findings in "What the 2020 electorate looks like by party, race and ethnicity, age, education and religion" by John Gramlich in October 2020. Unless otherwise noted, all findings are based on registered voters.

Party identification

Around a third of registered voters in the U.S. (34%) identify as independents, while 33% identify as Democrats and 29% identify as Republicans, according to a Center analysis of Americans' partisan identification based on surveys of more than 12,000 registered voters in 2018 and 2019.

Most independents in the U.S. lean toward one of the two major parties. When taking independents' partisan leanings into account, 49% of *all* registered voters either identify as Democrats or lean to the party, while 44% identify as Republicans or lean to the GOP.

Party identification among registered voters hasn't changed dramatically over the past 25 years, but there have been some modest shifts. One such shift is that the Democratic Party's advantage over the Republican Party in party identification has become smaller since 2017. Of course, just because a registered voter identifies with or leans toward a particular party does not necessarily mean they will vote for a candidate of that party (or vote at all). In a study of validated voters in 2016, 5% of Democrats and Democratic leaners reported voting for Trump, and 4% of Republicans and GOP leaners reported voting for Hillary Clinton.

Non-Hispanic White Americans make up the largest share of registered voters in the U.S., at 69% of the total as of 2019. Hispanic and Black registered voters each account for 11% of the total, while those from other racial or ethnic backgrounds account for the remainder (8%).

White voters account for a diminished share of registered voters than in the past, declining from 85% in 1996 to 69% ahead of this year's election. This change has unfolded in both parties, but White voters have consistently accounted for a much larger share of Republican and Republican-leaning registered voters than of Democratic and Democratic-leaning voters (81% vs. 59% as of 2019).

Generation, sex, and race

Younger generations overwhelmingly pick Biden over Trump

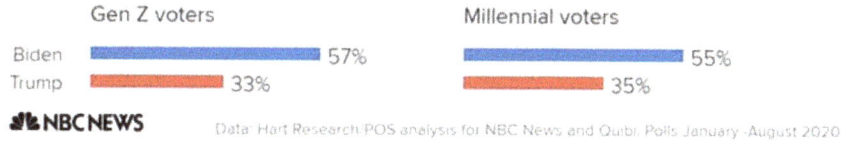

Gen Z voters		Millennial voters	
Biden	57%	Biden	55%
Trump	33%	Trump	35%

NBC NEWS Data: Hart Research/POS analysis for NBC News and Quibi. Polls January -August 2020

Young women break big for Biden. Among men, it's close.

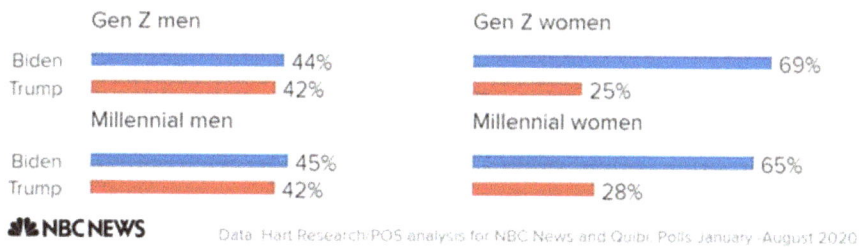

Gen Z men		Gen Z women	
Biden	44%	Biden	69%
Trump	42%	Trump	25%
Millennial men		Millennial women	
Biden	45%	Biden	65%
Trump	42%	Trump	28%

NBC NEWS Data: Hart Research/POS analysis for NBC News and Quibi. Polls January -August 2020

Young voters of color are more likely to reject Trump

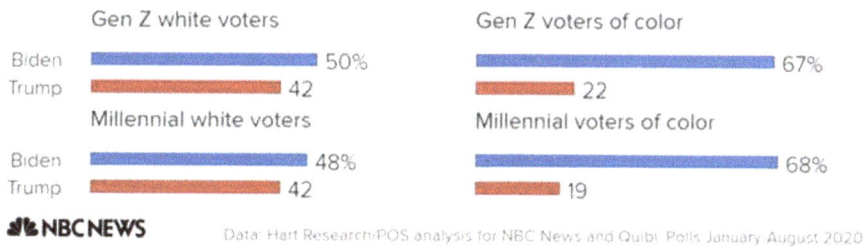

Gen Z white voters		Gen Z voters of color	
Biden	50%	Biden	67%
Trump	42	Trump	22
Millennial white voters		Millennial voters of color	
Biden	48%	Biden	68%
Trump	42	Trump	19

NBC NEWS Data: Hart Research/POS analysis for NBC News and Quibi. Polls January -August 2020

The racial and ethnic composition of the electorate looks very different nationally than in several key battleground states, according to a Center analysis of 2018 data based on eligible voters–that is, U.S. citizens ages 18 and older, regardless of whether or not they were registered to vote.

White Americans accounted for 67% of eligible voters nationally in 2018, but they represented a much larger share in several key battlegrounds in the Midwest and Mid-Atlantic, including Wisconsin (86%), Ohio (82%), Pennsylvania (81%) and Michigan (79%). The reverse was true in some battleground states in the West and South. For example, the White share of eligible voters was below the national average in Nevada (58%), Florida (61%) and Arizona (63%).

Age and generation

The U.S. electorate is aging: 52% of registered voters are ages 50 and older, up from 41% in 1996. This shift has occurred in both partisan coalitions. More than half of Republican and GOP-leaning voters (56%) are ages 50 and older, up from 39% in 1996. And among Democratic and Democratic-leaning voters, half are 50 and older, up from 41% in 1996.

Another way to consider the aging of the electorate is to look at median age. The median age among all registered voters increased from 44 in 1996 to 50 in 2019. It rose from 43 to 52 among Republican registered voters and from 45 to 49 among Democratic registered voters.

Despite the long-term aging of registered voters, 2020 marks the first time that many members of Generation Z–Americans born after 1996–will be able to participate in a presidential election. One-in-ten eligible voters this year are members of Generation Z, up from just 4% in 2016 according to Pew Research Center projections. (Of course, not all eligible voters end up registering and actually casting a ballot.)

Education

Around two-thirds of registered voters in the U.S. (65%) do not have a college degree, while 36% do. But the share of voters with a college degree has risen substantially since 1996, when 24% had one.

Voters who identify with the Democratic Party or lean toward it are much more likely than their Republican counterparts to have a college degree (41% vs. 30%). In 1996, the reverse was true: 27% of GOP voters had a college degree, compared with 22% of Democratic voters.

Religion

Christians account for the majority of registered voters in the U.S. (64%). But this figure is down from 79% as recently as 2008. The share of voters who identify as religiously unaffiliated has nearly doubled during that span, from 15% to 28%.

The share of white Christians in the electorate, in particular, has decreased in recent years. White evangelical Protestants account for 18% of registered voters today, down from 21% in 2008. During the same period, the share of voters who are White non-evangelical Protestants fell from 19% to 13%, while the share of White Catholics fell from 17% to 12%.

Around eight-in-ten Republican registered voters (79%) are Christians, compared with about half (52%) of Democratic voters. In turn, Democratic voters are much more likely than GOP voters to identify as religiously unaffiliated (38% vs. 15%).

Why Aren't Generations X Y Z Becoming More Sapient and Conservative Over Time?

According to comprehensive polling from the Pew Research Center, Gen Z is trending to the left. Their views mirror those of Millennials. The conservative magazine *Commentary* warns, "Generation Z is a liberal tsunami" as reported on in their October 2019 post "Is Generation Z more conservative or less conservative than other generations?" by Rachel Alexander at The Christian Post.

They believe in even higher numbers than Millennials that government should do more to solve problems, 70%. Only 30% approve of President Trump's job performance, barely more than

Millennials at 29%. In contrast, 38% of Generation X approves of his performance, 43% of Boomers and 54% of the Silent Generation.

When it comes to climate change, Gen Z is very similar to the Millennials and not that much different from Gen X. Over 50% of Gen Z and Millennials believe the earth is getting warmer due to human activity. Gen X isn't far behind, with 48% believing that.

Gen Z is also very similar to the Millennials when it comes to how great they think the U.S. is. Only 14% think the U.S. is the greatest country in the world, and only 13% of Millennials. In contrast, 20% of Gen X believes the U.S. is the greatest country in the world, 30% of Boomers, and 45% of the Silent Generation.

Of course, Pew always muddles their polls with artificial questions and breakdowns (they love splitting evangelicals between white evangelicals and non-white evangelicals, which is ridiculous since they're not that far apart, it's just stoking the racial flames). The poll asked whether more racial/ethnic diversity is good for society. Gen Z and the Millennials both said yes in higher percentages than the older generations. But that's no surprise.

Democrats supported Jim Crow laws last century and fought passage of the Civil Rights Act of 1964. The older generations are still tainted by that. Changing people's minds on that is not less conservative. It's less Democrat.

There are some exceptions to Gen Z becoming more liberal. Business Insider surveyed Gen Z and found that a majority did not identify as liberal or conservative. The remaining Gen Zers were about evenly split between the right and the left.

The Harris Poll took a survey on behalf of the LGBTQ advocacy group GLAAD and found that the percentage of young people who are comfortable interacting with LGBGQ people dropped from 53% in 2017 to 45% in 2018. That's further down from 63% in 2016. Other age groups did not have similar drops.

The Hispanic Heritage Foundation found that eight out of 10 Gen Zers identify as fiscal conservatives. This could be because they watched their parents live through the economic decline in the late 2000s.

While only 18% of Millennials attend church, 41% of Gen Z does. Of course, this could be due in part to the fact Gen Z is still living with their parents. The Pew survey found that Gen Z views single mothers raising kids similarly to the older generations. Almost half believe it has no effect on society. Over a third believe it has a bad effect.

It makes sense that Gen Z is turning out liberal. They were raised by Gen X parents, who brought them up in a hands-off manner, so they were heavily influenced instead by the public schools and social media. The big tech companies lean to the left and don't try to hide their bias. Social media is the top way Generations' X, Y and Z get their news. Business Insider conducted a survey with SurveyMonkey Audience partner Cint and found that more than half of Gen Z checks Snapchat, YouTube, or Instagram daily.

As Gen Z increasingly ages past 18, we are going to feel the effects of their politics at the polls more and more. It does not bode well for conservatives in the future. Of course, many who are liberal in their youth become more conservative as they age. The cycle will likely continue with future generations starting out liberal and becoming conservative in later years.

But with a more powerful and long-term influence on Generations' X, Y and Z from big tech and social media—that might be an unsapient conclusion.

Voter Turnout and Registrations by the Generations

For the past few decades, presidential elections have been dominated by voters of the Baby Boom and previous generations, who are estimated to have cast a majority of the votes. But their election reign ended io November 3, 2020 as predicted by the "This may be the last presidential election dominated by Boomers and prior generations" report by Richard Fry at the Pew Research Center in August 2016.

Baby Boomers and prior generations have cast the vast majority of votes in every presidential election since 1980, data from the Census Bureau's November Current Population Survey voting supplement show. In 2012, Boomers and previous generations accounted for 56% of those who said they voted. And these generations dominated earlier elections to an even greater degree.

But the ranks of Generation Z, Millennials and Generation X eligible voters have been growing, thanks to the aging-in of earlier generations and naturalizations among foreign-born adults. These generations matched Boomers and previous generations as a share of eligible voters in 2012 and are now estimated to outnumber them. As of July, an estimated 126 million Millennial and Gen X adults were eligible to vote (56% of eligible voters), compared with only 98 million Boomers and other adults from prior generations, or 44% of the voting-eligible population.

Although the electorate is increasingly comprised of younger generations, this does not imply that the electorate as a whole is getting younger.

Perhaps more importantly, eligible voters don't necessarily translate into actual voters–that all depends on who shows up to vote on Election Day. Whether Zillennials, Millennial and Generation X adults outnumber Boomers and other generations in November will hinge on voter turnout.

In the 2012 election an estimated 70% of eligible voters in the Baby Boom, Silent and Greatest generations voted. Turnout among these generations was similar in 2004 (70%) and 2008 (69%).

In the 2012 election, 53.9% of Millennial and Gen X eligible voters turned out. Turnout among these generations was even higher in 2004 (54.2%) and higher still in 2008 (56.6%).

Historical patterns of voter turnout by generation also suggest the likely end of dominance by Boomers and prior generations. In general, as a generation ages, turnout rises, hits a peak, and then declines.

Among those in the oldest living generation, the Greatest Generation, turnout crested in the 1984 election at 76% before declining. Similarly, turnout among eligible voters in the Silent Generation peaked at 76% in the 1992 election.

Providing the Census Bureau With the Time to Produce a Complete and Accurate Census

The Census Bureau has been collecting citizen population data since the 1820 Census, which had the first citizenship question on a Census form. It currently collects that data through the American Community Survey (ACS), which also has a citizenship question. The Citizen Voting Age Population (CVAP) data is essential to effective enforcement of Section 2 of the VRA when implementing remedies in vote dilution cases.

The Census Bureau has the right to collect citizenship data as noted in the October 2020 report "Providing the Census Bureau with the Time to Produce a Complete and Accurate Census' from The Heritage Foundation. In fact, even the United Nations recommends that its member countries ask a citizenship question on their census surveys, and countries ranging from Australia to Germany to Indonesia all ask this question.

Only in the U.S. is this considered at all controversial—and it shouldn't be.

Collection of citizenship data is also vital to establish a consensus on national immigration policy. Without citizenship data, it is not possible to have an informed debate and discussion over what U.S. policy should be and how to successfully implement it. The collection of citizenship data by the Census Bureau from available executive branch agency records is required for effective enforcement of the Voting Rights Act.

On July 11, 2019, President Trump issued Executive Order on Collecting Information about Citizenship Status in Connection with the Decennial Census, E.O. 13880, directing all federal agencies to provide the Census Bureau with administrative records "showing citizenship data."

This executive order followed a fragmented 2019 Supreme Court decision holding that the executive branch has both the constitutional and statutory authority to reinstate a citizenship question on the Census form, but that the Department of Commerce had not followed the proper procedure to do so under the Administrative Procedure Act.

This was a flawed decision; the administration followed the correct procedures and, as Justice Clarence Thomas wrote in his dissent, the Court should have stopped its analysis when it determined that the citizenship question is both constitutional and within the legal authority of the Secretary of the Department of Commerce.

Thus, when a court finds a violation of Section 2, the remedy is to draw a district—whether it is a town council, school board, county commission, state legislative, or congressional district—in which minority voters constitute a majority of the voters (known as a majority/minority district) such that they can elect their candidates of choice. Citizen population data is essential to drawing an effective voting district for minority voters.

For example, if a group of minority voters constitutes 51 percent of a district, then they will be able to elect their candidates of choice as the majority of the electorate in that district. But if a district is drawn using total population data, which includes both citizens and noncitizens, to draw a district in which Hispanics, for example, constitute 51 percent of the district, eligible Hispanic voters—citizens—may not constitute 51 percent of the voting electorate in that district. Thus, the Hispanics who can vote may only be a minority of the electorate and therefore are not able to elect their candidate of choice. Using total population rather than citizen population will not cure a Section 2 violation.

Basing apportionment on total population that includes large numbers of illegal aliens is fundamentally unfair to American citizens and dilutes and diminishes the value of their votes.

Finally, including aliens in apportionment not only dilutes the votes of individual citizens, but also damages the distribution of representation of state governments in our federal republic. In 2015, the Congressional Research Service analyzed how seats in the House would have been apportioned using the estimated citizen population instead of the 2010 total population Census count. Louisiana, Missouri, Montana, North Carolina, Ohio, Oklahoma, and Virginia would have all gained one congressional representative.

California, Florida, New York, and Texas would have lost seats. These latter states have gained congressional seats based on noncitizen populations, particularly large numbers of illegal aliens in states like California, at the expense of the representation to which Louisiana, Missouri, Montana, North Carolina, Ohio, Oklahoma, and Virginia are entitled.

Why Not Fewer Voters?

The 159.8 million cast ballots for the 2020 election represent the highest number of voters in a U.S. presidential election in history. In 2016, the total stood just above 136.6 million votes, a 23.2 million increase! Around 239.2 million Americans were eligible to vote in 2020, according to the U.S. Elections Project. NBC News' projected 159.8 million ballots cast in 2020 would constitute about a 66.8% voter turnout rate among eligible citizens—the highest since 1900.

If you cannot put in the time, research, and sapience when voting—why bother—just don't vote. Kevin D. Williamson, a fellow at the *National Review* Institute, and their roving correspondent who brings up an interested point that deserves recognition and further discussion as follows:

In his provocative April 2021 "Why Not Fewer Voters?" article in the *National Review*: Much of the discussion about proposed changes to voting laws backed by many Republicans and generally opposed by Democrats begs the question and simply asserts that having more people vote is, *ceteris paribus*, a good thing.

Why should we believe that? Why shouldn't we believe the opposite? That the republic would be better served by having fewer—but better—voters?

Many Americans, being devout egalitarians, recoil from the very notion of better voters as a matter of rhetoric—even as they accept qualifications for most every endeavor in life as a matter of fact.

However, all eligibility requirements risk excluding somebody who might make a good voter, or a better voter than someone who is eligible. There are plenty of very smart and responsible 16-year-olds who would make better voters than their dim and irresponsible older siblings or their parents. That doesn't mean we should have 16-year-old voters—I'd be more inclined to raise the voting age to 30—it means only that categorical decision-making by its nature does not account for certain individual differences.

Similarly, asking for government-issued photo ID at the polls seem to me obviously the right thing to do, even if it would result in some otherwise eligible voters not voting. I'm not convinced that having more voters is a good thing in any case, but, even if I were, that would not be the only good, but only one good competing with other goods, one of which is seeing to it that the eligibility rules on the books are enforced so that elections may be honestly and credibly regulated.

We could verify eligibility at the polls rigorously and easily, if we wanted to, just as we have the ability to verify who is eligible to enter the country or to drive a car. Of course that would put some burdens on voters. So, what? We expect people, including poor and struggling people, to pay their taxes—why shouldn't we also expect them to keep their drivers' licenses up-to-date? If voting really is the sacred duty that we're always being told it is, shouldn't we treat it at least as seriously as filing a 1040EZ?

There would be more voters if we made it easier to vote, and there would be more doctors if we didn't require a license to practice medicine. The fact that we believe unqualified doctors to be a public menace but act as though unqualified voters were just stars in the splendid constellation of democracy indicates how little real esteem we actually have for the vote, in spite of our public pieties.

One argument for encouraging bigger turnout is that if more eligible voters go to the polls then the outcome will more closely reflect what the average American voter wants. That sounds like a wonderful thing—if you haven't met the average American voter.

Voters—individually and in majorities—are as apt to be wrong about things as right about them, often vote from low motives such as bigotry and spite, and very often are contentedly ignorant. That is one of the reasons why the original constitutional architecture of this country gave voters a narrowly limited say in most things and took some things—freedom of speech, freedom of religion, etc.—off the voters' table entirely.

The real case—generally unstated—for encouraging more people to vote is a metaphysical one: that wider turnout in elections makes the government somehow more legitimate in a vague moral sense. But legitimacy is not popularity and popularity is not consent. The entire notion of representative government assumes that the actual business of governing requires fewer decision-makers rather than more.

To vote is only to register one's individual, personal preference, but democratic citizenship imposes broader duties and obligations. When we fail to meet that broader responsibility, the result is dysfunction: It is no accident that we are heaping debt upon our children, who cannot vote, in order to pay for benefits dear to the most active and reliable voters. That's what you get from having lots of voting but relatively little responsible citizenship.

Progressives and populists like to blame lobbyists, special interests, "the Swamp," insiders, "the Establishment," vested interests, shadowy corporate titans, and sundry boogeymen for our current straits, but the fact is that voters got us into this mess. Maybe the answer isn't more voters.

13 – 2020 Voter Polls, Election Results & Analysis and Georgia Vote Lawsuit

Credit: MANDEL NGAN/Contributor/Getty Image - Texas' attorney general, Ken Paxton, has begun the process to file a complaint against four states' elections.

The 2020 election year was like no other that we have ever seen, President Trump and America faced the challenges of impeachment, a global pandemic, depression level unemployment, a breakdown of law and order with rioting and looting, bitter media bias, big tech censorship—and now an extremely close election count, and probable recounts, where the media has proclaimed Joe Biden the winner prior to the legal state certification of the votes.

Voters who backed former Vice President Joe Biden are more likely to say they supported him because they didn't want to vote for President Donald Trump, according to an exit poll. According to a Morning Consult exit poll, Biden voters were twice as likely as Trump voters to say their vote was more about the other candidate than the one they supported.

Poll results pulled from the "Morning Consult Exit Poll: More Biden Voters Wanted to Vote Against Trump" article in *Newsmax* by Marisa Herman in November 2020 show:

- 75% of Trump voters say their vote was more of a vote for Trump, while only 22% say it was more of a vote against Biden.

- 54% of Biden voters say their vote was in support of Biden, while 44% say it was a vote against Trump.

The poll also found that Biden backers are looking to support a candidate that possesses good judgment, is trustworthy, honest, and stable. For Trump supporters, they want a president who has good mental fitness, is effective, has strong leadership, and judgment.

The poll, which was ongoing between Oct. 30 and Nov. 3, 2020, surveyed 10,870 voters who already cast their ballot. The poll has a margin of error of plus or minus one percentage point.

Trump-Biden Was Worst Presidential Polling Miss in 40 Years, Panel Says

Surveys overstated Democrats' support up and down the ballot, as some voters were less inclined to participate in polls as noted in the May 2021 "Trump-Biden Was Worst Presidential Polling Miss in 40 Years, Panel Says" article in the *Wall Street Journal* by Aaron Zitner.

Public opinion surveys ahead of the 2020 presidential election were the most inaccurate in 40 years, according to an expert panel convened by the main trade group for pollsters, which said its work hadn't yet pointed to a way to correct the error.

In the aggregate, the panel said, polls overstated support for Democratic nominee Joe Biden by 3.9 percentage points in the national popular vote in the final two weeks of the campaign. That was a larger error than the 1.3-point overstatement in 2016 surveys for Hillary Clinton, who won the popular vote but lost in the Electoral College.

It was the most substantial error in polling since 1980, when surveys found it hard to measure the size of Ronald Reagan's impending landslide and overstated support for President Jimmy Carter by 6 percentage points.

The 2020 polls overstated Democratic support "in every type of contest we looked at: the national popular vote, the state-level presidential vote as well as senatorial and gubernatorial elections," said Joshua D. Clinton, a professor of political science at Vanderbilt University who led the review for the American Association for Public Opinion Research.

"This was true no matter how respondents were polled. It didn't matter whether you're doing online or telephone surveys and polls. A similar level of error was pervasive," said Clinton.

Unsapient Young, Female & Diverse Voters Fueled Biden Victory Over Trump

As young voters age, their responsibility is to build on the momentum of 2020. They remain a rich target demographic for both parties—nearly half of voting-eligible young people did not cast a ballot this election cycle—but their patriotic duty is to be engaged and informed.

Nonetheless, a diverse coalition of young and new voters propelled President Biden to victory in November, according to a major new study of the 2020 electorate, while former President Trump made inroads among Hispanic voters in key states as reported in the May 2021 "Young, diverse voters fueled Biden victory over Trump" article in *The Hill* by Reid Wilson.

The report, from the Democratic data analytics firm Catalist, found the most diverse electorate in American history showed up to vote in last year's elections. Twenty-eight percent of voters last year were nonwhite, up 2 percentage points from the 2016 presidential election.

More than 159 million Americans voted in 2020, the largest turnout in history. The number of nonwhite participants skyrocketed, including by 31 percent among Latino voters and 39 percent among Asian American and Pacific Islander voters. For the first time, Latino voters made up 10 percent of the electorate.

Black turnout rose by 14 percent, outpacing the total growth among white voters with a college degree, up 13 percent, and among whites without a college degree, up 11 percent.

The number of new Black voters was key to Biden's win in several swing states. Biden won nearly 200,000 more Black votes in Georgia than did former Democratic presidential nominee Hillary Clinton in 2016, far more than his 11,779-vote margin of victory in the state. Biden scored 28,000 more Black votes in Arizona, another state where those votes alone account for more than his margin of victory.

Biden's margins among all Black voters were larger than his overall wins in Wisconsin, Pennsylvania, Nevada and Michigan, the foundational swing states he won to capture the White House.

Overall, 61 percent of voters who chose Biden were white, while 39 percent were voters of color. Among Trump supporters, 85 percent were white.

Biden took 44 percent of the two-party vote share among white voters, a 3-point increase over Clinton's performance in 2016. He improved on Clinton's performance, especially among college-educated white men, among whom Biden won 50 percent of the two-party vote, 5 points better than Clinton.

Democrat Share of Vote Fell by 8 Points Between 2016-20 Due to Rising Independent Voters

Despite Nancy Pelosi's unsapient assessment that the Republican Party is doomed due to America's changing demographics, the Democrat share of the vote fell by 8 points between 2016 and 2020 as Trump captured a growing share of the emerging young electorate in states like Florida, Texas, Wisconsin, and Nevada in 2020. Pelosi's prognosis is also at odds with Republican gains in the House and a dead heat in the Senate.

Amongst various non-white demographics, Trump did best among voters of Cuban and Puerto Rican descent and worst with voters of Chinese ancestry. While Biden performed well among Asian Americans, double that of Trump's share with 63 to 31 percent, the data suggest that Trump didn't lose support with this varied group, overall, and increased his share of black voters by approximately 50% from 8 to 12 percent, a relatively huge shift by black American voting standards.

In a measure of just how rapidly the Hispanic vote is growing, more than 1 in 5 Hispanic voters—22 percent—cast their first ballots in 2020. Forty percent of Hispanic voters had never voted in a presidential election before, compared with 29 percent of the overall electorate.

The 2020 elections also marked the first presidential contest in which Millennials and members of Generation Z combined to eclipse the voting power of Generation X. Members of the two youngest generations accounted for 31 percent of the electorate, up 8 points from four years earlier, while 26 percent were members of Generation X.

Biden won 60 percent of the vote among voters between the ages of 18 and 29, and 56 percent among those between 30 and 45, both significant increases over Clinton's performance. Trump improved his performance marginally among both groups, and far fewer people across all generations opted for a third-party candidate.

Trump performed best among baby boomers and those in older generations, but those generations are rapidly losing influence in the electorate. Those in and older than the baby boom generation accounted for 44 percent of the electorate in 2020, down from 51 percent in 2016 and 61 percent in 2008, when Barack Obama won the White House.

Last year's elections "accelerated a massive change in the composition of the electorate, with Millennials and Gen Z taking an increasingly prominent role in the future of American elections—a demographic change that is functionally permanent," the authors wrote.

Many of those younger voters cast a ballot for the first time or voted in their first presidential election—especially in swing states. More than a third of voters in Nevada, Arizona, and Texas and nearly a third of voters in Georgia voted for president for the first time. The researchers estimate that Biden won 56 percent of new voters and 62 percent of new voters under 30 years old.

More 2020 Post Election Poll Analysis of an Election Like No Other

Despite the record 2020 turnout, millions of Americans who are eligible to cast ballots remained on the sidelines, the report found. More than 70 million people who were eligible to vote opted not to in 2020, including about a quarter of whites, more than a third of Black residents and half of Latinos.

Full disclosure from John McLaughlin and Jim McLaughlin who conducted the polls below: "We worked for President Trump in 2016 and in 2020 and this earned us the derision and enmity of the anti-Trump, liberal, mainstream media. As we challenged their biased anti-Trump polling for under polling Republicans and Trump voters, we were repeatedly attacked. Even CNN's Chris Cuomo and CNN's legal counsel (appropriately named David Vigilante) defended their skewed and biased polling by personally attacking our firm.

Nonetheless, let's look at their extensive and unbiased polling data and results from the "2020 Post Election Poll Analysis of an Election Like No Other" report by John McLaughlin and Jim McLaughlin from November 2020 compared to fake news, false narratives, and mediacrat news and survey sources (that some of you may have been exposed to, like the CNN examples below):

- Among the most egregious examples, CNN manufactured a national poll in June by saying that the President was losing by 14 points—55% to 41%.

- Right before election day CNN doubled down on the same methodology and their final October national poll said the president would lose in a landslide by 12 points—54% to 42%.

Mediacrat Pollsters Continually Underrepresent Republicans in Their Samples

McLaughlin's main battle with media and Democratic pollsters was that their polls among adults or registered voters had polled only 26%, 25% or even fewer Republicans in their samples.

The 2016 media exit polls and the 2018 exit polls both had Republicans at 33% to 37% Democrat. Many of their so called polling experts defended the lack of Republicans in the polls. Ironically, CNN's 2020 exit poll now says the actual national electorate was 36% Republican and 37% Democrats!

It was pretty clear to McLaughlin that they were under polling the Republicans and Trump voters to create media narrative that the president was losing badly and would lose the election in a "Biden landslide" and "blue wave" to discourage President Trump's supporters and voters.

CNN seemed to know that the president's voters preferred to vote in person and that Joe Biden's voters would prefer to vote early by mail and if they could discourage Trump voters from actually showing up on election day, their predictions would have come true, and their polls would be right.

McLaughlin's post-election poll also showed that:

- Only one third, 36%, of the voters, voted on election day. Among the election day voters, they voted for President Trump 62% to 36%.

- Among the two thirds, 64% who voted early before election day by mail, drop-off or in person, they voted for Joe Biden 58% to 40%.

- Breaking apart those who voted early in person, they were almost evenly split Biden 51% - Trump 49%.

However, it's clear if President Trump had not had a strong turnout on Election Day, there would have been a Biden blue wave. President Trump, after recovering from the virus, rebounded with a very, strong debate performance, a strong contrast against Joe Biden and Sen. Kamala Harris, D-California, on the issues, and daily vigorous campaigning defying the biased media polls that had forecast a double digit loss for him.

In McLaughlin's latest March 2021 national survey of 1,000 likely voters, the polarization of the American electorate has not ended with the elections of 2020. Instead, in spite of all the promises and rhetoric political division and disunity continues into 2021.

Ironically, President Trump left a recovering economy and historic vaccine to the benefit of President Biden, but the country remains about evenly polarized by partisan politics. This roughly equal division defines virtually every issue and the voters' political outlooks.

Key Survey Results From McLaughlin's Polls

Going back to McLaughlin's November 2021 polling surveys, here is what the electorate had to say with their votes in those surveys:

- Voters who decided their vote in the last week preferred Trump 58% - 40%. (10% of all voters.)

- Fortunately for Joe Biden almost three in ten voters, 27% of all voters, were not aware of the alleged corruption charges against Joe Biden.

- Voters who were aware of Joe Biden's corruption, voted for President Trump 55% - 44%. (73% of all voters.)

- Voters who were not aware of Joe Biden's family corruption voted for Biden 66% - 31%. (27% of all voters.)

- Voters who approve of the job the president is doing, they voted for him 86% - 12 percent. (53% of all voters approved of the job the president is doing.)

- Voters who disapprove of the job the president is doing, they voted for Biden 93% – 6%. (47% of all voters disapprove of the job the president is doing.)

- Fully 7% of all voters approved the job the president was doing but did not vote for him. Instead 88% of that group voted for Biden. So you could like the job the president was doing, but some voted for Biden.

- Among all men they voted for Trump 53% - 45%. Women voted for Biden 54% - 44%.

- Working men voted for Trump 55% - 43%. Working women went for Biden 54% - 45%. Retired men voted for Trump 53% - 46%.

If You Liked Trump You Voted For Him. If You Disliked Him, You Voted For Biden

The key point in this section appears to be if you liked Trump you voted for him. If you disliked him, you voted for Biden—even though you may like the job that Trump is doing.

- President Trump's personality was more of a vote determinant than his job approval.

- Among the 49% of the voters who were favorable to President Trump, they voted for him 89% to 10%. Among the 50% who were unfavorable to president, they voted for Biden 89 % to 10%. This is an almost perfect inverse relationship.

- Voters who were favorable to both Trump and Biden, voted for Trump 61% - 36 %. (They were 10% of all voters.) If you liked Trump, it didn't matter you liked Biden, because most voted for Trump.

- Voters who are unfavorable to both Trump and Biden, voted Biden 52% - 38%. (They were 8% of all voters.). If you disliked Trump and Biden chances are you voted for Biden, because your dislike of Trump was more dominant.

When Trump voters were asked what the single most important reason that they voted for President Trump, 55% of the answers were related to the president's character and personal traits. 37% were related to issues. The leading responses were: stand on the economy 13%, dislike Biden/Harris 10%, good/like 9%, good job/record 6%, good views/positions 5%, MAGA/Patriotic 5%, and dislike socialism 5%.

- The overwhelming support was more a positive vote for Trump, 84%, rather than a negative vote against Biden only 15%.

When Biden votes were asked the single most important reason that they voted for Joe Biden, 74% cited a character or personality related trait, mostly anti-Trump rather than pro-Biden. Only 21% cited an issue. Leading responses why they voted for Biden were: disliked Trump 32%, Biden better choice 6%, Covid/pandemic 6%, honesty/character 6% and for the people 5%.

- Only six in ten of Biden's voters, 61%, said their vote was more a positive vote for Biden, while almost four in ten, 37% said their vote was more a negative vote against Trump.

The Biden campaign did a better job running a negative campaign against the president than the president's campaign did against Joe Biden. The paid television advertising advantage of the Biden campaign and biased media coverage drove this result.

Other Interesting Results From McLaughlin's Polls

Most of the results below are fairly typical of previous polls as well as those from the 2016 presidential election between Trump and Hillary Clinton.

- By party affiliation Republicans voted for President Trump 89% to 10%.

- Democrats voted for an identical Biden 89% to 10%.

- Independents were evenly split Trump 48%, Biden 49%. Independent men voted for Trump slightly 50% - 46%. Independent women slightly preferred Biden 50% - 47%.

- By ideology liberals chose Biden 82% - 16%. Moderates supported Biden 62% - 36%. Conservatives voted for Trump 85% - 15%.

- Anti-abortion voters supported Trump 64% - 34%. Pro-abortion rights voters voted for Biden 65% - 34%.

- Married voters went for Trump 56% - 42%. Single voters voted for Biden 65% - 33%.

- Veteran households voted for Trump 57% to 42%. Active military households voted for Trump 59% to 38%.

- Labor union households including teachers and public service unions preferred Biden 50% to 46%.

- By race white voters voted for Trump 59% to 40%. Hispanics voted for Biden 64%, but Trump received 32%. Black voters voted for Biden 81%, but 18% voted for Trump.

- There was a significant generational gap with Biden winning voters under 40, 57% - 41%. Trump won middle-aged voters ages 41-55, 53% - 45%, and voters over 55 years, 51% - 48%.

- Urban voters voted for Biden 56% - 42%. Suburban voters were close, Biden 51% - Trump 47%. Small town, rural voters voted strongly for Trump 60% - 40%.

Religious Affiliation or None Showed in the Surveys

Many of these trends reinforce the same Republican-Democratic voting patterns of much of the 21st century. The same with this pattern: The more frequently somebody attends worship, the more likely that voter went Republican, and vice versa.

- Protestants voted for Trump 53% - 36%.

- Catholics were slightly favored Trump 50% to 48% for Biden.

- Evangelicals chose Trump 62% - 36%; white Evangelicals voted Trump 79% - 19%.

- All voters who regularly attend church or religious services voted for Trump 53% - 45%.

- Voters who do not regularly attend services chose Biden 54% - 45%.

- For Joe Biden who says he's a practicing Catholic, his fellow practicing Catholics who attend church voted for Trump 54% - 43%, while non-church going Catholics voted for Biden 53% - 46%.

A Deeper Dive Into Voter Responses

Regarding the vote for Congress, it appears that the Republicans were able to gain seats due the foundation that President Trump provided Republican candidates for the House. Trump voters voted Republican for Congress 90% - 7%, while Biden voters went for Democrats 89% - 8%.

Although Biden has a lead in the national popular vote, when the voters were asked: "Regardless of your vote for president who do you think most of your friends and neighbors voted for?", an even 50% said most of their friends and neighbors voted for Trump while 50% said they voted for Biden. Notably 12% of the Biden voters and 15% of the Democrats said most of their friends voted for Trump.

On election day voters' opinions of President Trump were evenly split 49% favorable, 50 % unfavorable. Joe Biden was a net positive 52% favorable, 45% unfavorable.

Mike Pence was a net favorable 49% favorable, 44% unfavorable. Kamala Harris was slightly net positive 47% favorable, 43% unfavorable.

Speaker Nancy Pelosi was a huge negative only 36% favorable, 54% unfavorable while socialist Rep. Alexandria Ocasio-Cortez, D-New York, is widely known by 89% of all voters and is a net negative 31% favorable to 42% unfavorable.

- Among all voters six in ten, 61% say they are better off now than four years ago.
- Only 38% say that they are worse off.
- Trump voters were more likely to say that they were better off 85% - 15%.
- Biden voters said that they were worse off today 60%, but 39% said better off.

Fully 20% of all voters thought they were better off today than four years ago and did not vote for President Trump. It seems that there were not enough voters who believed that they would be worse off under Joe Biden going forward.

The majority thought that President Trump would do a better job rebuilding the economy 54 percent–46 percent and restoring law and order 52 % - 48%.

However, the majority thought that Joe Biden would do a better job: uniting America and improving race relations 55% - 45%, dealing with the Coronavirus 55% - 45%, and restoring honesty and integrity to government 53% - 47%.

The majority blamed the Democrats for rioting, looting and unrest in our cities 54% to 45 % who blamed Republicans. Trump voters blamed the Democrats 81% - 19% and 28 % of Biden voters blamed the Democrats as well.

The majority preferred free market capitalism 76% over big government socialism 24%. Trump voters were more supportive of capitalism 85% – 15% and Biden voters preferred capitalism 67% - 32%.

The majority also favored smaller government with fewer services 53% over larger government with more services 46%. Trump voters favored smaller government 68% to 31 % while Biden voters prefer larger government 61% to 37%.

Regarding the economy 59 percent think that the economy is still in recession, while 41% say it's not. However, voters are more closely split in their perception that it's getting better 48% to getting worse 52%. Trump voters say that the economy is getting better 75% - 25 %, while Biden voters believe the economy is getting worse 77% - 23%.

Almost half the voters, 48%, say that the media coverage was unfair and biased against President Trump. Only 36% said the media coverage of the race was fair and not biased and only 16% said that it was unfair and biased against Joe Biden. 85% of Trump voters say that the media coverage was unfair and biased against him.

Looking ahead to the presidential primaries in 2024 without either President Trump or Joe Biden, the Republicans are strongly the party of Trump and the Democrats are the party of

Obama. These are the base of their parties. When Democratic primary voters were asked their preference for 2024, the leading candidates are Michelle Obama 25%, Kamala Harris 18%, Pete Buttigieg 8%, Andrew Cuomo 8%, and Alexandria Ocasio-Cortez 6% with others getting less and undecided at 28%.

- Among Republicans the leaders are clearly tied to President Trump, Mike Pence 30% and Donald Trump, Jr., 20%, followed by Nikki Haley 8%, Ted Cruz 5%, and Mitt Romney 5%.

- Others received fewer votes and 21% were undecided.

- Three in ten voters, 29%, followed the president on Twitter, Facebook or Instagram and they voted for the president 60% - 37%.

- If they do not follow the president on social media they voted for Biden 55% - 44%.

- The majority, 52%, watched or followed news reports of the president's rallies and they voted for President Trump 66% - 33%. Four in 10 voters, 39%, never watched or followed the president's rallies and they voted for Biden 76% - 23%.

Voter Fraud and Stolen Election Leanings

On Election Day, before the polls closed, 70% of all voters said that the election would be decided honestly. However, 30% thought that there was significant fraud in the election. Trump voters were more likely to believe that there was fraud, 38%.

Only 22% of Biden voters though there was fraud.

Among Republicans, 37% and Independents 34%, were more likely to think there was significant fraud. Only 20% of Democrats thought that there was fraud. Voters who voted in person on election day, 35%, and voters who voted early in person, 39%, were more likely to say that there was fraud. Voters who voted early by mail only 20% said there was fraud.

Suspicions of fraud seems to have been higher among those who preferred to vote in person.

Among all voters they split the blame for fraud evenly between the parties—Republicans 51%, Democrats 49%. However, it will be interesting how post-election developments may change this perception.

Vote Smart, formerly called Project Vote Smart, is a non-profit, non-partisan research organization that collects and distributes information on candidates for public office in the United States. It covers candidates and elected officials in six basic areas: background information, issue positions (via the Political Courage Test), voting records, campaign finances, interest group ratings, and speeches and public statements.

This information is distributed via their web site, a toll-free phone number, and print publications. The president of the organization since its founding is Richard Kimball. PVS also provides records of public statements, contact information for state and local election offices, polling place and absentee ballot information, ballot measure descriptions for each state (where applicable), links to federal and state government agencies, and links to political parties and issue organizations.

A Serious Georgia Lawsuit Is Filed

The Georgia Supreme Court had previously ruled that challengers to an election don't need to show definitive fraud with particular votes, just that there were enough irregular ballots or violations of election procedures to place doubt in the result as noted in the March 2021 "Media's Entire Georgia Narrative Is Fraudulent, Not Just The Fabricated Trump Quotes" article by Mollie Hemingway in *The Federalist*:

Judges never want to overturn the results of an election, but under Georgia law, the remedy for showing enough problems to cast doubt was that a new election be held. One was already scheduled for early January for Senate runoff races. Trump's lawsuit argued that it appeared votes had come from:

- 2,560 felons.

- 66,247 underage registrants.

- 2,423 people who were not on the state's voter rolls.

- 4,926 voters who had registered in another state after they registered in Georgia, making them ineligible.

- 395 people who cast votes in another state for the same election.

- 15,700 voters who had filed national change of address forms without re-registering.

- 40,279 people who had moved counties without re-registering.

- 1,043 people who claimed the physical impossibility of a P.O. Box as their address.

- 98 people who registered after the deadline, and, among others.

- 10,315 people who were deceased on election day (8,718 of whom had been registered as dead before their votes were accepted).

Unlike so much of the Trump campaign's legal efforts, outside observers agreed that this lawsuit was serious. The 64-page complaint is a linear, cogently presented description of numerous election-law violations, apparently based on hard data. If true, the allegations would potentially disqualify nearly 150,000 illegal votes in a state that Biden won by only 12,000.

But as legitimate as the lawsuit was, it entered a Kafkaesque (or circle jerk) world where it couldn't get heard because the election code in Georgia requires that an election contest has to be served to defendants by the sheriff. The clerk is supposed to quickly give special notice to the relevant sheriffs that it needs to be served, since election lawsuits need extremely quick resolution and require a hearing within 20 days.

Lawyers for Trump had to keep asking the clerk to give that special notice to the sheriffs where the defendants lived. In one case, a county sheriff waited until the end of January of 2021 before asking if he should serve it.

A Circle Jerk of Monumental Proportions

With no hearing in sight, the Trump team—desperate to get to a court date before the Electoral College convened—appealed to the Georgia Supreme Court, asking it to grant immediate review of that interim order slow-walking the case, as well as the judge. That court said they couldn't do anything about the interim order because they lacked final jurisdiction.

They did get a liberal senior judge from Cobb County, Adele Grubbs, to handle the case. She set a date for a hearing of Jan. 8, which was of no help to the Trump team as it was after Jan. 6, when Congress would process the Electoral College vote.

In the midst of all this, the Trump team also had a federal case before Judge Mark Cohen on Jan. 5. That case dealt with the Trump team's view that they had not gotten their day in Fulton County Superior Court, which they perceived as a due process violation.

While he dismissed the case, noting that they'd soon have a hearing before Grubbs, Cohen also noted that the power and authority to do anything about the election dispute lies with Congress, not the court.

This brings us back to Trump's phone calls and we now know that the account of Trump's call to an investigator was based on false quotes. Another call with Raffensperger was also leaked to the press to harm those who opposed Raffensperger's handling of the election, days before another pivotal election.

Much of the angst over the calls was about Trump saying he needed the secretary of state to "find" votes. This was always characterized as him asking Raffensperger to commit fraud or do something unethical, not the intent—which was to find (i.e., locate from the voting records) problematic votes. It even made it into the article of impeachment that Democrats supported.

Anyone familiar with the lawsuit knew Trump was saying his team had already "found" nearly 150,000 irregular or fraudulent votes and simply needed the secretary of state's office to agree. He was saying they didn't need to agree that all 150,000 were bad, just that fewer than 10 percent of them were problematic.

The secretary of state and his team kept asserting that Trump's figures were wrong. Trump's legal team kept asking Raffensperger to provide the state data and information that would enable them to see for themselves. For some reason, Raffensperger and his team have never been willing to share their data or reports.

For months, the Trump team tried desperately to get a hearing in court to make their case, and the court dockets prove that. In fact, they kept getting into trouble for how aggressively they were trying to get a hearing. Trump attorneys were on record saying they wanted the hearing so they might get access to Raffensperger's information. The information was really what they were after.

They issued a statement after the leak to the *Washington Post* saying Raffensperger's office "has made many statements over the past two months that are simply not correct, and everyone involved with the efforts on behalf of the President's election challenge has said the same thing: show us your records on which you rely to make these statements that our numbers are wrong."

Raffensperger's office finally said, after that infamous phone call, that they'd share state data and information "on the condition" that the Trump team drop their lawsuit. They agreed to that. Instead of turning over the data that would settle the issue, Fuchs and Raffensperger issued a press release that said, "on the eve of getting the day in court they supposedly were begging for, President Trump and Chairman David Shafer's legal team folded and voluntarily dismissed their election contests against Secretary of State Brad Raffensperger rather than submit their evidence to a court and to cross-examination." Voting madness!

Georgia Judge Decides to Unseal Absentee Ballots in Fulton County for Review

A judge in Georgia on May 21, 2021 ruled to unseal absentee ballots submitted in the 2020 presidential election. Petitioners in an ongoing case will be able to go to where the ballots are stored in Fulton County, Henry County Superior Court Judge Brian Amero said at the conclusion of a hearing. Amero plans to issue an order soon that will set forth protocols governing a fresh scanning of the ballots, which will be done by county workers while petitioners and their experts observe.

Per a recent May 2021 report "Georgia Judge Decides to Unseal Absentee Ballots in Fulton County for Review" in the *Epoch Times* by Zachary Stieber: A group of voters filed a petition last year asking for a forensic inspection of mail-in ballots that were sent in for the 2020 election. The petition alleged an abnormal vote increase for Democrat presidential candidate Joe Biden and an abnormal reduction in President Donald Trump's tabulation, among other alleged abnormalities.

Amero allowed the petitioners in March access to scanned images of the ballots, but attorneys for the petitioners argued in court that the resolution, 200 dots per inch (DPI), was too low to perform proper analysis. The petitioners asked for images at 600 DPI or higher, and access to the ballots themselves.

David Sawyer, a forensics expert, testified for the petitioners. He said he identified a discrepancy in the number of batches that were received by petitioners and the number that Georgia Secretary of State Brad Raffensperger's office listed as having been examined in a risk-limiting audit. He told the judge that direct access to ballots would be best "because that's the original evidence, and that's the best evidence."

Lawyers for Fulton County and Georgia Attorney General Chris Carr, a Republican, argued that letting the petitioners examine the ballots outside of the presence of county workers would violate federal law. They also said a "citizen audit" wasn't provided for in state law. If the judge allowed such an audit, he should pick the auditing team or allow the parties to reach an agreement on which firms should do the audit, they added.

Amero assured them he was largely of the same mind. "I have no inclination at all to release these ballots to anyone other than the clerk or the county," he said. But he pushed back on the notion that petitioners did not have the ability to get better scans of the ballots or visually inspect them. "That seems to be something that they have the authority and the right to do," he said.

"I have never seen in this case a motion to dismiss from anyone for any reason and in the absence of considering things in that way then this does take the form of a civil case where there is some discovery" under state law, he said.

The parties are scheduled to meet at the Fulton County ballot storage location on May 28.

Raffensperger told *The Epoch Times* via email: "From day one I have encouraged Georgians with concerns about the election in their counties to pursue those claims through legal avenues. Fulton County has a long standing history of election mismanagement that has understandably weakened voters' faith in its system. Allowing this audit provides another layer of transparency and citizen engagement."

14 – Stop the Steal, State Courts & Legislatures Rulings and Maricopa County Audit

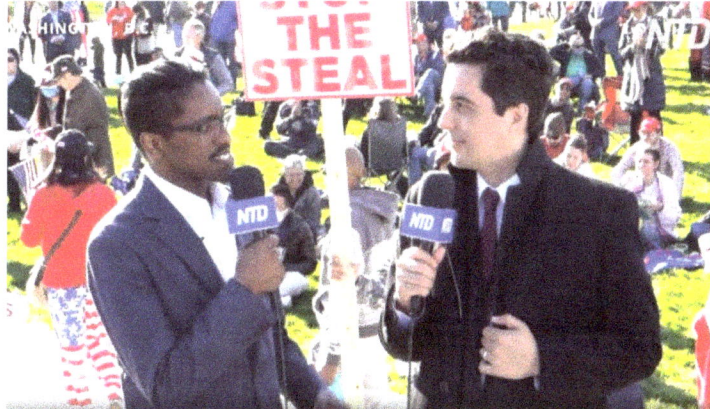

Credit: NTD - Ali Alexander, the "Stop the Steal" organizer (left), speaks to NTD reporter (right) at a peaceful rally in Washington D.C., on Dec. 12, 2020.

Five people died during the January 6, 2021 Capitol Riot, which experts have estimated caused $30 million dollars in damage and could have been prevented by a well prepared and functioning Capitol security force. The death toll and cost of damages still pales in comparison to the 2020 BLM and Antifa instigated riots as covered in detail in *Crime Rate Madness*.

Even though then President Trump offered to send additional security forces ahead of the January 6th session of Congress that was held to validate the election, his offer was denied—and the storming of the Capitol and the violence and loss of life that took place there without a doubt are a dark stain on American history as noted above—and also because it also deprived the American people of a substantive discussion in Congress about election integrity in America.

FBI Director Christopher Wray said the agency divided the pro-Trump ralliers and those who engaged in rioting during the Capitol breach into three different groups (which I will refer to as the good, bad, and ugly), while suggesting that the majority of protesters on Jan. 6 were peaceful. The good!

Per Wray, "The first group—the largest group, the group that we need to spend the least time talking about—is peaceful, maybe rowdy, protesters, but who weren't violating the law," he told lawmakers.

The second group consists of individuals who might have come to the rally to peacefully protest but got caught up in the events of the day. Describing these individuals as "opportunistic," Wray noted that breaching the Capitol grounds is "still criminal conduct." The bad!

The third group is the smallest "numerically," and they "breached the Capitol grounds and engaged in violence against law enforcement, who attempted to disrupt the members of Congress and the conduct of their constitutional responsibilities," Wray went on to say.

The Truth About the 'Stop the Steal' Organization and Its Rallies

Ali Alexander is the national organizer of the "Stop the Steal" movement (not the fringe groups that are the focus of fake news media) and he spoke to NTD's "Focus Talk" about, "What we're working on right now is lobbying members in the House and members in the Senate."

Alexander said, "that at least three senators will stand with President Donald Trump and that he has talked to more than 30 House members that will also object to the certification of the Electoral College votes on Jan. 6, which will trigger a debate over the voter fraud allegations."

He emphasized that the constitutional process is of utmost importance and that they want to urge Congress to stand for voter integrity. "It's a time of the people, the people want their Congress to do the right thing," said Alexander. "We don't care about bureaucratic deadlines or silly judges, what we care about is that the right thing is done, and we all know that there's voter fraud in this country, all of us."

Alexander and the Stop the Steal movement were not responsible for the Capitol Riot, where more than 400 people have been charged in connection to the breach on January 6, 2021, which occurred as members of Congress were voting to certify the 2020 presidential election.

John Earle Sullivan, a political activist who reportedly attended Black Lives Matter protests in 2020 and who allegedly agitated rioters inside the Capitol, was charged with weapons charges, and the Department of Justice (DOJ) seized $90,000 from the Utah man who sold footage of rioter Ashli Babbitt being shot during the Capitol breach, according to court filings per the May 2021 "DOJ Seizes $90,000, Charges Black Lives Matter Supporter Who 'Stormed Capitol,' Sold Footage to News Outlets" Jack Phillips on the *Epoch Times*.

According to the court filings, Sullivan portrayed himself as an independent journalist who was reporting on the chaos, but he actually encouraged other participants to "burn" the building and engage in violence.

Second Trump Impeachment Trial For Incitement Is a Distraction

Per Robert Natelson, a former constitutional law professor, is a senior fellow in constitutional jurisprudence at the Independence Institute in Denver, and a senior adviser to the Convention of States movement, "The public furor over the illegal Capitol break-in is a diversion. Those who tried to turn the Capitol incident into a President impeachment for incitement knew there's no time, or grounds, for impeachment."

Per Natelson's January 2021 article "Don't Be Fooled! Don't Let Them Divert Us From Ensuring Electoral Integrity!" in the *Epoch Times*: They also know then President Donald Trump didn't incite illegal behavior. Anyone can see that by reading his allegedly objectionable words below, courtesy of Snopes, a left-leaning website. Here is verbatim what Trump said during his speech. You be the judge:

"After this, we're going to walk down—and I'll be there with you—we're going to walk down, we're going to walk down—anyone you want, but I think right here—we're going to walk down to the Capitol, and we're going to cheer on our brave senators and congressmen and women.

And we're probably not going to be cheering so much for some of them. Because you'll never take back our country with weakness, you have to show strength, and you have to be strong. We have come to demand that Congress do the right thing, and only count the electors who have been lawfully slated—lawfully slated. I know that everyone here will soon be marching over to the Capitol building to peacefully and patriotically make your votes heard today. …

"The best is yet to come. We're going to, we're going to walk down Pennsylvania Avenue—I love Pennsylvania Avenue—and we're going to the Capitol. And we're going to try and give—the Democrats are hopeless, they never vote for anything, not even one vote—but we're going to try to give our Republicans, the weak ones because the strong ones don't need any of our help; we're going to try and give them the kind of pride and boldness that they need to take back our country. So let's walk down Pennsylvania Avenue."

The goals of this unsapient and Democratic Party diversion apparently are to (1) move public attention away from election irregularities and the legitimacy of the Biden presidency, (2) forestall honest investigation into those irregularities, and (3) prevent corrective action. But we mustn't be diverted states Natelson:

Instead, as constitutionally bound Americans, we can adopt changes that will reduce greatly many of the problems that bedeviled the 2020 election and also begin to ameliorate dysfunctions and divisions in our political system by focusing on state legislatures.

Problems In Governance Are Acknowledged Across the Political Spectrum

Irregularities in the 2020 presidential election left the winner in doubt in six states. In that situation, federal law (3 U.S.C. Section 2) explicitly invites the state legislature to arrange for appointment of their state's presidential electors.

All six contested states were certified for the Democratic ticket. In five of those states, the legislative assemblies were controlled by Republicans. Yet none acted. Most failed to investigate.

Surprised? No. A pattern of state legislative abdication has prevailed for more than a century, and like other members of the public, are unaware that the Constitution places them near the center of our political system.

There's no hope of making much progress at the federal level, where the system—and perhaps the elections themselves—has been corrupted. In Washington, the power and incentives are stacked against the responsible and productive Americans who make up our country's backbone.

In most states, the playing field is very different than at the federal level. Moreover, in the 2020 election, while Donald Trump reluctantly conceded victory to Joe Biden, at the state level conservatives were gaining. Republicans (admittedly, not all of whom are conservative) now control both legislative chambers and the governorship in 23 states. In at least seven more, they control both houses of the legislature without the governorship."

And while it's not widely known, state legislatures are near the heart of our constitutional system. They have power to force changes in federal operations—in some cases, even without the consent of their governors. What follows are the four agenda items proposed by Rob Natelson to improve and enhance election and voter integrity:

Item 1: Constituents must educate state lawmakers about their constitutional role and motivate them to fulfill that role. As mentioned above, state lawmakers have important constitutional responsibilities. They govern the presidential election process, they have much to say about the congressional election process, and they can control the constitutional amendment procedure. State legislatures have been neglecting these duties. That must change.

Item 2: Reform state election laws. After the 2020 election, the need for this is evident. The details to be addressed vary from state to state (and the *National Review* and others have clearly listed them). However, it's clear that the promiscuous use of mail-in ballots is dysfunctional, as well as unconstitutional. That being said, it's clear that election law change can't cure all corruption. That's the reason for Item 3.

Item 3: This applies in states with histories of big-city or university town-vote corruption. These include six swing states with Republican legislatures: Arizona, Georgia, Michigan, North Carolina, Pennsylvania, and Wisconsin. Their legislatures should adopt resolutions whereby those states' presidential electors are chosen by congressional district rather than at large.

Two states—Maine and Nebraska—do this already, and the Supreme Court has upheld that approach. The consent of the governor isn't necessary. This reform would effectively cage local corruption to a few congressional districts rather than allow it to infect the presidential election in the entire state.

Item 4: Persuade as many state legislatures as possible to endorse the "Convention of States" application for constitutional amendments. These amendments would impose federal term limits and restrain federal power. Over the long term, this is the most important of the four agenda items.

Certain problems in our current system of governance are acknowledged across the political spectrum:

- Severe division among citizens; enormous special interest influence.
- Poorly functioning, and sometimes abusive, government.
- Excessive centralization.
- An oligarchy ("deep state" or "swamp") not subject to popular control.

Only a convention of states—or, in the Constitution's phrase, a "convention for proposing amendments"—would have both the will and power to propose constitutional reforms to address those problems. Only the state legislatures can ensure a convention is called.

Each of those four goals is achievable on a playing field where sapient Americans, rather than so-called "progressive" interests, have the advantage. And each is a relatively small change with big potential effects.

2020 – By the Numbers: President Donald Trump's Failed Efforts to Overturn the Election

President Donald Trump spent much of the 2020 presidential campaign insisting that he could only lose if the election was rigged against him, and he has spent nearly every day since his defeat claiming his dire predictions of fraud had come to pass reports the January 2021 article "By the numbers: President Donald Trump's failed efforts to overturn the election" by William Cummings, Joey Garrison and Jim Sergent of *USA Today*.

But just as he cried foul before a single vote was cast–something he also did in 2016–Trump has maintained he was robbed of victory without any credible evidence to support that belief. Despite assurances from his own departments of Justice and Homeland Security that no serious fraud occurred, Trump has raged against the election result and mounted a relentless campaign to reverse President-elect Joe Biden's 306-232 Electoral College win.

Biden finished with a record 81,281,502 votes nationally, defeating Trump in the popular vote by a sizable 7 million votes. With 51.3% of the national popular vote, Biden won with the highest share of the vote for a challenger of an incumbent president since Franklin D. Roosevelt in 1932. Trump won 46.8% of the vote nationally.

The president and his allies filed 62 lawsuits in state and federal courts

Trump and allies filed scores of lawsuits, tried to convince state legislatures to take action, organized protests and held hearings. When the last lawsuit was judicated, none of it worked.

The president and his allies filed 62 lawsuits in state and federal courts seeking to overturn election results in states the president lost, according to Marc Elias, a Democratic election lawyer who is tracking the outcomes. Out of the 62 lawsuits filed challenging the presidential election, 61 have failed, according to Elias.

Some cases were dismissed for lack of standing and others based on the merits of the voter fraud allegations. The decisions have come from both Democratic-appointed and Republican-appointed judges–including federal judges appointed by Trump.

State Supreme Courts in Arizona, Nevada, and Arizona each rejected or declined to hear Trump's appeals to overturn results in those states, while the Pennsylvania and Michigan supreme courts denied multiple lawsuits.

A Trump-appointed federal judge in Texas dismissed a lawsuit from Rep. Louie Gohmert, R-Texas, that argued Vice President Mike Pence has the conditional power to decide which states' Electoral College votes to count. Another federal judge dismissed a lawsuit filed by voters in Wisconsin, Pennsylvania, Georgia, Michigan, and Arizona that argued state legislatures should have met after the election to certify votes.

These were 60th and 61st losses for the Trump team and they had one lone victory and it was a small one. A Pennsylvania judge sided with the Trump campaign, ruling that voters could not go back and "cure" their ballots if they failed to provide proper identification three days after the election. The ruling affected few votes and did not change the outcome in Pennsylvania, which Biden won by 81,660 votes.

The vast majority of the lawsuits were in six pivotal battleground states that Biden won: Arizona, Georgia, Michigan, Nevada, Pennsylvania, and Wisconsin. Trump won five of the states four years ago in his victory over Hillary Clinton, but Biden flipped each to the Democratic column.

The U.S. Supreme Court twice refused to take up Trump-endorsed lawsuits that sought to overturn the results of the Nov. 3 election.

In a one-sentence denial, the Supreme Court on Dec. 8, 2020, rejected a request from Pennsylvania Republicans that sought to overturn Biden's win in the state. The challenge led Rep. Mike Kelly, R-Pennsylvania, claimed that the Republican-led state legislature's expansion of absentee voting violated the state's constitution.

Three days later, the Supreme Court refused to let Texas challenge the election results in four battleground states critical to Trump's defeat. The court said Texas did not demonstrate "a judicially cognizable interest in the manner in which another state conducts its elections."

The number of electoral votes that changed as the result of Trump's effort was zero and in the end, Biden and Harris were inaugurated and sworn in as the next POTUS and VPOTUS at noon on January 20, 2021 by Chief Justice John G. Roberts.

A 2020 Election Redo in 4 States? Here Are the Details About Texas Lawsuit

The state of Texas filed an unprecedented motion with the U.S. Supreme Court in December 2020, asking for leave to file a complaint with the court against the states of Pennsylvania, Georgia, Michigan, and Wisconsin over the 2020 presidential election.

Per the December 2020 "A 2020 Election Redo in 4 States? Here Are the Details About Texas Lawsuit" by Hans von Spakovsky for The Daily Signal: The motion alleges that changes made in election rules governing absentee ballots in those states by "non-legislative actors" violated the Constitution and "cumulatively preclude knowing who legitimately won the 2020 election and threaten to cloud all future elections."

In a nutshell, Texas is saying these four states' elections were unconstitutional—and therefore, invalid. The Lone Star State's complaint, filed by state Attorney General Ken Paxton, asks that Georgia, Pennsylvania, Michigan, and Wisconsin to conduct new elections to determine their electors for the Electoral College.

The motion filed by Texas includes the 41-page complaint and a 35-page brief making the legal arguments for why the Supreme Court should grant approval of the filing of the lawsuit, since Article III, Section 2 of the Constitution gives the Supreme Court—not lower federal courts—original jurisdiction over "controversies between two or more States."

The complaint goes into great detail describing what happened in each state as follows:

Pennsylvania: The complaint accuses Pennsylvania Secretary of State Kathy Boockvar of, among other things, "without legislative approval, unilaterally abrogating" Pennsylvania statutes that require "signature verification for absentee or mail-in ballots." These changes were "not ratified" by the Pennsylvania legislature.

Georgia: Similarly, the complaint describes how Georgia's Secretary of State, Brad Raffensperger, also "without legislative approval, unilaterally abrogated Georgia's statute governing the signature verification process for absentee ballots."

Michigan: The complaint states that Michigan Secretary of State Jocelyn Benson "abrogated Michigan election statutes related to absentee ballot applications and signature verification."

Wisconsin: Lastly, the Wisconsin's elections commission made similar changes in state laws without the permission of the legislature that "weakened, or did away with, established security procedures put in place by the Wisconsin legislature to ensure absentee ballot integrity."

The complaint catalogues these and numerous other changes made in all four states by government officials, not the state legislatures (which is in violation of the Constitution). According to Texas, these "amendments to States' duly enacted election laws" violated the Electors Clause of the Constitution, Art. II, § 1, Cl. 2, which vests "state legislatures with plenary authority regarding the appointment of presidential electors."

In other words, while the state legislatures have the authority to set the rules for presidential elections in their states—and thus could have made all of these changes if they had wanted to—other government officials in those states, including judges, did not have the constitutional authority to make these changes.

This is an "unprecedented lawsuit," and the Supreme Court may be extremely leery and disinclined to take any actions regardless of the merits that could upset the results of a presidential election. Texas does a good job of describing what happened in each state and why the actions of government officials making unauthorized, unilateral changes in the rules may have violated the Constitution and affected the outcome of the election.

But by almost any measure, this is the legal equivalent of a Hail Mary pass. While the questions raised are serious ones, the Supreme Court rejected the lawsuit on December 11, 2020. Nonetheless, as Texas points out, these issues will likely be repeated in future elections. If the Supreme Court does not take up these issues now, they may well have another opportunity in the future.

Supreme Court's Decision Not to Hear Elections Cases Could Have Serious Repercussions

With the U.S. Supreme Court's "baffling" refusal in March 2021 to grant review of the Pennsylvania election cases that had been appealed to the justices, the majority of the court is—to quote Justice Clarence Thomas' dissent—"leaving election law hidden beneath a shroud of doubt" and "inviting further confusion and erosion of public confidence" in our elections as noted in the February 2021 "Supreme Court's Decision Not to Hear Elections Cases Could Have Serious Repercussions" article by The Heritage Foundation writers and researchers Zack Smith and Hans von Spakovsky.

Who can forget the chaos of this past election season? Attempts to change election rules and procedures began before any ballots had even been cast. In some cases, state executive branch officials changed the rules; in others, judges made the changes. But under the U.S. Constitution, neither had the authority to do so.

As Justice Neil Gorsuch wrote in late 2020, "[t]he Constitution provides that state legislatures—not federal judges, not state judges, not state governors, not other state officials—bear primary responsibility for setting election rules … [a]nd the Constitution provides a second layer of protection, too. If state rules need revision, Congress is free to alter them."

Notable instances during and after the 2020 election where this procedure wasn't followed occurred in Pennsylvania. There, the state's Supreme Court ordered election officials to accept late-arriving mail-in ballots up to three days after Election Day and to count them even if they didn't have a postmark showing they had been mailed by Election Day.

What's particularly problematic about the Pennsylvania Supreme Court's decision is that the Pennsylvania legislature had explicitly decided not to extend the ballot-receipt deadline past Election Day.

The authority the Pennsylvania court cited for overriding state law was what Thomas called a "vague clause" in the state's constitution providing that elections "shall be free and equal." Apparently, requiring absentee ballots to be received by Election Day is somehow not a "free and equal" election, but allowing ballots to come in three days after Election Day is a "free and equal" election.

That Was the Ludicrous Justification Used By the State Court

The U.S. Supreme Court was asked to enjoin (or stop) the Pennsylvania Supreme Court's ruling from taking effect, but the justices deadlocked 4-4 because Justice Ruth Bader Ginsburg had passed away and Justice Amy Coney Barrett had not yet joined the court. Thus, the decision remained in place.

Later, the state Republican Party and others asked the high court to hear the cases on the merits, but to do so on an expedited basis. Again, the court declined—meaning, the cases proceeded according to the court's normal procedures, which has now led to it declining to review the case at all.

That prompted blistering dissents from Justices Thomas and Samuel Alito, with Justice Gorsuch joining Alito's dissent.

Disappointingly, neither Justice Brett Kavanaugh, nor Barrett joined them in getting the court to accept a very important case on a fundamental issue, as described by Alito, that could affect all future federal elections and has divided the lower courts; namely, "whether the Elections or Electors Clause of the United States Constitution … are violated when a state court holds that a state constitutional provision overrides a state statute governing the manner in which a federal election is to be conducted."

They did not, of course, explain why. Should the issue arise again, as seems likely, perhaps Kavanaugh and Barrett will be less reticent to take up the issue then. One can only hope.

The election may be over, but Thomas pointed out that the court now had even more reason to hear this case because the 8th Circuit Court of Appeals had reached the opposite result from the Pennsylvania Supreme Court and had enjoined the Minnesota secretary of state from extending the ballot-receipt deadline that state's legislature had set.

Thomas made the commonsense point: "Unclear rules threaten to undermine [the electoral system]. They sow confusion and ultimately dampen confidence in the integrity and fairness of elections." That shouldn't be controversial, but apparently it is," Thomas went on to say.

Officials Dispute Who Has Authority To Set Or Change Those Rules

An election system lacks clear rules when, as here, different officials dispute who has authority to set or change those rules. This kind of dispute brews confusion because voters may not know which rules to follow. Even worse, with more than one system of rules in place, competing candidates might each declare victory under different sets of rules.

According to Justice Thomas, the country was "fortunate that the Pennsylvania Supreme Court's decision to change the receipt deadline for mail-in ballots does not appear to have changed the outcome in any federal election. … But we may not be so lucky next time."

In fact, he pointed out that the Pennsylvania Supreme Court's decision to change another rule did make a difference in a state election. The state Supreme Court "nullified" a state law requiring a voter to write the date on his mail-in ballot. One candidate for a state Senate seat was the winner under the applicable state law, but her opponent was declared the winner under the "contrary rule—that violated state law—announced by the Pennsylvania Supreme Court."

As Thomas said in his spirited dissent, "If state officials have the authority they have claimed, we need to make it clear. If not, we need to put an end to this practice now before the consequences become catastrophic." The Heritage Foundation and the SAPIENT Being agree.

We also agree with Thomas that "because the judicial system is not well suited to address these kinds of questions in the short time period available immediately after an election, [the court] ought to use available cases outside that truncated context to address these admittedly important questions."

Justice Alito agreed, saying that now that "the election is over," there was "no reason for refusing to decide the important questions that these cases pose."

These cases seemed to provide the perfect opportunity for the court to do so. Yet, it inexplicably declined the opportunity. Thomas ended with a sharp rejoinder to his colleagues:

One wonders what this Court waits for. We failed to settle this dispute before the election, and thus provide clear rules. Now we again fail to provide clear rules for future elections. The decision to leave election law hidden beneath a shroud of doubt is baffling. By doing nothing, we invite further confusion and erosion of voter confidence. Our fellow citizens deserve better and expect more of us. I respectfully dissent.

While we all hope Thomas' words don't prove to be prophetic, they may well be. By refusing to take these cases, the Supreme Court is—for the time being anyway—giving state government officials free rein to make unauthorized changes in election rules and to override election laws set by state legislatures.

Even if states set clear rules well in advance of their next elections by enacting commonsense reforms (as many Republican law makers are now doing) to protect the integrity of their electoral processes, those rules may be voided by partisan officials with no respect for the Constitution and the rule of law.

2020 Election: Justice Dept. Finds No Evidence of Fraud to Alter Election Outcome

In the most prominent break from President Donald Trump's attempt to overturn the election, Attorney General William Barr said December 1, 2020 that the Justice Department has not found evidence of widespread voter fraud that would change the outcome of the vote.

Barr's comments in an interview with The Associated Press represented an especially public retreat from Trump's repeated claims of voter fraud by one of the president's closest allies in the administration. He said federal prosecutors and the FBI had reviewed specific complaints, but they have uncovered no evidence that would change the outcome of the election.

Per the December 2020 article "Attorney General Barr: Justice Dept. finds no evidence of fraud to alter election outcome" by Kevin Johnson of *USA Today* with Associated Press contributing, "To date, we have not seen fraud on a scale that could have affected a different outcome in the election," Barr told the AP, even as Trump continued to pursue legal challenges to an election he has yet to concede to President-elect Joe Biden.

Barr's remarks prompted a swift response from Trump's legal team, led by Rudy Giuliani and Jenna Ellis. "With all due respect to the Attorney General, there hasn't been any semblance of a Department of Justice investigation," Giuliani and Ellis said in a written statement. "We have gathered ample evidence of illegal voting in at least six states, which they have not examined ...

"Again, with the greatest respect to the Attorney General, his opinion appears to be without any knowledge or investigation of the substantial irregularities and evidence of systemic fraud," the Trump attorneys said.

Barr's remarks were also striking since he had raised the prospect of widespread fraud prior to the election as a result of the increased switch to mail-in ballots during the coronavirus pandemic because voters feared casting their ballots in person.

As recently as a week after the election, with Trump scrambling to contest the victory claimed by Biden, the attorney general issued a two-page memorandum authorizing federal prosecutors to pursue allegations of voting irregularities before election results have been certified. The action bucked decades of Justice Department policy that prohibited interventions that could influence election results. And it opened the department to claims of partisan interference that could delay the traditional post-election transfer of power, prompting rebukes from outside and inside the department.

The most stinging admonishment, however, came from the Justice Department's own director of the Election Crimes Branch, Richard Pilger, who resigned his post shortly after Barr issued the directive.

The Trump campaign team led by Giuliani has alleged a widespread conspiracy by Democrats to dump millions of illegal votes into the system. They have filed multiple lawsuits in battleground states alleging that partisan poll watchers didn't have a clear enough view at polling sites in some locations and therefore something illegal must have happened. The claims have been repeatedly dismissed including by Republican judges who have ruled the suits lacked evidence. Local Republicans in some battleground states have followed Trump in making similar claims.

Trump has railed against the election in tweets and interviews, though some members of his own administration has said the 2020 election was the most secure ever. So many contradictions in so many different ways! Too many voter fraud and election irregularities investigation have not yet concluded as of the May 2021 publication of *Voting Madness*. So much more still needs to be reported on, evaluated, and said.

Arizona's Maricopa County Recount and Audit

The May 2021 Maricopa County ballot recount comes after two election audits found no evidence of widespread fraud throughout the state of Arizona. However a faction of Arizona Republicans is actively feuding with the GOP-led Arizona Senate over the audit of the 2020 presidential election results in Maricopa County, with county officials battling Senate President Karen Fann over claims of "serious issues" uncovered by examiners as per the May 2021 "Sparks Fly in Arizona Recount" *Newsmax* article by Brian Trusdell.

The rhetorical war has been brewing since December when the Arizona Senate decided to audit election results from only Maricopa County, whose population of approximately 4.5 million represents more than 60% of the state's residents and whose registered Republicans outnumber Democrats by more than 100,000 as of last October 2020.

Joe Biden defeated Trump by more than 45,000 votes in the county, which resulted in an 10,000-vote victory statewide for Biden. County officials went to court to block the Senate from taking control of election records and equipment needed to conduct the audit, *The New York Times* reported.

The Maricopa County board is also controlled by a Republican majority of four with just one Democrat member. The battle escalated in May 2021 when auditors sought, and the Senate threatened with more subpoenas to enforce, passwords and other access to computers, routers, and other equipment that Dominion Voting Systems refused to provide.

The most recent flare-up ignited when Fann sent a letter May 12. 2021 to the Maricopa County Board of Supervisors complaining of the county's failure to comply with the first round of subpoenas. Auditors also had discovered problems regarding a chain of custody with ballots and evidence of database files being deleted from the election management computer, Phoenix ABC affiliate KNXV reported.

Jack Sellers, the Maricopa County Board of Supervisors chairman, quickly released a statement refuting the claims, and accused the firm hired by the Senate to conduct the audit, Sarasota, Florida-based CyberNinjas, as "in over their heads."

Critics of CyberNinjas note the firm has little experience in conducting election audits and members of the firm have made partisan statements. Dominion Voting Systems, contracted by the county to conduct the election, also has blasted the company, claiming it is not certified by the federal Election Assistance Service and that it has "demonstrated incompetence."

Since the election, no evidence has surfaced suggesting the voting software was manipulated in Arizona or elsewhere. Arizona auditors appear to be focused on missing and potentially fraudulent mail-in ballots.

Besides Maricopa County Recorder Stephen Richer's statement, the county board of supervisors met on May 17, 2021, and declared they would not comply with the Senate's demands. "This board is done explaining anything," Sellers said after a special meeting of the five-member board "People's ballots and money are not make-believe. It's time to be done with this craziness and get on with this county's critical business."

A forensic auditor helping conduct an audit of 2020 election machines in Arizona's largest county disputed on May 20, 2020, reports claiming he backtracked on allegations that files were deleted from one of the machines.

"My testimony on May 19th before the AZ Senate is being taken out of context by some media outlets. To confirm: the 'Databases' directory on the EMS Primary Server WAS deleted containing the voting databases. I was able to recover the deleted databases through forensic data recovery processes," Ben Cotton, founder of CyFIR, said in a statement emailed to *The Epoch Times* by the audit's liaison.

Arizona Secretary of State Katie Hobbs (D) advised Maricopa County officials to replace all voting machines that were turned over to the private contractor carrying out an audit of the 2020 presidential election.

A poll by HighGround Inc., an Arizona public affairs firm, found that 78% of Arizona Republicans believe fraud was a factor in Biden's victory, a figure backed up by other national polls showing strong GOP support for such claims.

15 – The Unsapient H.R. 1 the "For the People Act" vs. the Sapient Convention of States Movement

Credit: Business Insider.

There are many vulnerabilities in the American election system they need to be fixed. Now! Unfortunately, H.R. 1—the "For the People Act of 2021," which recently passed in the House without a single Republican vote and is now before the Senate in June 2021 as S. 1—are not the way to do it.

Indeed, H.R. 1 and S. 1would make things much worse, usurping the role of the states, wiping out basic safety protocols, and mandating a set of rules that would severely damage the integrity of the election process. This chapter will cover in more detail the pros and cons of the bills and use and focus on H.R. 1 as a working example.

If H.R. 1 is not stopped, then Americans may never be able to trust the fairness and credibility of future election outcomes as explained in March 2021 "Election Integrity Is a National Imperative" in The Daily Signal by former Vice-President Mike Pence:

To assure the integrity of future elections, a far better approach is to prod states, which have primary constitutional responsibility for the administration of elections, to fix the holes in their election laws and rules to ensure both eligible voter access and ballot security.

Those are the two essential principles of the election process and, unlike what the left believes, you cannot have one without the other. H.R. 1 would federalize and micromanage the election process administered by the states, imposing unnecessary, unwise, and unconstitutional mandates on the states, and reversing the decentralization of the American election process—which is essential to the protection of our liberty and freedom.

It would implement nationwide the worst changes in election rules that occurred during the 2020 election and go even further in eroding and eliminating basic security protocols that states have in place. The bill would interfere with the ability of states and their citizens to determine the qualifications and eligibility of voters, to ensure the accuracy of voter registration rolls, to secure the fairness and integrity of elections, to participate and speak freely in the political process, and to determine the district boundary lines for electing their representatives.

H.R. 1's proposed changes to election laws do exactly the opposite of creating trust.

Under H.R. 1, no one has to prove they are who they say they are in order to vote. It essentially outlaws voter ID laws and other identity verification procedures. It severely restricts the ability of states to check the eligibility of individuals registering to vote. It prevents states from participating in programs that compare state voter registration lists to detect individuals registered in multiple states. And it keeps them from removing many ineligible voters from their voter rolls.

H.R. 1 would mandate same-day and automatic voter registration and encourage vote trafficking of absentee ballots. It would eviscerate state voter ID laws and limit the ability of states to verify the accuracy of their voter registration lists. This would institutionalize the worst changes in election rules that occurred during the 2020 election. But H.R. 1 would go even further in increasing the security weaknesses inherent in the current "honor" voter registration and voting system that exists in states across the country.

The Facts About H.R. 1: The So-Called "For the People Act of 2021"

H.R. 1 would federalize and micromanage the election process administered by the states, imposing unnecessary, unwise, and unconstitutional mandates on the states, and reversing the decentralization of the American election process—which is essential to the protection of our liberty and freedom as explained by the February 2021 "The Facts About H.R. 1: The "For the People Act of 2021" report from The Heritage Foundation.

It would (among other things) implement nationwide the worst changes in election rules that occurred during the 2020 election; go even further in eroding and eliminating basic security protocols that states have in place; and interfere with the ability of states and their citizens to determine the qualifications and eligibility of voters, ensure the accuracy of voter registration rolls, secure the fairness and integrity of elections, and participate and speak freely in the political process.

H.R. 1 Legislation is Designed to Rig the Election System in Favor of Democratic Politicians

A key law in this regard being pushed by Democrats is H.R. 1, or the "so called" For the People Act of 2021. It passed the Democrat-controlled House in April 2021 on a largely party-line vote of 220–210, with all Republicans voting against it.

The comprehensive scope of the bill prompted House Rules Committee Ranking Minority Member Tom Cole (R-OK) to remark during debate that, "this is a bill that's about preserving the present Democratic majority. It is a bill by the majority, for the majority, and is intended to entrench the majority in power for years to come."

If HR1 is approved in the Senate the individual states and their voters will become the "have nots" while the bureaucrats in Congress will become the "haves." This simple concept violates the sanctity of our Republic and undermines the sapience of our Constitution. Sapient beings cannot let that happen.

The controversial election reform package, which spans nearly 800 pages, seeks to impose requirements on voting procedures across the entire country. Its provisions include transferring authority over how elections are administered to the federal government from states, mandating automatic voter registration in all 50 states, and legalizing nationwide vote-by-mail without the need to provide photo ID to obtain an absentee ballot.

Heritage Action, in one of its key election integrity policy fights, called H.R. 1 "Speaker Nancy Pelosi's signature piece of legislation to rig the election system in favor of Democratic politicians by undermining America's electoral process."

The organization argues that the bill "interferes with the ability of states and their citizens to determine qualifications for voters, to ensure the accuracy of voter registration rolls, to secure the integrity of elections, to participate in the political process, and to determine the district boundary lines for electing their representatives."

H.R. 1 Enshrines Into Law Dubious Electoral Practices That Enable & Encourage Fraudulent Behavior

"The end goal of H.R. 1 is clear—to enshrine into law dubious electoral practices that enable and encourage fraudulent behavior, such as ballot harvesting, false voter registrations, duplicate voting, and ineligible voting," Heritage Action states.

The Biden administration, which has pushed for the bill, praised its passage, saying the legislation is "urgently needed to protect the right to vote and the integrity of our elections, and to repair and strengthen American democracy."

Biden has said he would sign the bill into law if it reached his desk, which may be a tall order since the proposed legislation would need 60 votes to overcome the Senate filibuster, meaning 10 Republicans would have to buy in.

Republicans have roundly denounced the bill, with governors and state legislators across the country saying it would kneecap election integrity efforts. A previous version of the bill had passed the Democrat-controlled House 234–193 at the beginning of the 116th Congress in 2019 but ultimately wasn't taken up in the Republican-controlled Senate.

H.R. 1 would eliminate those safeguards and prevent states from implementing new, needed reforms. Polling shows that large numbers of Democrats did not trust the outcome of the 2016 election and that large numbers of Republicans still do not trust the outcome of the 2020 election.

We have to do everything we can to change that and ensure that the American people, no matter which political party they favor, have confidence in the fairness and security of the election process

States Would Count Every Mail-in Vote Arriving Up to 10 Days after Election Day!

States would be required to count every mail-in vote that arrives up to 10 days after Election Day. States must also allow ballot harvesting—where paid political operatives collect absentee ballots from places such as nursing homes—exposing our most vulnerable voters to coercion and increasing the risk that their ballots will be tampered with.

At the same time, state and local election officials would be stripped of their ability to maintain the accuracy of voter rolls, barred from verifying voter eligibility, and voter ID would be banned from coast to coast.

Congressional districts would be redrawn by unelected, unaccountable bureaucrats. Illegal immigrants and law-abiding American citizens would receive equal representation in Congress. Felons would be able to vote the moment they set foot out of prison.

Leftists and Democrats not only want you powerless at the ballot box, they want to silence and censor anyone who would dare to criticize their unconstitutional power grab.

H.R. 1 is also loaded with ill-advised changes to federal campaign laws that would impose onerous legal and administrative burdens on candidates, civic groups, unions, nonprofit organizations, and ordinary citizens who want to exercise their First Amendment rights to engage in political speech, including on public policy issues that are vital to the life of our nation.

Under H.R. 1, donations to many private organizations would be made public, exposing millions of Americans to the radical left's cancel culture crusade.

Every single proposed change in . .serves one goal, and one goal only: to give Democrats and leftists a permanent, unfair, and unconstitutional advantage in our political system.

H.R. 1 would turn a blind eye to very real problems at the state level, exacerbate existing vulnerabilities, and further undermine the American people's confidence in the principle of "one person, one vote."

Election reform is a national imperative, but under our Constitution, election reform must be undertaken at the state level. Our Founders limited Congress' role in conducting our elections for good reason: They wanted elections to be administered closest to the people, free from undue influence of the national government.

Hidden H.R.1 Horrors That Should Scare All Honest Voters

H.R. 1 mandates the most questionable and abuse-prone election rules nationwide, while banning commonsense measures to detect, deter, and prosecute election fraud as noted in the March 2021 "Hidden HR1 Horrors That Should Spook All Honest Voters" by *Newsmax* writer Larry Bell.

The bill would force states to adopt universal mail-in ballots, early voting, same-day voter registration, online voter registration, and automatic voter registration for any individual listed in state and federal government databases, such as the Department of Motor Vehicles and welfare offices, ensuring duplicate registrations and that millions of illegal immigrants are quickly registered to vote.

Most particularly, the nearly 800-page package is stuffed with an uber-progressive wish-list of provisions that, if passed by the Senate, would institutionalize, and expand conditions surrounding the 2020 elections which have undermined public confidence and produced contested outcomes.

Here is a Summary of H.R. 1 Wish Lists

The Federalization of Elections:

H.R.1 will override a constitutional guarantee that state legislatures, not the federal government, will establish election practices.

Passage of the bill will override all state laws requiring validation of legitimate mail-in voters to be notarized or signed by witnesses from having to submit "any form of identification as a condition of obtaining an absentee ballot," except a signature or "affirmation."

In other words, whereas personal ID verification is required in order to fly on an airline—or to attend a Democratic convention—it is somehow deemed to be an unnecessarily intrusive requirement in exercising a constitutional right and privilege to influence who will represent our electorate.

Delayed and Contested Results:

Such undocumented mail-in ballots would be issued to anyone who requests one with no excuses necessary, and if postmarked in time, late-arriving ballots would continue to be considered valid nationwide for 10 days after "Election Day."

But don't expect the federal government to hold some state elections to even that restriction. New York's 22nd Congressional District didn't determine a victor for 97 days, resulting instead in an "Election Quarter."

An alarming 6.6% of 10,097 late-arriving Pennsylvania 2020 ballots lacked legible postmarks to establish when they were submitted, and a state Senate seat outside Pittsburgh turned on whether, or not, to count mail ballots that voters neglected to date.

One county tallied them. The neighboring county didn't.

Conflicting Federal/State Requirements:

Similar H.R.1 questions hold for state conflicts with other federal mandates. For example, would mail ballots be accepted 10 days late in the race for president, but not for a governor?

The bill also says that convicted felons who have been released from prison can't be denied the right to vote in federal elections. This would seem to be incongruent with the Fourteenth Amendment of the Constitution which allows certain individuals to be barred from voting for "participation in rebellion, and other crimes."

Some felons, however, would still be eligible to vote in state elections. This begs another practical question of whether county election officials would be required to maintain two sets of voter lists and two sets of ballots.

A Ballot Harvesting Bonanza:

H.R.1 would also overrule all state ballot harvesting restrictions, allowing Americans nationwide to "designate any person" to return a vote so long as the carrier "does not receive any form of compensation based on the number of ballots."

The bill also mandates that states "may not put any limit on how many voted and sealed absentee ballots any designated person can return." This will still allow hourly-billed partisan operatives to collect thousands of door-to-door or nursing home votes.

Violating a Separation of Powers:

H.R.1 would allow Congress to create a commission to determine a "code of conduct" for judges of the Supreme Court. This will serve as an open invitation for federal House and Senate partisans to gin up ethics complaints and phony calls demanding recusals from decisions that they believe run counter to their desired outcomes.

We have already watched this ugly and unconstitutional scene play out in a transparently bogus impeachment campaign against Justice Brett Kavanaugh. As a co-equal branch of government, Congress cannot set standards for the actions of another co-equal branch.

First Amendment Encroachments:

The American Civil Liberties Union (ACLU), an organization that most typically supports Democratic Party policies, opposes H.R.1 because many of its provisions would "unconstitutionally impinge on the free speech rights of American citizens and public interest organizations. They will have the effect of harming our public discourse by silencing necessary voices that would otherwise speak out about the public issues of the day."

Among these free speech impingements, H.R.1 gives federal bureaucrats powers to control political speech through a new category of regulations called "campaign-related disbursements" which apply to nonprofit advocacy groups and others interested in communicating about public policy issues.

Such restrictions would include public communications that mention a specific candidate for federal office and attacks or supports that candidate without regard to whether the communication expressly advocates a vote for or against the candidate.

Included are all public communications that meet the current law's definition of "electioneering communications." Radio and TV adds that merely mention a candidate or officeholder by name would be subject to significant new regulatory compliance costs involving all internet political speech that doesn't constitute paid advertising.

Follow the Money:

H.R.1 would create a scheme of public funds to match small political contributions at a 6-to-1 rate, whereby a $200 donation would be eligible get an additional $1,200 from "the government." The match money would come from a 4.75% surcharge on fines and penalties paid by businesses or corporate officers.

Sure, small donors are the salt of democracy. But nevertheless, why should this entitle the recipients for gigantic subsidies paid for by other taxpayers who may very well strongly disagree with their policies and qualifications?

Incidentally, the top-five list for share of funds coming in from small donors includes two socialists, Alexandria Ocasio-Cortez, and Bernie Sanders.

No, despite its lofty-sounding moniker, the "For the People Act," is not about people like you and me. Rather, it is for politicians who are bent upon seizing powers to limit our constitutional rights and control us.

The Sapient Solution Is a Convention of the States

For more than 80 years, Americans who love their country have been fighting a defensive political battle to preserve the values and traditions that made our country great. But we have suffered one defeat after another. Even the incremental successes of the Reagan and Trump administrations have been wiped away in the "progressive" tide, like sandcastles on the seashore.

The American Founders weren't superhuman, but they were very wise. They understood that the day might come when the federal government exceeded and abused its powers and the electoral system had failed to remedy the problems. So they inserted an additional remedy in the Constitution: the amendment process.

We usually think of constitutional amendments as responses to changed conditions. But the founding generation recognized that we can use amendments to cure constitutional drafting defects, resolve constitutional disputes, overrule bad Supreme Court decisions, and restrain federal power.

As per February 2021 "The Solution Is a Convention of the States" article in the *Epoch Times* by Rob Natelson: In subsequent years, Americans have used the constitutional amendment process to institutionalize other reforms: abolishing slavery, protecting minorities from state oppression, ensuring that women can vote, and imposing term limits on the president.

Each of these amendments was ratified by the requisite three-quarters of the states. Before they could be ratified, however, they had to be proposed. In each case, Congress proposed them. But that was back when the necessary two-thirds of each house of Congress still had some sense of honor.

Today, however, Congress is abusive. It revels in its power. And as an entity, it's mendacious: Despite repeated promises over many years, Congress still refuses to propose amendments favored by towering majorities of the American people. These include amendments requiring a balanced budget except in genuine emergencies, imposing term limits on members of Congress and on the Supreme Court and curbing undemocratic and unfair regulations.

Constitution's Article V Provision Effectively Grants State Legislatures Equal Power With Congress

Anticipating this, the Founders included in the Constitution's Article V a provision effectively granting state legislatures equal power with Congress to propose amendments. Upon the "applications" (resolutions) of two-thirds of the state legislatures, Congress must call "a Convention for proposing Amendments." This is a task force of state delegations with authority to propose pre-specified amendments that Congress refuses to propose.

A convention for proposing amendments is a type of "convention of the states"—a very old mechanism employed many times for other purposes. However, special-interest groups have prevented such a convention from being used to formally propose constitutional amendments. They have done so primarily through an effective disinformation campaign that began during the 20th century.

In the 1970s, it appeared that the states might force a convention to reverse liberal-activist Supreme Court decisions on a wide range of subjects. (The most famous is the abortion case of *Roe v. Wade*.) Liberal establishment figures—academics, politicians, "journalists," and others— were determined to prevent the American people from overriding the court. So they decided to frighten people away from the convention route by publicizing scare stories.

They claimed, for example, that a convention of states would be almost unprecedented and that its procedures and composition were unknown. They simultaneously argued both that it would be an uncontrollable "constitutional convention" and that Congress could control it.

Mainstream media outlets, particularly *The New York Times* and The Washington Post, readily spread these falsehoods.

Today, the campaign continues, largely carried on by groups funded by progressive financier George Soros. Left-wing professors, none of whom has ever published any scholarly research on the subject, work with these groups. They use their unique access to the mainstream media to publicize their disinformation. A handful of naïve conservatives provide them political "cover" on the right.

In 2009, Rob Natelson started researching the Constitution's provision for a "convention for proposing amendments" and published his conclusions in scholarly articles, thereby subjecting them to the review of other academics—several of whom have confirmed his core findings.

Since Natelson began publishing his research, more state lawmakers have come to understand why we need a convention. Indeed, a majority of state legislatures have now adopted "applications" (resolutions) to force Congress to call one. Resolutions of this kind need not be signed by the governor.

Perhaps the most prominent convention-advocacy group today is the "Convention of States" movement. It urges state legislatures to pass applications for a convention limited to proposing amendments by:

- Restraining federal power.
- Imposing fiscal restraints.
- Adopting term limits on federal officials.

Of course, any proposed amendments would have to be ratified by three-quarters of the states (38) before they became effective.

But once ratified, these amendments can't be reversed by any president, Congress, or federal bureaucrats. As explained above, amendments historically have very long life expectancies, longer even than the original Constitution itself—and this is a step we can encourage state lawmakers to take and that no one in the federal government can block.

By using the Constitution's convention procedure, we can enact the reforms necessary to save the country—and we can make them permanent.

Protecting the Constitution—Or Destroying It

It is foolish to think that the principles of the U.S. Constitution can be compromised without eventually destroying America by continual decay of those principles. The principles of America are established in our Declaration of Independence and our Constitution of the United States. Those who stretch and change the meanings of those documents without the due process for change as defined in those documents are traitors to America.

Our Constitution is what makes the USA a republic. Our republic is what provides the freedoms of religion, speech, and all other freedoms. We are a republic only if we can keep it as long as the contract between we the people and our government-the Constitution-is maintained.

This oath is what is stipulated in the Constitution for our political leaders and military leaders: (I) will to the best of my ability, preserve, protect, and defend the Constitution of the United States.

There is no middle ground. Loyalty must be to the Constitution, to the dream... and not loyalty to political leaders or political parties or political ideology.

We have a republic if all Americans force our leaders to keep the oath that they took to preserve, protect, and defend the Constitution of the United States. If you only believe as Edmund Burke did, that "the only thing necessary for the triumph of evil is for good men (and women) to do nothing... (paraphrased); then sapient constitutionalists need to take action.

Constitutionalism is a compound of ideas, attitudes, and patterns of behavior elaborating the principle that the authority of government derives from and is limited by a body of fundamental law. Constitutionalism is descriptive of a complicated concept, deeply embedded in historical experience, which subjects the officials who exercise governmental powers to the limitations of a higher law. Constitutionalism proclaims the desirability of the rule of law as opposed to rule by the arbitrary judgment or mere fiat of public officials.

It may therefore be said that the touchstone of constitutionalism is the concept of limited government under a higher law.

Protecting the Vote, the Republic, and the Constitution With Constitutionalism

The Constitution is the contract between the government and the people, and it limits the authority of the federal government through a check and balance between the legislative branch, the executive branch, the judicial branch, and the states.

The authority of the federal government is limited by processes defined in the Constitution, which are meant to be cumbersome to slow down the actions of the federal government, and by defining what the federal government can do and cannot do.

The Founding Fathers wisely created a republic, a Constitution, and Bill of Rights intended for most domestic laws to be handled by the individual states.

Americans need to be wary of anyone who would speed legislation through the process, of anyone who would deny a full hearing about actions by our leaders, of anyone who would add powers to the federal government that are not specifically stated in the Constitution, and of anyone who would encroach on the rights of free speech, religious expression, or gun ownership. The last amendment in the Bill of Rights, the Tenth amendment, is clear:

The powers not delegated to the United States by the Constitution, nor prohibited by it to the States, are reserved to the States respectively, or to the people.

The Tenth Amendment is part of the Bill of Rights. It is a right of "we the people" and the individual states. So violations to that amendment are violations to our rights and to the rights of the state governments. Those violations upset the balance of power between the federal government and the states as established in the Constitution.

Today, many supposed government intellectuals think that there are only three elements to the government balance of power-legislative, executive, and judicial. They forget that the states are part of the balance of power, and that those violations to the tenth amendment are no different than violating rights based on race or gender. They are violations to rights and, today, the federal government-the judicial branch, the executive branch, and the legislative branch-are all in violation to the contracted rights of the states and "we the people:'

"We are in a fight for our survival as a Constitutional Republic like no other time since our founding in 1776. The conflict is between supporters of Socialism and Marxism vs. supporters of Constitutional freedom and liberty," stated the letter signed by 124 former generals and admirals, released by Flag Officers 4 America.

From the May 2021 "120 Retired Generals, Military Officers Sign Letter Warning of Conflict Between Marxism and 'Constitutional Freedom'" article by Jack Phillips of the *Epoch Times*: The letter also posited that opposition to proposed bills and laws that would strengthen election initiatives has troublesome implications.

"Election integrity demands insuring there is one legal vote cast and counted per citizen. Legal votes are identified by State Legislature's approved controls using government IDs, verified signatures, etc. Today, many are calling such commonsense controls 'racist' in an attempt to avoid having fair and honest elections," the letter added.

According to the Flag Officers 4 America website, it is a group of former military leaders who "pledged to support and defend the Constitution of the United States against all enemies," who are "domestic" and "foreign."

By now after covering almost 15 chapters—you know who the "domestic enemies" in the eyes of the Constitution are.

Get Politically Involved. Start Early. Be Sapient About It

Today, activists and interest groups recognize that primary elections are where the action is, and they increasingly realize that they need to groom candidacies from the very earliest stages. According to Mark Bauerlein's March 2021 *Epoch Times* article "An America-First George Soros," by the time the primary ballot is printed, it's often too late as explained below:

Political analysts sometimes refer to the process by which candidacies emerge and test their viability as the invisible primary. Although the term is often used to designate pre-primary fundraising, it properly also includes a wider range of activities: candidate recruitment, training, networking, team-building, grassroots cultivation, and more. Compared to electoral dynamics, the invisible primary has received little study and analysis. Yet in recent years, it has changed— and it continues to change, with far-reaching effects.

Per Bauerlein, the Soros strategy of hitting local races fits perfectly with the leftist playbook of institution-conversion by changes in personnel. It says: You don't need to reform an institution to alter its values or philosophy or goals—just get the right people in place and the other transformations will follow. That goes for city councils, school boards, human rights commissions, election bodies, and so on.

Per Bauerlein, with leftist money and strategy planting leftists into lower posts in states and cities across the nation, a Republican governor will have the same Swamp problem President Donald Trump faced every time. November 2016 was a conservative triumph at the top alone. It's all too clear that a wider strategy is needed: a Soros network for the right.

Conservatives, on the other hand, believe that rules and norms hold those institutions to a firm course. They respect traditions and suspect the progressivist impulse to "evolve."

However, using the same Soros analogy of "just get the right people in place and the other transformations will follow" noted in the preceding paragraph—conservatives should be deeply concerned that Generations X Y Z will overwhelm and dominate the voter rolls (which they did in 2020) with their "regressive" ideologies in the name of "so called" Progressivism madness.

Trump has the money and popularity, the energy and charisma, too to reserve these trends. Imagine sapient conservative campaigns starting with:

- Protecting and promoting voter and election integrity by utilizing all the benefits the Constitution has to offer.

- Opposing high school and college curriculums adding the controversial Critical Race Theory and "The 1619 Project."

- Exposing the false narratives and fake news of systemic police brutality and racism and the idiocracy of defunding the police.

- Opposing new corporate progressive and cancel culture policies now implementing implicit bias training and racial quotas.

- Exposing fake news mainstream media, free speech suppression of big tech, and leftist Democratic Party polices (i.e., mediacrats).

The list of maddening issues to address go on and on—but they can only be addressed if you're willing to get involved and take a stance. At the SAPIENT Being there are dozens of issues to choose from and our 50 *MADNESS* series of textbooks can help provide the ammunition to get you started.

Sapient conservatives must show to all of Americans of every race, ethnicity, religion, sexual orientation, political ideology, generation, and so on that the sapient principles of the Constitution transcends all of our uniqueness and qualities that we bring to the American experiment of a Democratic Republic with one unifying and socially cohesive construct that we all know so well:

"I pledge allegiance to the flag of the United States of America, and to the republic for which it stands, one nation under God, indivisible, with liberty and justice for all."

If that pledge means anything to you—you must be the spark to ignite the flame of sapience—or do nothing and become a useful idiot. It's your choice. If the "God" part concerns you—take it out—but keep the rest.

Conclusion

Please keep in mind that *Voting Madness* has only touched upon the many ongoing investigations and disputed topics that will continue to develop after publication in May 2021. We sincerely hope and encourage our readers to contribute to the second edition in the months and years to come with updates and further research.

At the SAPIENT Being, we do not promote and/or demote any particular political party's ideology, policies, and practices—unless they are sapient and/or unsapient in regards to the book topic they impact—such as this one in *Voting Madness*. We do encourage you to protect and validate by following the link in the Appendix to the Voter Integrity Project for their Election Observer Training Program.

Also taken into consideration is if each party is being honest, forthright, and truthful in reporting and promoting their party ideology, policies, and practices; whether or not they protect and strengthen election and voter integrity; plus if they protect and honor the Constitution or if they weaken and destroy them, or parts of it.

As your voyage of sapience concludes with this final chapter, it should be apparent and obvious my now which of the two major political parties in America (at this particularly point in time in 2021) is the defender of election and voter integrity and a champion of the constitution and the democracy and republic it stands for.

It's time for sapient beings of all races, ethnicities, religions, sexual orientations, political ideologies, generations, and so on to recognize the one common denominator we can all agree on and respect as Americans—the Constitution of the United States of America. It's the sustaining article of enlightenment and freedom that nourishes our republic and protects our democracy.

Hold it in high esteem and dig deep if you must—to find the conviction, content of character, and patriotism to lead and fight for the republic, and the democratic principles for which it stands, so that United States of America can continue its self-fulfilling journey as the greatest democracy the world has ever seen or known.

Furthermore, we must never forget it's "we the people" our elected leaders, appointed officials, and governments serve—not the other way around—and that our lasting legacy must shine for our children and grandchildren and all the generations to follow.

Appendix

50 *MADNESS* Textbook Titles: https://www.fratirepublishing.com/madnessbooks
- *Fake News Madness*
- *Crime Rate Madness*
- *Voting Madness*

Ballotpedia: https://ballotpedia.org/Voter_identification_laws_by_state

Convention of States (COS): https://conventionofstates.com/take_action

Election Observer Training Program - Voter Integrity Project: https://voterintegrityproject.com/vip-launches-election-observer-training/

Executive Order on Collecting Information about Citizenship Status in Connection with the Decennial Census, E.O. 13880, July 11, 2019: https://www.whitehouse.gov/presidential-actions/executive-order-collecting-information-citizenship-status-connection-decennial-census/

H.R. 1 – For the People Act of 2021: https://www.congress.gov/bill/117th-congress/house-bill/1/text

H.R. 1 (2021) Studies and Reference Materials - PILF: https://publicinterestlegal.org/reports/

Here is the Evidence - Crowdsourcing Analyzer for Journalists: https://hereistheevidence.com/

HERITAGE FOUNDATION, THE:
- **Destroying the Electoral College - The Anti-Federalist National Popular Vote Scheme:** https://www.heritage.org/sites/default/files/2020-02/LM260.pdf
- **Election Fraud Database:** https://www.heritage.org/voterfraud
- **Election Integrity Articles:** https://www.heritage.org/election-integrity
- **Four Stolen Elections - The Vulnerabilities of Absentee and Mail-In Ballots:** https://www.heritage.org/election-integrity/report/four-stolen-elections-the-vulnerabilities-absentee-and-mail-ballots
- **Heritage Leads the Way to Protect Integrity of Elections:** https://www.heritage.org/election-integrity/impact/heritage-leads-the-way-protect-the-integrity-elections
- **How the Electoral College Protects and Nurtures Our Republic:** https://www.heritage.org/election-integrity/report/how-the-electoral-college-protects-and-nurtures-our-republic
- **Safeguarding the Electoral Process:** https://www.heritage.org/election-integrity/heritage-explains/safeguarding-the-electoral-process
- **Standards for Absentee Ballots and All-Mail Elections: Doing It Right...and Doing It Wrong:** https://www.heritage.org/election-integrity/report/standards-absentee-ballots-and-all-mail-elections-doing-it-rightand-doing
- **The Essential Electoral College:** https://www.heritage.org/electoralcollege
- **The Facts About Election Integrity and the Need for States to Fix Their Election Systems:** https://www.heritage.org/election-integrity-facts

- **The Facts About H.R. 1 - The "For the People Act of 2021":** https://www.heritage.org/election-integrity/report/the-facts-about-hr-1-the-the-people-act-2021
- **The National Popular Vote - Misusing an Interstate Compact to Bypass the Constitution:** https://www.heritage.org/civil-rights/report/the-national-popular-vote-misusing-interstate-compact-bypass-the-constitution
- **Vote Harvesting - A Recipe for Intimidation, Coercion, and Election Fraud:** https://www.heritage.org/sites/default/files/2019-10/LM253_0.pdf

Judicial Watch: https://www.judicialwatch.org/

Navarro Reports, The - Volumes 1, 2 & 3: https://peternavarro.com/the-navarro-report/

Presidential Election Process: https://www.usa.gov/election

Save Our States: https://saveourstates.com/

Semi-Comprehensive List of 2020 Election Fraud Allegations: https://art19.com/shows/the-sharyl-attkisson-podcast/episodes/bc8992f4-d987-43c8-a70e-40ac468975cc

What Happened in Atlanta on Election Night - Timeline of Events on the Night of Nov. 3 at the State Farm Arena in Atlanta: https://infogram.com/timeline-of-events-on-the-night-of-nov-3-at-the-state-farm-arena-in-atlanta-1h9j6qggy0zjv4g?fbclid=IwAR0ZilNxrIpu49MMoViBr2hTcea5l0s-kyOutEn1Cm8lXiMtUH8ssiP9UpY

SAPIENT BEING PROGRAMS:
- **Make Free Speech Again On Campus (MFSAOC) Program:** https://www.sapientbeing.org/programs
- **Sapient Conservative Textbooks (SCT) Program:** https://www.sapientbeing.org/programs
- **World Of Writing Warriors (WOWW) Program:** https://www.sapientbeing.org/programs
- **World Of Writing Warriors (WOWW) Journalism Code of Ethics, Practical Logic & Sapience Guidelines:** https://www.sapientbeing.org/resources

The S.A.P.I.E.N.T. Being: https://www.fratirepublishing.com/books

Thomas More Society - The Legitimacy and Effect of Private Funding in Federal and State Electoral Processes: https://got-freedom.org/wp-content/uploads/2020/12/HAVA-and-Non-Profit-Organization-Report-FINAL-W-Attachments-and-Preface-121420.pdf

Vote Integrity: Data Analytics For Election Integrity by Vote P. Analysis: https://votepatternanalysis.substack.com/people/20957397-vote-integrity

Voter's Defense Manual – 2020 Edition: https://static.votesmart.org/static/pdf/2020_VSDM.pdf

Glossary

Abrogating – To abolish or annul by formal means; to repeal; put aside; cancel; revoke; rescind; nullify: to abrogate a law.

Absentee Ballot Vote Fraud – A person attempts to fill out and turn in an absentee ballot containing false information. For example, this can occur when a person attempts to fill out and turn in an absentee ballot with the name of a false or non-existent voter. The term can extend to manipulation, deception, or intimidation of absentee voters.

Algorithmic unfairness – A social media term describes systematic programing and repeatable errors that create unfair outcomes, such as privileging one arbitrary group of users over others.

Ballot Stuffing – Casting illegal votes or submitting more than one ballot per voter.

Civil Rights Act of 1964 – Outlawed discrimination on the basis of race, color, religion, sex, or national origin, required equal access to public places and employment, and enforced desegregation of schools and the right to vote.

Consent Decree – Is an agreement or settlement that resolves a dispute between two parties without admission of guilt (in a criminal case) or liability (in a civil case).

Democracy – A government in which the supreme power is vested in the people and exercised by them directly or indirectly through a system of representation usually involving periodically held free elections; a political unit that has a democratic government.

Disparate impact – Refers to practices in employment, housing, and other areas that adversely affect one group of people of a protected characteristic more than another.

Electioneering – Ignoring restrictions that usually include limiting the display of signs, handing out campaign literature, water, or soliciting votes within a pre-determined distance of a polling place.

Electoral College – Is the group of presidential electors in the U.S. required by the Constitution to form every four years for the sole purpose of electing the president and vice president.

Ephemeral Experiences – Are brief online moments by search engine Google where information is generated instantaneously, such as search suggestions. They are not stored anywhere and can't be tracked.

Fascism – A political philosophy, movement, or regime (as that of the Fascisti) that exalts nation and often race above the individual and that stands for a centralized autocratic government headed by a dictatorial leader, severe economic and social regimentation, and forcible suppression of opposition; a tendency toward or actual exercise of strong autocratic or dictatorial control.

Felon Vote Fraud – The casting of a ballot by a person convicted of a felony who is not eligible to vote as a result of the conviction.

Filibusters and Cloture – The Senate tradition of unlimited debate has allowed for the use of the filibuster, a loosely defined term for action designed to prolong debate and delay or prevent a vote on a bill, resolution, amendment, or other debatable question. In 1917 the Senate adopted a rule to allow a two-thirds majority to end a filibuster, a procedure known as "cloture." In 1975 the Senate reduced the number of votes required for cloture from two-thirds of senators voting to three-fifths of all senators duly chosen and sworn, or 60 of the 100-member Senate.

Fraud by Election Officials – Manipulation of ballots by officials administering the election, such as tossing out ballots or casting ballots in voters' names, deleting voting data, removing flash drives, altering voting machine settings.

Idiocracy – An idiocracy is a disparaging term for a society run by or made up of idiots (or people perceived as such). Idiocracy is also the title of 2006 satirical film that depicts a future in which humanity has become dumb.

Illiberalism – The 21st century term is used to describe an attitude that is close-minded, intolerant, and bigoted.

Intellectual Humility – A mindset that encompasses empathy, trust, and curiosity, viewpoint diversity gives rise to engaged and civil debate, constructive disagreement, and shared progress towards truth.

Intersectionality – A theoretical framework for understanding how aspects of one's social and political identities might combine to create unique modes of discrimination.

Intervenor Defendant – Is a nonparty who intervenes in a case is called an intervenor. The intervener joins the suit by filing a motion to intervene.

Jim Crow – Racial segregation laws up to 1965, that were enacted and enforced in the South in the late 19th and early 20th centuries by white Southern Democrat-dominated state legislatures to disenfranchise and remove political and economic gains made by blacks during the Reconstruction period.

Judicial Fiat – Refers to an order or a decree especially an arbitrary one.

Libertarian - An advocate of the doctrine of free will; a person who upholds the principles of individual liberty especially of thought and action; a member of a political party advocating libertarian principles.

Mainstream Media (MSM) – Traditional forms of mass media, as television, radio, magazines, and newspapers, as opposed to online means of mass communication.

Marxism – The political, economic, and social principles and policies advocated by Marx and a theory and practice of socialism including the labor theory of value, dialectical materialism, the class struggle, and dictatorship of the proletariat until the establishment of a classless society.

Municipal Elections – Elections for sub-state municipalities, such as county government or city government. Mayors, councilmembers, city attorneys, school boards, and sheriffs are some of the people who may be elected by municipal elections.

Open Inquiry – Is the ability to ask questions and share ideas without risk of censure.

Political Correctness – A term used to describe language, policies, or measures that are intended to avoid offense or disadvantage to members of particular groups in society.

Politiquerias – In the Rio Grande Valley of Texas, for example, ballot harvesters roam Spanish speaking communities, preying on the most vulnerable and limited-English speaking voters and voting their ballots for them.

Preclearance – Is defined as the process of seeking U.S. Department of Justice approval for all changes related to voting.

Progressivism – A political philosophy in support of social reform based on the idea of progress in which advancements in science, technology, economic development, and social organization are vital to improve the human condition.

Republic – A government having a chief of state who is not a monarch and who in modern times is usually a president; a political unit (as a nation) having such a form of government; a government in which supreme power resides in a body of citizens entitled to vote and is exercised by elected officers and representatives responsible to them and governing according to law.

Sapience – Also known as wisdom, is the ability to think and act using knowledge, experience, understanding, common sense and insight. Sapience is associated with attributes such as intelligence, enlightenment, unbiased judgment, compassion, experiential self-knowledge, self-actualization, and virtues such as ethics and benevolence.

Social Justice – A political and philosophical theory which asserts that there are dimensions to the concept of justice beyond those embodied in the principles of civil or criminal law, economic supply and demand, or traditional moral frameworks.

Social Media – Websites and other online means of communication that are used by large groups of people to share information and to develop social and professional contacts.

Socialism – Any various economic and political theories advocating collective or governmental ownership and administration of the means of production and distribution of goods. A system of society or group living in which there is no private property. A system or condition of society in which the means of production are owned and controlled by the state. A stage of society in Marxist theory transitional between capitalism and communism and distinguished by unequal distribution of goods and pay according to work done.

Useful Idiot – Is attributed to Vladimir Lenin. It describes naïve people who can be manipulated to advance a political cause.

Viewpoint Diversity – Viewpoint diversity occurs when members of a group or community approach problems or questions from a range of perspectives.

Vote-Buying – Agreements between voters and others to buy and sell votes, such as a candidate paying voters to vote for him or her.

Voter Impersonation – A person claims to be someone else when casting a vote.

Voter Registration Fraud – Filling out and submitting a voter registration card for a fictional person or filling out a voter registration card with the name of a real person but without that person's consent and forging his or her signature on the card.

Voter Suppression – An artificially created term that unfairly condemns any perfectly legal election reform with which liberal critics disagree. It is a linguistic trick designed to taint reasonable and commonsense safeguards that protect voters by lumping these policies together with illegal activities like poll taxes and literacy tests that did occur in the Democratic South prior to the Civil Rights Act of 1964 and Voting Rights Act of 1965.

Votes Cast in the Names of Deceased People – The name of a deceased person remains on a state's official list of registered voters and a living person fraudulently casts a ballot in that name.

Voting Rights Act of 1965 – The Voting Rights Act of 1965 expanded the 14th and 15th amendments by banning racial discrimination in voting practices. The act was a response to the barriers that prevented African Americans from voting for nearly a century.

References

28.3 Million Mail Ballots Went Missing from 2012 - 2018 Elections. Public Interest Legal Foundation (PILF). April 13, 2020. https://publicinterestlegal.org/press/report-28-million-mail-ballots-went-missing-in-past-decade/.

Adams, J. Christian. "The Myth of 'Voter Suppression'." Inside Sources. March 17, 2020. https://insidesources.com/the-myth-of-voter-suppression/.

Alexander, Rachel. "Is Generation Z more conservative or less conservative than other generations?" Christian Post. October 3, 2019. https://www.christianpost.com/voices/is-generation-z-more-conservative-less-conservative-than-other-generations.html.

Alkhouri, Dana. "Pandemic's mental health burden heaviest among young adults. In a recent survey, almost two-thirds of 18-to-24-year-olds reported symptoms." ABC News. February 21, 2021. https://abcnews.go.com/Health/pandemics-mental-health-burden-heaviest-young-adults/story?id=75811308.

Allegri, Samuel, and Bowen Xiao contributing. "Big Tech Employees and PACs Gave 12 Times More Money to Democrats Than to GOP." April 2, 2021. Epoch Times. https://www.theepochtimes.com/mkt_breakingnews/big-tech-employees-and-pacs-gave-12-times-more-money-to-democrats-than-to-gop-report_3759975.html.

Allegri, Samuel. 'Over a Million People' Will Rally in Washington to Pressure Congress: 'Stop the Steal' Organizer. Epoch Times. December 30, 2020. https://www.theepochtimes.com/over-a-million-people-will-rally-in-washington-to-pressure-congress-stop-the-steal-organizer_3637839.html.

Anomalies in Vote Counts and Their Effects on Election 2020 A Quantitative Analysis of Decisive Vote Updates in Michigan, Wisconsin, and Georgia on and after Election Night. Vote Integrity. Nov 24, 2020. https://votepatternanalysis.substack.com/p/voting-anomalies-2020.

Ball, Molly with reporting by Mariah Espada and Abby Vesoulis. "How COVID-19 Changed Everything About the 2020 Election." Time. August 6, 2020. https://time.com/5876599/election-2020-coronavirus/.

Bauerlein, Mark. "An America-First George Soros." March 21, 2021. Epoch Times. https://www.theepochtimes.com/an-america-first-george-soros_3734799.html.

Bell, Larry. "Hidden HR1 Horrors That Should Spook All Honest Voters." March 3, 2021. Newsmax. https://www.newsmax.com/larrybell/hr1-voting-elections-free-speech/2021/03/03/id/1012267/.

Billingsley, Lloyd. "The Senator Nobody Voted for Has Curious Plan for Joe Biden's America." Epoch Times. April 28, 2021. https://www.theepochtimes.com/the-senator-nobody-voted-for-has-a-curious-plan-for-joe-bidens-america_3788840.html?utm_source=pushengage.

Bozell to Levin: Survey Shows 4.6% of Democrats Would Not Have Voted for Joe Biden Had They Known Hunter Biden Story. The Spectator, November 12, 2020. https://thespectator.info/2020/11/11/bozell-to-levin-survey-shows-4-6-of-democrats-would-not-have-voted-for-joe-biden-had-they-known-hunter-biden-story/.

Carlson, J.R. "The Legitimacy and Effect of Private Funding in Federal and State Electoral Processes." Prepared for Phill Kline: Thomas More Society Authored by Stillwater Technical Solutions (STS). December 14, 2020. https://got-freedom.org/wp-content/uploads/2020/12/The-Legitimacy-and-Effect-of-Private-Funding-in-Federal-and-State-Electorial-Processes-1.pdf.

Carlson, Jeff. *Time* Magazine Details the 'Shadow Campaign' Against Trump. *Epoch Times.* March 11, 2021. https://www.theepochtimes.com/time-magazine-article-points-to-a-controlled-election_3688393.html.

Carpenter, Matt. "Voters Should Have an ID to Vote and States are Leading the Way to Make Sure They Do." Mar. 26, 2021. LifeNews.com. https://www.lifenews.com/2021/03/26/voters-should-have-an-id-to-vote-and-states-are-leading-the-way-to-make-sure-they-do/.

Critical Condition: American Voter Rolls Filled with Errors, Dead Voters, and Duplicate Registrations. Public Interest Legal Foundation (PILF). September 16, 2020. https://publicinterestlegal.org/reports/critical-condition-american-voter-rolls-filled-with-errors-dead-voters-and-duplicate-registrations/.

Cummings, William, Joey Garrison, and Jim Sergent. "By the numbers: President Donald Trump's failed efforts to overturn the election." *USA Today.* Jan. 6, 2021. https://www.usatoday.com/in-depth/news/politics/elections/2021/01/06/trumps-failed-efforts-overturn-election-numbers/4130307001/.

DeSilver, Drew. "Election night marks the end of one phase of campaign 2020 –and the start of another." Pew Research Center. Oct. 28, 2020. https://www.pewresearch.org/fact-tank/2020/10/22/election-night-marks-the-end-of-one-phase-of-campaign-2020-and-the-start-of-another/.

Devlin, Meagan, and Hans von Spakovsky. "Hundreds of Illegal Voters Revealed in Philadelphia." September 24, 2017. The Daily Signal. https://www.dailysignal.com/2017/09/24/hundreds-of-illegal-voters-revealed-in-philadelphia/.

Dinan, Stephen. "Trump cancels voter fraud commission; says cost of legal battles was too much. Orders Homeland Security Department to take up investigation. *The Washington Times.* January 3, 2018. https://www.washingtontimes.com/news/2018/jan/3/donald-trump-dissolves-voter-fraud-commission/.

Fry, Richard. "This may be the last presidential election dominated by Boomers and prior generations." Pew Research Center. August 29, 2016. https://www.pewresearch.org/fact-tank/2016/08/29/this-may-be-the-last-presidential-election-dominated-by-boomers-and-prior-generations/.

Gramlich, John. "What the 2020 electorate looks like by party, race and ethnicity, age, education, and religion." Pew Research Center. October 23, 2020. https://www.pewresearch.org/early-voting-begins-in-florida-5/.

Haq, Masooma. "Sen. Graham Supports Denying Quorum If Democrats End Filibuster." *Epoch Times.* April 22, 2021. https://www.theepochtimes.com/sen-graham-supports-denying-quorum-if-democrats-end-filibuster_3787149.html?utm_source=pushengage.

Hemingway, Mollie. "Media's Entire Georgia Narrative Is Fraudulent, Not Just The Fabricated Trump Quotes." *The Federalist.* March 17, 2021. https://thefederalist.com/2021/03/17/medias-entire-georgia-narrative-is-fraudulent-not-just-the-fabricated-trump-quotes/.

Herman, Marisa. "Morning Consult Exit Poll: More Biden Voters Wanted to Vote Against Trump." *Newsmax.* November 3, 2020. https://www.newsmax.com/politics/trump-biden-election-exit-poll/2020/11/03/id/995221/.

Johnson, Kevin. "Attorney General Barr: Justice Dept. finds no evidence of fraud to alter election outcome." *USA Today.* Dec. 1, 2020. Associated Press contributing. https://www.usatoday.com/story/news/politics/elections/2020/12/01/attorney-general-barr-no-evidence-widespread-election-fraud/3783305001/.

Levine, Jon. "Joe Biden spent decades warning of voter fraud—now called a myth by Dems." *New York Post.* September 19, 2020. https://nypost.com/2020/09/19/biden-spent-years-warning-of-voter-fraud-now-call-a-myth/.

Loudon, Trevor. "Pro-China Communists Working to Mobilize 40 Million New Voters Against Trump." *Epoch Times.* July 22, 2019. https://www.theepochtimes.com/pro-china-communists-working-to-mobilize-40-million-new-voters-against-trump_2983985.html.

Lucas, Fred. "15 Election Results That Were Thrown Out Because of Fraudulent Mail-In Ballots." The Daily Signal. April 21, 2020. https://www.dailysignal.com/2020/04/21/15-election-results-that-were-thrown-out-because-of-fraudulent-mail-in-ballots/.

Lucas, Fred. "7 Ways the 2005 Carter-Baker Report Could Have Averted Problems With 2020 Election." November 20, 2020. The Daily Signal. https://www.dailysignal.com/2020/11/20/7-ways-the-2005-carter-baker-report-could-have-averted-problems-with-2020-election/.

Luo, Irene, and Jan Jekielek. "Robert Epstein: How Big Tech Bias Threatens Free and Fair Elections." *Epoch Times.* October 5, 2019. https://www.theepochtimes.com/robert-epstein-how-big-tech-bias-threatens-free-and-fair-elections_3077681.html.

Masket, Seth. "How Much Did COVID-19 Affect The 2020 Election? Not as much as one might expect." FiveThirtyEight.com. Jan. 27, 2021. https://fivethirtyeight.com/features/how-much-did-covid-19-affect-the-2020-election/.

McLaughlin, John, and Jim McLaughlin. "2020 Post Election Poll Analysis of an Election Like No Other." November 12, 2020. https://www.newsmax.com/mclaughlin/men-women-catholics-evangelicals/2020/11/12/id/996748/.

Morrison, Micah. "Judicial Watch Cleans Up Dirty Voter Rolls." Judicial Watch. October 15, 2020. https://www.judicialwatch.org/investigative-bulletin/ballot-update-judicial-watch-cleans-up-dirty-voter-rolls/.

Morrison, Micah. "Judicial Watch's Campaign for Clean Elections." Judicial Watch. April 22, 2020. https://www.judicialwatch.org/investigative-bulletin/judicial-watchs-campaign-for-clean-elections/.

Murdock, Deroy. "The vote fraud that Democrats refuse to see." July 14, 2017. *New York Post.* https://nypost.com/2017/07/14/the-vote-fraud-that-democrats-refuse-to-see/.

Natelson, Rob. "Don't Be Fooled! Don't Let Them Divert Us From Ensuring Electoral Integrity!" January 12, 2021. *Epoch Times.* https://www.theepochtimes.com/dont-be-fooled-dont-let-them-divert-us-from-ensuing-electoral-integrity_3651042.html.

Natelson, Rob. "The Solution Is a Convention of the States." *Epoch Times.* February 25, 2021. https://www.theepochtimes.com/the-solution-is-a-convention-of-the-states_3669475.html.

Navarro, Dr. Peter. *The Navarro Report: Volumes 1, Dec. 5, 2020; Volume 2, Jan. 5, 2021; and Volume 3, February 2, 2021.* https://peternavarro.com/the-navarro-report/.

Noncitizens Discovered in New Jersey Voter Registration System. September 11, 2017. Public Interest Legal Foundation (PILF). https://publicinterestlegal.org/blog/report-noncitizens-discovered-new-jersey-voter-registration-system/.

Noyes, Rich. "Study: 150 Times More Negative News on Trump than Biden." NewsBusters: Media Research Center (MRC). August 17, 2020. https://www.newsbusters.org/blogs/nb/rich-noyes/2020/08/17/study-150-times-more-negative-news-trump-biden.

Ozimek, Tom. "Conservative Nonprofit to Launch $10 Million Campaign to Strengthen Election Integrity." *Epoch Times.* March 8, 2021. https://www.theepochtimes.com/conservative-nonprofit-to-launch-10-million-campaign-to-strengthen-election-integrity-report_3724693.html.

Pan, GQ. "Poll Shows Overwhelming Support for Photo ID Voting Requirement." April 3, 2021. *Epoch Times.* https://www.theepochtimes.com/mkt_morningbrief/poll-shows-overwhelming-support-for-photo-id-voting-requirement_3760454.html?utm_source=morningbriefnoe&utm_medium=email&utm_campaign=mb-2021-04-03&mktids=9ee1d300d8b4cbd8671a4f3e9e27f0a7.

Payne, Daniel. "Zuckerberg pours $250 million into group funding voting drives in Wisconsin Democratic strongholds." Just the News. September 5, 2020. https://justthenews.com/politics-policy/elections/zuckerberg-pours-250-million-group-funding-voting-drives-wisconsin.

Pence, Mike. "Election Integrity Is a National Imperative." The Daily Signal. March 3, 2021. https://www.dailysignal.com/2021/03/03/election-integrity-is-a-national-imperative/.

Pentchoukov, Ivan. "Senate Intelligence Committee Releases Final Volume of Russia Report." *Epoch Times.* August 21, 2020. https://www.theepochtimes.com/senate-intelligence-committee-releases-final-volume-of-russia-report_3466170.html.

Pero, Colleen. "Hijacking Justice: The Well-Funded Campaign to Replace Judicial Elections with Selection by Liberal Special Interests." September 9, 2010. The Heritage Foundation. https://www.heritage.org/election-integrity/report/hijacking-justice-the-well-funded-campaign-replace-judicial-elections.

Phillips, Jack. "120 Retired Generals, Military Officers Sign Letter Warning of Conflict Between Marxism and 'Constitutional Freedom'." *Epoch Times.* May 12, 2021. https://www.theepochtimes.com/mkt_breakingnews/120-retired-generals-military-officers-sign-letter-warning-of-conflict-between-marxism-and-constitutional-freedom_3813043.html

Phillips, Jack. "DOJ Seizes $90,000, Charges Black Lives Matter Supporter Who 'Stormed Capitol,' Sold Footage to News Outlets." *Epoch Times.* May 23, 2021. https://www.theepochtimes.com/doj-seizes-90000-charges-black-lives-matter-supporter-who-stormed-capitol-sold-footage-to-news-outlets_3827441.html.

Phillips, Jack. "FBI Dividing Pro-Trump Ralliers Involved in Capitol Breach Into 3 Different Groups: Wray." March 4, 2021. *Epoch Times.* https://www.theepochtimes.com/fbi-dividing-pro-trump-ralliers-involved-in-capitol-breach-into-3-different-groups-wray_3720745.html.

Phillips, Jack. "Florida Gov. DeSantis Signs GOP-Backed Election Bill Limiting Mail-In Voting, Drop Boxes." *Epoch Times.* May 6, 2021. https://www.theepochtimes.com/florida-gov-desantis-signs-gop-backed-election-bill-limiting-mail-in-voting-drop-boxes_3805245.html.

Phillips, Jack. "Texas House Passes GOP-Backed Election Integrity Bill." *Epoch Times.* May 7, 2021. https://www.theepochtimes.com/texas-house-passes-gop-backed-voting-restrictions-bill_3807171.html.

Providing the Census Bureau with the Time to Produce a Complete and Accurate Census. The Heritage Foundation. Oct. 14, 2020. https://www.heritage.org/testimony/providing-the-census-bureau-the-time-produce-complete-and-accurate-census.

Raffensperger, Brad. "Setting the Record Straight on Georgia's New Voter-Access Law." *National Review.* April 6, 2021. https://www.nationalreview.com/2021/04/setting-the-record-straight-on-georgias-new-voter-access-law/?utm_source=recirc-desktop&utm_medium=article&utm_campaign=river&utm_content=top-bar-latest&utm_term=third.

Riedl, Brian, "The 'Facts' We Take on Faith: How do we know our political convictions are based in reality?" *City Journal.* January 14, 2021. https://www.city-journal.org/the-facts-we-take-on-faith.

Roarty, Alex. "Did the pandemic sink Trump's chances? Not as much as his opponents expected." November 12, 2020. *McClatchy* DC Bureau. https://www.mcclatchydc.com/news/politics-government/election/article247141899.html.

Schoffstall, Joe. "Soros Pours Record $50 Million Into 2020 Election." The Washington Free Beacon. July 27, 2020. https://freebeacon.com/elections/soros-pours-record-50-million-into-2020-election /.

Sherman, Amy. "Why Arizona Republicans are auditing election results." May 6, 2021. Poynter. https://www.poynter.org/fact-checking/2021/why-arizona-republicans-are-auditing-election-results/.

Slattery, Elizabeth, and Jason Snead. "Here Are 4 Egregious Ways the Left Wants to Transform American Politics." Mar. 26, 2019. The Daily Signal. https://www.dailysignal.com/2019/03/26/here-are-4-ways-egregious-ways-the-left-wants-to-transform-american-politics/.

Smith, Bradley, Josiah H. Blackmore II and Shirley M. Nault. "How the Electoral College Protects and Nurtures Our Republic." May 11, 2020. The Heritage Foundation. https://www.heritage.org/election-integrity/report/how-the-electoral-college-protects-and-nurtures-our-republic.

Smith, Zack, and Hans von Spakovsky. "Supreme Court's Decision Not to Hear Elections Cases Could Have Serious Repercussions." Feb. 24, 2021. The Heritage Foundation. https://www.heritage.org/election-integrity/commentary/supreme-courts-decision-not-hear-elections-cases-could-have-serious.

Snead, Jason. "More Proof That Voter Fraud Is Real, and Bipartisan." The Daily Signal. Aug. 27, 2019. https://www.dailysignal.com/2019/08/27/more-proof-that-voter-fraud-is-real-and-bipartisan/.

Stieber, Zachary. "Arizona Lawmakers Tell Maricopa Officials to Turn Over Routers or Face Subpoenas." *Epoch Times.* May 9, 2021. https://www.theepochtimes.com/turn-over-routers-or-face-subpoenas-arizona-lawmakers-tell-maricopa-county_3807631.html.

Stieber, Zachary. "Georgia Judge Decides to Unseal Absentee Ballots in Fulton County for Review." *Epoch Times.* May 21, 2021. https://www.theepochtimes.com/georgia-judge-decides-to-unseal-absentee-ballots-in-fulton-county-for-review_3825366.html.

Strom, Roy. "Snubbing Trump, Lawyers Doling More Cash to Democrats." Bloomberg Law. Nov. 20, 2019. https://news.bloomberglaw.com/business-and-practice/snubbing-trump-lawyers-doling-more-cash-to-democrats.

Svab, Petr. "Google Engineer Leaks Nearly 1,000 Internal Documents, Alleging Bias, Censorship." *Epoch Times.* August 14, 2019. https://web.archive.org/web/20190814222428/https://www.theepochtimes.com/google-engineer-leaks-nearly-1000-internal-documents-alleging-bias-censorship_3042234.html.

Svab, Petr. "Statistical Anomalies in Biden Votes, Analyses Indicate." *Epoch Times.* April 10, 2021. https://epochtimes.today/statistical-anomalies-in-biden-votes-analyses-indicate/.

The 4 Biden vote dumps that changed the 2020 election. Gray's Economy. December 1, 2020. https://grayseconomy.com/2020/12/01/the-4-biden-vote-dumps-that-changed-the-2020-election/.

The Facts About Election Integrity and the Need for States to Fix Their Election Systems. February 1, 2021. The Heritage Foundation. https://www.heritage.org/election-integrity-facts.

The Facts About H.R. 1: The "For the People Act of 2021." Feb. 21, 2021. The Heritage Foundation. https://www.heritage.org/election-integrity/report/the-facts-about-hr-1-the-the-people-act-2021.

Trusdell, Brian. "Sparks Fly in Arizona Recount." *Newsmax.* May 18, 2021. https://www.newsmax.com/newsfront/arizona-audit-republicans-feud/2021/05/18/id/1021871/.

Vadum, Matthew. "Google Awards Grants to Left-Wing Media Outlets, Critics Say." *Epoch Times.* October 30, 2019. https://www.theepochtimes.com/google-awards-grants-to-left-wing-media-outlets-critics-say_3132658.html.

Van Dyke, Tyler. "'The Art of the Steal': Peter Navarro releases 'Volume Two' of report on voter fraud allegations." *Washington Examiner.* January 5, 2021. https://www.washingtonexaminer.com/news/peter-navarro-releases-volume-two-report-voter-fraud.

Viebeck, Elise. "More than 500,000 mail ballots were rejected in the primaries. That could make the difference in battle ground states this fall." *The Washington Post.* August 23, 2020. https://www.washingtonpost.com/politics/rejected-mail-ballots/2020/08/23/397fbe92-db3d-11ea-809e-b8be57ba616e_story.html.

von Spakovsky, Hans "Allowing Felons to Vote While Incarcerated Is Reckless." The Heritage Foundation. Oct. 15, 2019. https://www.heritage.org/election-integrity/commentary/allowing-felons-vote-while-incarcerated-reckless.

von Spakovsky, Hans "Stolen Elections Show the Vulnerabilities of Absentee Ballots." The Heritage Foundation. July 24, 2020. https://www.heritage.org/election-integrity/commentary/stolen-elections-show-the-vulnerabilities-absentee-ballots.

von Spakovsky, Hans "Vote Harvesting a Recipe for Coercion and Election Fraud." *The Washington Times.* Oct. 28, 2019. https://www.washingtontimes.com/news/2019/oct/28/vote-harvesting-a-recipe-for-coercion-and-election/.

von Spakovsky, Hans "Why Safeguarding Our Elections Matters." The Daily Signal. Nov. 1, 2020. https://www.dailysignal.com/2020/11/01/why-safeguarding-our-elections-matters/.

von Spakovsky, Hans and Caleb Morrison. "New Study Confirms Voter ID Laws Don't Hurt Election Turnout." The Daily Signal. Feb. 27, 2019. https://www.dailysignal.com/2019/02/26/new-study-confirms-voter-id-laws-dont-hurt-election-turnout/.

von Spakovsky, Han, J. Christian Adams, and Cleta Mitchell. "von Spakovsky, Adams & Mitchell: Coronavirus and elections—changes increase risk of voter fraud." Fox News. April 1, 2020. https://www.foxnews.com/opinion/coronavirus-election-fraud-von-spakovsky-adams-mitchell.

von Spakovsky, Hans and J. Christian Adams. "Adams & von Spakovsky: America's hidden voting epidemic? Mail ballot failures." Fox News. Apr. 17, 2020. https://www.foxnews.com/opinion/voting-epidemic-mail-ballot-failures-christian-adams-hans-von-spakovsky.

von Spakovsky, Hans and J. Christian Adams. "COVID-19 and Ebola: What We Can Learn from Prior Elections." The Heritage Foundation. May 1, 2020. https://www.heritage.org/sites/default/files/2020-08/IB5066.pdf.

von Spakovsky, Hans and J. Christian Adams. "Vote-by-Mail Makes Fraud and Errors Worse." *The Washington Times.* Mar. 31, 2020. https://www.washingtontimes.com/news/2020/mar/31/vote-by-mail-for-2020-election-will-make-fraud-and/.

von Spakovsky, Hans and Kaitlynn Samalis-Aldrich. "Tens of Thousands of Cases of Possible Vote Fraud Cited in New Report." The Daily Signal. Oct 6, 2020. https://www.heritage.org/election-integrity/commentary/tens-thousands-cases-possible-vote-fraud-cited-new-report.

von Spakovsky, Hans and Kaitlynn Samalis-Aldrich. "The Heritage Foundation's Election Fraud Database Tops 1,300 Cases." The Daily Signal. Dec. 11, 2020. https://www.dailysignal.com/2020/12/11/the-heritage-foundations-election-fraud-database-tops-1300-cases/.

von Spakovsky, Hans. "A 2020 Election Redo in 4 States? Here Are the Details About Texas Lawsuit." The Daily Signal. Dec. 8, 2020. https://www.dailysignal.com/2020/12/08/a-2020-election-redo-in-4-states-here-are-the-details-about-texas-lawsuit/.

von Spakovsky, Hans. "Against the John Lewis Voting Rights Advancement Act." *National Review.* October 15, 2020. https://www.nationalreview.com/magazine/2020/11/02/against-the-john-lewis-voting-rights-advancement-act/.

von Spakovsky, Hans. "Coronavirus Is No Reason for the Feds to Take Over the Election Process. The Heritage Foundation. Mar. 27, 2020. https://www.heritage.org/election-integrity/commentary/coronavirus-no-reason-the-feds-take-over-the-election-process.

von Spakovsky, Hans. "Despite Predictions, *Shelby v. Holder* Did Not Lead to Voter Suppression." *Newsweek.* Dec. 8, 2020. https://www.newsweek.com/despite-predictions-shelby-v-holder-did-not-lead-voter-suppression-opinion-1552941.

von Spakovsky, Hans. "Ensuring the Integrity of Our Election System." The Daily Signal. Oct. 5, 2020. https://www.dailysignal.com/2020/10/05/ensuring-the-integrity-of-our-election-system/.

von Spakovsky, Hans. "The Left Versus the Vote." The American Mind. Aug. 25, 2020. https://americanmind.org/essays/democrats-versus-the-vote/.

von Spakovsky, Hans. "The Left's 'Jim Crow' Rhetoric Is Absurd, Insulting, and Dishonest." The Daily Signal. Mar. 30, 2021. https://www.dailysignal.com/2021/03/30/the-lefts-jim-crow-rhetoric-is-absurd-insulting-and-dishonest/.

von Spakovsky, Hans. "U.S. Election Fraud is Real—And It Is Being Ignored." *The National Interest.* Oct. 24, 2020. https://nationalinterest.org/feature/us-election-fraud-real%E2%80%94and-it-being-ignored-171188.

Walsh, Michael, and David Kahane. *Rules for Radical Conservatives: Beating the Left at Its Own Game to Take Back America.* Don Congdon Associates, Inc. New York, NY. 2010.

Weaver, Corinne. "Censorship Insanity: Twitter Goes After Trump and Campaign 194 Times." Nov. 16, 2020. MRC NewsBusters. https://www.newsbusters.org/blogs/techwatch/corinne-weaver/2020/11/16/censorship-insanity-twitter-goes-after-trump-and-campaign.

Why Do Democrats Pretend Voter Fraud Doesn't Exist?. Nov. 2, 2018. *Investor's Business Daily.* https://www.investors.com/politics/editorials/voter-fraud-midterm-elections/.

Williamson, Kevin D. "Why Not Fewer Voters?" *National Review.* April 6, 2021. https://www.nationalreview.com/2021/04/why-not-fewer-voters/?utm_source=onesignal&utm_medium=push&utm_campaign=article.

Wilson, Reid. "Young, diverse voters fueled Biden victory over Trump." *The Hill.* May 10, 2021. https://thehill.com/homenews/campaign/552605-young-diverse-voters-fueled-biden-win-study?userid=396709.

Xiao, Bowen. "Google Will 'Actively Interfere' in 2020 Elections, Researcher Says." *Epoch Times.* August 8, 2019. https://www.theepochtimes.com/google-will-actively-interfere-in-2020-elections-researcher-says_3033230.html.

Zitner, Aaron. "Trump-Biden Was Worst Presidential Polling Miss in 40 Years, Panel Says." *Wall Street Journal.* May 13, 2021. https://www.wsj.com/articles/trump-biden-was-worst-presidential-polling-miss-in-40-years-panel-says-11620909178?mod=searchresults_pos1&page=1.

Index

E

F

Author Bio

Author: Corey Lee Wilson.

Corey Lee Wilson was raised an atheist by his liberal *Playboy* Bunny mother, has three Anglo-Hispanic siblings, a brother who died of AIDS, baptized a Protestant by his conservative grandparents, attended temple with his Jewish foster parents, baptized again as a Catholic for his first Filipina wife, attends Buddhist ceremonies with his second Thai wife, became an agnostic on his own free will for most of his life, and is a lifetime independent voter.

Corey felt the sting of intellectual humility by repeating the 4th grade and attended eighteen different schools before putting himself through college at Mt. San Antonio College and Cal Poly Pomona University (while on triple secrete probation). Named Who's Who of American College Students in 1984, he received a BS in Economics and won his fraternity's most prestigious undergraduate honor, the Phi Kappa Tau Fraternity's Shideler Award, both in 1985. In 2020, he became a member of the Heterodox Academy and in 2021 a member of the National Association of Scholars and 1776 Unites.

As a satirist and fraternity man, Corey started Fratire Publishing in 2012 and transformed the fiction "fratire" genre to a respectable and viewpoint diverse non-fiction genre promoting practical knowledge and wisdom to help everyday people navigate safely through the many hazards of life. In 2018, he founded the SAPIENT Being to help promote freedom of speech, viewpoint diversity, intellectual humility and most importantly advance sapience in America's students and campuses.

The SAPIENT Being has three programs: Make Free Speech Again On Campus (MFSAOC), World of Writing Warriors (WOWW) and the Sapient Conservative Textbooks (SCT) all working together to promote its mission and vision of sapience. The WOWW program plans to self-publish 50 *MADNESS* non-fiction textbooks in partnership with Fratire Publishing over the span of the 2020 decade in alliance with the MFSAOC program to start 50 chapters on America's high school and college campuses by 2030.

If you're interested in the MFSAOC Program and starting a S.A.P.I.E.N.T. Being club, chapter, or alliance please got to https://www.SapientBeing.org/start-a-chapter, e-mail SapientBeing@att.net, or call (951) 638-5562 for more information.

If you're interested as an author or journalist in the WOWW Program and their 50 MADNESS series of textbooks from the S.A.P.I.E.N.T. Being, please check them out at https://www.FratirePublishing.com/madnessbooks, e-mail SapientBeing@att.net, or call (951) 638-5562 for more information.

If you're interested as an educator or marketer in the SCT Program and their 50 MADNESS series of textbooks from the S.A.P.I.E.N.T. Being, please check them out at https://www.FratirePublishing.com/madnessbooks, e-mail SapientBeing@att.net, or call (951) 638-5562 for more information.

Hopefully, this book was enlightening and your journey through it—along with mine—made you aware of the issues and challenges ahead of us. If it has, your quest and mine towards becoming a sapient being has begun. If it hasn't, there's no better time to start than now. Come join us in creating a society advancing personal intelligence and enlightenment now together (S.A.P.I.E.N.T.) and become a sapient being.

www.ingramcontent.com/pod-product-compliance
Lightning Source LLC
Chambersburg PA
CBHW040832040426
42336CB00034B/3457